The Clash of the Cultures

BOOKS BY
JOHN C. BOGLE

The Clash of the Cultures

Investment vs. Speculation

John C. Bogle

WILEY

John Wiley & Sons, Inc.

Published by John Wiley & Sons, Inc., Hoboken, New Jersey.
Published simultaneously in Canada.

For general information on our other products and services or for technical support, please contact our Customer Care Department within the United States at (800) 762-2974, outside the United States at (317) 572-3993 or fax (317) 572-4002.

Wiley also publishes its books in a variety of electronic formats. Some content that appears in print may not be available in electronic books. For more information about Wiley products, visit our website at www.wiley.com.

Library of Congress Cataloging-in-Publication Data:
ISBN 978-1-118-12277-8 (cloth)
ISBN 978-1-118-22474-8 (ebk)
ISBN 978-1-118-41438-5 (ebk)
ISBN 978-1-118-41437-8 (ebk)

Printed in the United States of America

10 9 8 7 6 5 4 3 2 1

*To all of those human beings who have helped to shape my character,
my values, and my career—my ancestors; my parents—especially my
beloved mother—and my brothers; my loving wife Eve and my
children and grandchildren; my teachers; my pastors; my classmates in
school and college; my bosses and mentors in finance; my guardian
angels in medical care; my truth-seekers in the academy; my colleagues
and believers at Vanguard; the Vanguard shareholder/owners, who
have given me their trust; and my friends from all walks of life.
"No man is an island, entire of itself."*

Contents

Foreword

By Arthur Levitt

There is a motto that Jack Bogle uses from time to time (and he uses it in this book): "Even one person can make a difference." And while he uses it to elevate and praise the contributions of a single, relatively powerless person, that motto applies uniquely to Jack Bogle.

Here is a man whose contribution to American finance was not just a well-executed idea—the index fund—but a well-executed philosophy of investing and life. It is a philosophy that has the dual merit of simplicity and proven success.

Having known Bogle for several decades, I have come to appreciate his unique ability to speak to investors in a language that is accessible, lyrical, and yet also bracing. He points out with clarity the inherent conflicts present throughout our financial markets, most notably between the investor's interests and those of many financial professionals.

This is a critical complaint in his discussion of mutual funds. Many investors are under the mistaken impression that mutual funds are a secure and relatively matter-of-fact way to gain the benefit of diversification at low cost. In reality, as Bogle richly details here and elsewhere, mutual funds have a large incentive to benefit from the economics of their businesses, rather than look after their investors' long-term wealth. Thus we see some mutual funds not only charge outsized fees, but also practice portfolio management strategies that leave investors behind market index averages and overexposed to certain equities, sectors, and strategies.

That Bogle has stood against such practices for decades is no surprise to anyone who knows this man. He is a person of great courage, wisdom, and forthrightness. He has never lost the zeal or ability to go against conventional wisdom, and is strengthened by those moments when he stands alone. Jack Bogle is brilliant and persuasive, and his ability to get to the heart of often complex issues of finance and markets is one of his greatest gifts.

He loves investing and loves what investing can do. He marvels at the miracles possible when corporations and their owners and managers jointly pursue long-term shareholder return to the exclusion of all else. He is the free market's greatest friend: a faithful ally. And yet when he sees the corridors of finance and investment turned into a den of speculation and greed, he does not hold his tongue. He knows the stakes are great.

The Clash of Cultures is definitional, and could well serve as a philosophic and academic grounding for investors of every age. Throughout, his language is disarmingly straightforward. Because of his respect for the investor, he sidesteps glibness and oversimplification. He defines the difference between risk-taking and recklessness. He correlates costs to returns. He explains why indexing works, and why active management usually doesn't. He traces the roots of today's markets to the rise of corporate agents and then investment managers—both of whom form an impenetrable and expensive "double-agency" layer separating the real investor-owners from active control over their assets.

While some Wall Street professionals may not agree with every word here—or even some of the words—I hope they read it. One of the greatest threats to the strength of financial markets is groupthink. When regulators, market professionals, investors, and policymakers all share the same assumptions, emerge from the same trading floors, nod to the same broad arguments, and expect the same outcomes, the result is as predictable as it is disastrous. Jack Bogle's iconoclasm is a useful tonic to groupthink. We need more like him.

There are many villains in this book: auditors, regulators, politicians, rating agencies, the Securities and Exchange Commission (which I led), the Federal Reserve, sell-side analysts, and the media. And their collective (as well as individual) sins have one primary victim: investors.

And he is right. Investors must remain the focus of any efforts to improve our financial markets. No matter the regulatory reform, the market practice or the new financial product, if the investor's interests don't trump all others, we ought to question what purpose we are serving. One thinks of rules requiring ever more volumes of disclosures. The result is not better-informed investors, but the opposite. The disclosures, written in legalese and printed in agate type, might as well not exist to most investors. What we need is transparency: ways for investors to see information, understand it, and weigh the potential risks and opportunities of their investment options.

Transparency is at the core of effective market regulation, precisely because it empowers investors. Sadly, most efforts to improve transparency are fought by a well-funded mutual fund lobby and its related allies. One recent SEC proposal, to have money market funds mark to market their holdings every day, is one such example. This basic idea would not only give investors greater insight into their holdings. It would also impose a healthy appreciation for liquidity among mutual fund managers. Yet the mutual fund industry predictably has fought the idea.

The industry would be wise to consider what Jack Bogle and others observe: If investors do not feel that mutual funds are protecting their interests, they will not participate in markets—and the markets themselves will suffer. If mutual funds wish to remain the gold standard for investor protections and stability, they ought to take seriously—and adopt—reforms and practices that add to those protections and stability. We are but three years removed from one of the biggest financial crises of history, brought about by an excess of risk-taking, leverage, and opaque financial products, combined with lax regulation. Surely mutual fund managers can see the value in avoiding a repeat of that catastrophic period. And if not, they can expect to reap what follows. Surely Jack Bogle and others inside the industry have done enough to raise the alarm.

Never is this clearer than in his insistence that fees and costs are draining all the promised value out of the pockets of investors. Investors must know that they inevitably earn the gross return of the stock market, but only before the deduction of the costs of financial intermediation are taken into account. If beating the market is a zero sum game before costs, it is a loser's game after costs are deducted. Which is why costs must be made clear to investors, and, one hopes, minimized. Pointing this out routinely surely cannot earn Jack Bogle many friends among Wall Street, which depends on the mystery surrounding financial innovations—as they are called euphemistically. But Bogle doesn't care much about "stirring the pot." His friends have long learned to appreciate that his truth-telling is the key to his personality.

Jack Bogle has spent a lifetime in study and active participation in financial markets. The amount of self-dealing and self-enrichment he has seen qualifies him to bear witness against not just a few individuals, but entire firms and certainly an entire industry. They should be glad that Jack Bogle is merely an expert witness, and not the judge and jury as well.

Acknowledgments

This book is my attempt to provide a living history—replete with personal anecdotes—of some of the most significant elements of an era in which the character of our financial system changed. And not for the better. We must understand what went wrong in finance in order to take the necessary steps toward building a better system. Only if we serve "individual and institutional investors in the most economical, efficient, and honest way possible"—a phrase from my 1951 Princeton senior thesis—can we again honor the standard of fiduciary duty that once largely prevailed among the trustees of Other People's Money.

Readers of my earlier books—nine in number—will hardly be unfamiliar with many of the themes that I sound in this tenth book. Indeed, I've deliberately reiterated not only some of the themes from earlier books, but even a few of the earlier passages. For readers of my earlier books, I reasoned that if I said it well then, why say it less well now? For new readers, there's no way to tell this story without doing so. Nonetheless, the vast majority of the material in *The Clash of the Cultures* breaks totally new ground—with additional data, up-to-date information about the continued deterioration in financial industry standards, and an author who has become rather more assertive and less fearful of candor.

I take this opportunity to thank the three members of my staff for their skill, their support, their patience, and their unflappability. Emily Snyder, who has now been at my side for 23 years, did her usual yeoman's job. So did Sara Hoffman, well-seasoned to the hurly-burly of our small office despite only seven years at her post. Michael Nolan, a 10-year Vanguard veteran who joined us only a year ago, has done a fantastic job in providing and checking the data, helping to edit my manuscript, and organizing my information sources. His remarkable skills in the use of information technology have been essential to the entire process of producing this book.

Special thanks, too, to Pamela van Giessen of John Wiley & Sons, my publisher, and to Leah Spiro, who served as editor. Leah's job was not an easy one, but she came through with flying colors, helping to make this book better than it otherwise would have been. My former assistants, Kevin Laughlin and Andrew Clarke, both now back in the Vanguard mainstream, also made valuable suggestions. I continue to be in debt to these two long-time friends.

Speaking bluntly is not always the way to please others, so I give special thanks to John Woerth, Vanguard principal in charge of public relations and my colleague for 25 years. John made a series of recommendations from the standpoint of the firm's policies, and I did my best to respond. Nonetheless, some of my opinions may not represent the opinions of Vanguard's present management. Sometimes reasonable people can disagree!

Contrarily, I fear that some readers will look at the over-all thrust of the book as too biased toward the firm that I founded, and that the book is some sort of Vanguard "commercial." To that criticism, I can only respond that I have been as objective as is humanly possible. The data are the data! More broadly, I hardly need apologize for the investment strategies and human values on which I founded Vanguard, for these strategies and values have met the test of time.

Please enjoy the book and let me know what you think. Read my blog at www.johncbogle.com.

JOHN C. BOGLE
Valley Forge, Pennsylvania
June, 2012

About This Book

In 1951, when I began my career, long-term investing was the mantra of the investment community. In 1974, when I founded Vanguard, that tenet still remained intact. But over the past several decades, the very nature of our nation's financial sector has changed—and not for the better. A culture of short-term speculation has run rampant, superseding the culture of long-term investment that was dominant earlier in the post–World War II era. These two very different cultures have existed in the world of capital markets and capital formation all through history. But today's model of capitalism has gotten out of balance, to the detriment of the investing public—indeed, to the ultimate detriment of our society.

As strategies focused on short-term speculation have crowded out strategies focused on long-term investment, the change has benefited financial sector insiders at the direct, arguably dollar-for-dollar, expense of their clients. In truth, that tension between investment and speculation is at the very heart of the great challenges we now face in Investment America and in Corporate America, challenges that could ultimately undermine the functioning of our financial markets and threaten the ability of our individual investor/citizens to build their wealth.

So, I'm deeply concerned with today's ascendance of a culture of speculation over a culture of investment in our financial markets. I'm concerned as a member of the financial community, I'm concerned as a member of the community of investors, and I'm concerned as a citizen of this nation. Inspired by the British author C. P. Snow, I describe this change as "The Clash of the Cultures." A half-century ago, C. P. Snow described a parallel contrast. In his book *The Two Cultures*, Snow focused on the ascendance of the culture of science—of precise measurement and quantification—over the culture of the humanities—of steady enlightenment and reason. Similarly, *The Clash of the Cultures* contrasts the culture of long-term investing—the rock of the intellectual, the philosopher, and the historian—with the culture of short-term speculation—the tool of the mathematician, the technician, and the alchemist.

Resisting this new dominance of speculation over investment might seem to fly in the face of our ever more scientific and technological world. After all, innovation, information, instant communications, and competition have brought great benefits to our society. But I see our financial system as somehow separate and distinct from the other business and commercial systems that permeate our world.

"Value-Creating" and "Rent-Seeking"

There is a difference—a difference in kind—between what economists describe as "value-creating" activities that add value to society and "rent-seeking" activities that subtract value from society on balance. One provides new and improved products and services, delivered through ever more efficient channels and at prices that are more competitive, and the other simply shifts economic claims from one set of participants to another. Think of the law: one side wins, the other loses, but the lawyers and the legal system profit, and diminish the amount of money that changes hands between the actual litigants. Government operates this way, too: Before being dispensed as expenditures, tax revenues are reduced by the intermediation costs of the bureaucracy. The financial system is the classic example, in which investors trade with each other and one is a winner and one a loser. But the costs of trading create an obvious economic drag that results, for investors as a group, in a net loss from trading activity.

Yes, today's financial system also creates value—innovation, real-time information, vast liquidity, and a certain amount of capital formation. But technology cannot eliminate the frictional costs of the system. While unit-trading costs have plummeted, trading volumes have soared, and total costs of the financial system continue to rise. Too many innovations have served Wall Street at the expense of its client/investors. Pressed to identify useful financial innovations created during the past quarter-century, Paul A. Volcker, former Federal Reserve Chairman and recent chairman of President Obama's Economic Recovery Board, could single out only one: "The ATM." (Mr. Volcker recently told me that if the period of evaluation had been the past 40 years, he would have also included the creation of the index mutual fund in 1975 as an important and positive innovation that has served investors well.)

A 60-Year Perspective

My primary purpose in writing this book is to sound the alarm about the shocking change in the culture of finance that I have witnessed firsthand during my now 60-year career in the financial field—the gradual but relentless rise of the modern culture of speculation, characterized by frenzied activity in our financial markets, complex and exotic financial instruments, and trading in derivatives of various securities (rather than in the securities themselves). These characteristics dominate today's burgeoning financial system, peppered as it is with self-interest and greed. Somewhere down the road—if not already—the consequences to our investors, our society, and our nation are almost certain to be extremely harmful.

This newly dominant culture of short-term speculation has made huge inroads into the traditional culture of long-term investment that I found in finance when I began my career in 1951. Actually, my work started early in 1950, when I began a study of the mutual fund industry for my Princeton senior thesis. I began by reading the four-volume, 1,059-page SEC report to the U.S. House of Representatives, chronicling the events that led to the passage of the Investment Company Act of 1940. That Act was the legislative response to the remarkably similar (as it turned out) transgressions in the investment company field during the 1920s, and the collapse that followed in the 1930s. While that history did not *repeat* itself during the recent crisis (to paraphrase Mark Twain's likely apocryphal formulation), it *rhymed*.

In midsummer 2011, as I began to write the manuscript for this book, I quickly came to realize that I had been more than a mere eyewitness to these six-plus decades of financial history. In fact, I was one of its most active participants. As it turns out, I was privileged to be in a position to actually influence many of the important issues that have been my focus during my long career. So I write out of a sense of history, lest the stories that are told by others who are mere observers come to dominate the discourse. *The Clash of the Cultures* is not another book on the financial crisis that began in 2007, but rather an examination of the tumultuous changes that have taken place over the long sweep of history in the business and financial sectors of our nation and of the world, within the context of free-market capitalism and capital formation.

The Big Picture

In Chapter 1, I begin with the ideas that culminated in the "Clash of the Cultures," an essay I wrote for the *Journal of Portfolio Management* in the spring of 2011, itself a product of my lecture at Wall Street's Museum of American Finance just a few months earlier. The essay focused on how a culture of short-term speculation came to dominate a culture of long-term investment. One example: In recent years, annual trading in stocks—necessarily creating, by reason of the transaction costs involved, negative value for traders—averaged some $33 trillion. But capital formation—that is, directing fresh investment capital to its highest and best uses, such as new businesses, new technology, medical breakthroughs, and modern plant and equipment for existing business—averaged some $250 billion. Put another way, speculation represented about 99.2 percent of the activities of our equity market system, with capital formation accounting for 0.8 percent.

Chapter 2 examines what I consider the proximate dual cause of the various failures of capitalism I've witnessed—the "Double-Agency

Society," in which our giant corporate manager/agents interact with our giant investment manager/agents in a symbiotic "Happy Conspiracy" to focus on the momentary fluctuations of evanescent stock prices rather than the building of long-term intrinsic corporate value. In our double-agency system, both our corporate manager/agents and our investment manager/agents have been unable to resist the temptation to look first to their own interests.

Alas, as I report in this chapter, our "Gatekeepers"—the courts, the Congress, the regulatory agencies, the public accountants, the rating agencies, the security analysts, the money managers, the corporate directors, even the shareholders—largely failed in honoring their responsibilities to call out what was going on right before their eyes. The wild and risky "innovative" securities of the era, financial shenanigans by some of our largest corporations, and Congressional sanctioning of excessive mortgage debt by ill-qualified homebuyers are but a few of the myriad examples.

In Chapter 3, "The Silence of the Funds," I describe the failure of our institutional money managers—mutual fund managers and their affiliated pension fund managers, which together manage the lion's share of our nation's pension fund assets—to step up to the plate and exercise the rights and responsibilities of corporate governance in the interests of the fund shareholders and plan beneficiaries whom they are duty-bound to serve. I use as examples two current issues to illustrate the shortfall of these managers of "Other People's Money"—the rampant abuses in executive compensation, and corporate political contributions. It's high time that these managers stand up and be counted and put the interests of their clients first.

Mutual Funds

Going, in a sense, from the general to the particular, I describe in Chapter 4 the change in the culture of the mutual fund industry, the focus of my career for the past 60 years. During that long span, fund assets increased by nearly 5,000-fold—from $2.5 billion to $12 trillion. A *profession* once focused largely on investing became a *business* largely focused on marketing. Of course such growth makes change inevitable. But the counterproductive form of change that developed was fostered by a sea change in the industry's culture, from private ownership to largely public ownership and the near-pervasive control of fund managers by financial conglomerates. For fund shareholders, it was a tragic change.

The creation of Vanguard and its truly *mutual* (fund-shareholder-owned) structure has been the so-far-single counterexample to this pattern. I explain why this structure has worked so well, and why it must ultimately become the dominant structure in the industry. To bring this once-fine industry back to its traditional roots, I propose in this chapter a change designed to fix what is broken: the establishment of a federal standard of fiduciary duty that places the interests of fund shareholders first.

Now, we all know what investment fiduciary duty means: *placing the interests of investor/principals who provide the firm's capital ahead of the interests of the manager/agents who invest it.* Since fiduciary duty may be difficult for investors to measure intuitively, Chapter 5 is designed to help mutual fund investors measure their own fund managers, evaluating them on 15 different points of judgment. This chapter will likely prove contentious, for I set down my own evaluations—flawed and subjective though they may be—of what I call the "Stewardship Quotient" for Vanguard and for three other fund managers.

The Index Fund

In 1975, I created the first index mutual fund, now known as Vanguard 500 Index Fund. Then, as now, I considered it the very paradigm of long-term investing, a fully diversified portfolio of U.S. stocks operated at high tax efficiency and rock-bottom costs, and designed to be held, well, "forever." It is now the world's largest equity mutual fund. In Chapter 6, I chronicle the Fund's formation, its investment advantages, its minimal costs, and its remarkable record of performance achievement. It is these factors that underlie the growth of index funds to their dominant position in today's mutual fund industry, holding 28 percent of total assets of equity funds.

But a funny thing happened on this long road toward the dominance of the index fund. Beginning in the early 1990s, a new kind of index mutual fund—one that could be traded "all day long, in real time" was created. In essence, the ETF (exchange-traded fund) makes it easy for investors to engage in short-term speculation—not only in the S&P 500 Index, the standard for the first ETF, but across a mind-boggling array of 1,056(!) different so-called indexes, sometimes hyped with high leverage risk. This focus stands in sharp contrast to the TIF (traditional index fund) that I designed for long-term investors all those years ago. In the second half of Chapter 6, I express my views on the manifestation of this radical and astounding change in the culture of indexing. The ETF is surely the greatest marketing idea in finance so far in the twenty-first century. Whether it proves to be a great—or even a good—idea for investors remains to be seen. (Remarkably, the assets of ETFs now exceed those of TIFs.)

Our Retirement System: Potential Train Wreck

America's retirement system, too, has been bitten by the speculative bug, though in ways ignored by many financial leaders who should have known better. As I explain in Chapter 7, the linchpin of the system is Social Security, and its participants really have little choice but to speculate on whether we have the national will to fix the system or face the consequences. (The simple fixes, which I identify, are hardly vast; they can be done in small increments. The failure of our politicians to act before it's too late is a disgrace.) Similarly, our corporate and local pension funds are speculating that they will earn annual future returns in the 8 percent range, a grand illusion ultimately fraught with severely negative economic consequences.

What's more, given the trend away from defined-benefit (pension) plans to defined-contribution (savings) plans, the choices being made by plan participants also reflect the dangers of speculation on (1) the returns the plans earn over the participant's lifetime; (2) which active managers will win; (3) the performance of the stock of a single company ("employer stock"), and even its survival; and (4) asset allocation. (Many participants are far too conservative; many are far too aggressive. That the average between these two polar extremes is quite sensible is, of course, irrelevant.) I conclude that unless we reform the very structure and implementation of both our public and our private retirement systems, we face a financial train wreck.

Wellington Fund

It is with both embarrassment and pride that I offer a firsthand example of the change in the culture of one of America's oldest, proudest, and now most successful mutual funds. In Chapter 8, I present the history of Wellington Fund. I joined the Fund when I graduated from college in 1951, and have stayed the course with Wellington to this day, first as an employee, then as an officer, then as CEO, finally moving to "honorary" status in 1999. Since its founding in 1928, Wellington Fund had held high its traditional culture of long-term investment ("a complete investment program in one security"), but, under new management in 1966, we gave way to the new culture of speculation reflected in the "Go-Go Years" of the stock market. As I acknowledge, this foolish change was in part my responsibility. But in a blistering memorandum that I wrote to the Fund's portfolio managers as the stock market peaked late in 1972, I railed against it.

The overheated stock market of that era, of course, would soon collapse, and Wellington's assets shriveled by almost 80 percent. I owed it to my career-long friend and mentor Walter L. Morgan, Wellington's founder, to restore the Fund's original culture and its hard-won reputation. In a 1978 memorandum, I articulated how to do exactly that, and, with the support of the fund's board, I forced a return to the culture of long-term investment. I articulated the new strategy, and even provided a sample stock portfolio. The fund's adviser accepted the change, and implemented it well. (Excerpts from both the 1972 and 1978 memos are included in this chapter.)

For readers of *The Clash of the Cultures*, I sought a clear, real-world confirmation that short-term speculation is apt to lead to failure and long-term investment to success. My career had placed me at the very heart of both sides of this issue; the history of Wellington Fund fit that mold perfectly. In 1966, I had made a huge error in succumbing to the foolish stock market passions of the day; I paid a large price (I was fired from my job); and in my new role at Vanguard was given an incredible opportunity to fix what I'd helped to break. The renaissance of Wellington Fund that followed has been one of the greatest joys of my long career.

"The Man in the Arena"

This book began as an historical tract by an interested observer. But it became, in major part, a personal memoir by an active participant in the world of finance. The many anecdotes that I have recounted in these chapters remind me once again of the incredible delight that I've experienced during my long career, the opportunity to reflect on the many challenges I've faced, and—despite my many weaknesses and the mistakes I've made along the way—the strength and determination I've brought to the task of building a better world for investors. Yes, even as I recognize that they were often born of the many defeats that I've suffered, I admit that I'm proud of the many victories I've won.

In this context, I cannot help but be reminded of "The Man in the Arena," the individual that President Theodore Roosevelt described with these classic and inspiring words:

> It is not the critic who counts; not the man who points out how the strong man stumbles, or where the doer of deeds could have done them better. The credit belongs to the man who is actually in the arena, whose face is marred by dust and sweat and blood; who strives valiantly; who errs, who comes short again and again, because there is no effort without error and shortcoming; but who does actually strive to do the deeds; who knows great enthusiasms, the great devotions; who spends himself in a worthy cause; who at the best knows in the end the triumph of high achievement, and who at the worst, if he fails, at least fails while daring greatly, so that his place shall never be with those cold and timid souls who neither know victory nor defeat.

Of course the jury is still out on my legacy. But I confess that I can't worry about how others may appraise it. Yes, I've erred. Yes, I've come up short more times than I care to count. But if, at the end, I'm deemed to have failed, at least I will have failed despite the rush of great enthusiasm; despite the high achievement of having my most important ideas—the *mutual* fund structure, the single-eye focus on rock-bottom costs, the index mutual fund, the abandonment of sales loads, and the creation of a new structure for bond funds—proven beyond doubt; and despite championing the worthy cause of serving our nation's citizen/ investors "economically, efficiently, and honestly"—the very words that I cited in my Princeton University thesis more than six decades ago. All too soon, it will be time for history to be the judge.

Some Investment Guidance

Yes, I've lived in an era where the many weaknesses of capitalism have come to the fore, and the challenges of building a better world for investors remain profound. Unless we undertake a serious reform of our financial system, the problems are likely to get even worse. So I conclude with the hope that this perspective on American capitalism, especially today's dominance of short-term speculation over long-term investment in the culture of finance, will help make you a more concerned citizen, a more aware investor, and a successful accumulator of assets for a more secure financial future.

But even despair over today's new culture of finance should not—*cannot*—preclude your participation in the world of investing. First, because *not* investing is the only way to guarantee that at the end of the line you'll have nothing. But second, beyond the crazy world of short-term speculation, there remain commonsense ways to invest for the long term and capture your fair share of the returns that are earned by our public corporations.

So for Chapter 9, the final chapter, I decided that the readers who have had the stick-to-itiveness to read through my ideas and histories and anecdotes deserve a modest reward: some rules (10, in fact) that will help those of you who are long-term investors reach your financial goals. The most important of these rules is the first one: the eternal law of reversion to the mean (RTM) in the financial markets. Most of us think that we can pick tomorrow's top funds by looking back to yesterday's winners. But I chart just eight examples of major mutual funds that once led the way in the mutual fund industry, only to falter, and even to die. (The same RTM principle prevails between the returns generated by the stock market itself and the investment returns earned by our public corporations, which I chart over the past century.) The only advice I have for short-term speculators is this warning: Stop!

Whether you endorse the theme of *The Clash of the Cultures* and seek a better financial system than the one we are stuck with today or whether you don't; whether you are satisfied or dissatisfied with the state of American capitalism today, *invest you must*. One day, we shall get our broken corporate/financial system fixed. For finally, "you can always count on Americans to do the right thing," as Churchill pointed out, "but only after they've tried everything else." So my final chapter offers some guidance intended to help you negotiate your way through the thicket that is today's financial system. My conclusion: "Stay the course."

So, if it meets your test of common sense and wisdom, please accept my advice for living through the coming era of booms and busts, where the debasement of ethical values and greed that enriches the insiders and diminishes the returns of investors will gradually recede. Then become part of the army of investors who will stand up and be counted, deal with the powerful challenges that await our society, and serve our great nation in the years ahead. "Press on, regardless."

Chapter 1

The Clash of the Cultures

When enterprise becomes the bubble on a whirlpool of speculation . . . [and] when the stock market takes on the attitude of a casino, the job [of capitalism] is likely to be ill-done.
                                                        —*John Maynard Keynes*

Throughout my long career, I've observed firsthand the crowding-out of the traditional and prudent culture of long-term investing by a new and aggressive culture of short-term speculation. But the personal experiences that I've outlined in the introduction to this book require deeper discussion—a broader view, an historical perspective, persuasive data—not only of the problems created by this change, but also of recommendations for fixing the nation's financial system. Those are the subjects that I intend to pursue in this chapter.

Let's begin by observing the consequences of the change in the culture of our financial system. When applied to the physical world, scientific techniques have been successfully used to determine cause and effect, helping us to predict and control our environment. This success has encouraged the idea that scientific techniques can be productively applied to all human endeavors, including investing. *But investing is not a science*. It is a human activity that involves both emotional as well as rational behavior.

1

Financial markets are far too complex to isolate any single variable with ease, as if conducting a scientific experiment. The record is utterly bereft of evidence that definitive predictions of short-term fluctuations in stock prices can be made with consistent accuracy. The prices of common stocks are evanescent and illusory. That's because equity shares are themselves merely *derivatives*—think about that!—of the returns created by our publicly held corporations and the vast and productive investments in physical capital and human capital that they represent.

Intelligent investors try to separate their emotions of hope, fear, and greed from their trust in reason, and then expect that wisdom will prevail over the long term. Hope, fear, and greed go along with the volatile market of short-term expectations, while trust in reason goes with the real market of long-term intrinsic value. In this sense, long-term investors must be philosophers rather than technicians. This difference suggests one of the great paradoxes of the financial sector of the U.S. economy today. Even as it becomes increasingly clear that a strategy of staying the course is inevitably far more productive than market timing, or than hopping from one stock—or a particular mutual fund—to another, the modern information and communications technology provided by our financial institutions make it increasingly easy for their clients and shareholders to engage in frequent and rapid movement of their investment assets.

The Rise of Speculation

The extent of this step-up in speculation—a word I've chosen as a proxy for rapid trading of financial instruments of all types—can be easily measured. Let's begin with stocks and their annual turnover rate, which is represented by the dollar value of trading volume as a percentage of market capitalization. When I entered this business in 1951, right out of college, annual turnover of U.S. stocks was about 15 percent. Over the next 15 years, turnover averaged about 35 percent. By the late 1990s, it had gradually increased to the 100 percent range, and hit 150 percent in 2005. In 2008, stock turnover soared to the remarkable level of 280 percent, declining modestly to 250 percent in 2011.

Think for a moment about the numbers that create these rates. When I came into this field 60 years ago, stock-trading volumes averaged about 2 *million* shares per day. In recent years, we have traded about 8.5 *billion* shares of stock daily—4,250 times as many. Annualized, the total comes to more than 2 trillion shares—in dollar terms, I estimate the trading to be worth some $33 trillion. That figure, in turn, is 220 percent of the $15 trillion market capitalization of U.S. stocks. To be sure, some of those purchases and sales are made by long-term investors. But even if we look at what are considered long-term investors, precious few measure up to that designation. In the mutual fund industry, for example, the annual rate of portfolio turnover for the average actively managed equity fund runs to almost 100 percent, ranging from a hardly minimal 25 percent for the lowest turnover quintile to an astonishing 230 percent for the highest quintile. (The turnover of all-stock-market index funds is about 7 percent.)

High-Frequency Trading

The numbers measuring stock market turnover include enormous trading through today's principal market makers: high-frequency traders (HFTs), who are said to presently constitute some 50 percent or more of the total market volume. These HFTs, in fairness, stand ready to provide liquidity to market participants, a valuable service offered for just pennies per share, with holding periods for their positions as short as 16 seconds. Yes, 16 seconds. (This multiple market system, however, has created significant inequities in order execution that demand a regulatory response.) The high demand for the services of HFTs comes not only from "punters"—sheer gamblers who thrive (or hope to thrive) by betting against the bookmakers—but from other diverse sources, as well. These traders may range from longer-term investors who value the liquidity and efficiency of HFTs to hedge fund managers who act with great speed based on perceived stock mispricing that may last only momentarily. This aspect of "price discovery," namely statistical arbitrage that often relies on complex algorithms, clearly enhances market efficiency, which is definitely a goal of short-term trading, but also benefits investors with a long-term focus.

Yes, HFTs add to the efficiency of stock market prices, and have slashed unit trading costs to almost unimaginably low levels. But these gains often come at the expense of deliberate investors, and expose the market to the risks of inside manipulation by traders with knowledge of future order flows. It is not yet clear whether the good aspects of HFT exceed the bad. But despite the claims that all this exotic liquidity is beneficial, one wonders just how much liquidity is actually necessary, and at what price? Paraphrasing Samuel Johnson on patriotism, I wonder if liquidity hasn't become "the last refuge of the scoundrel." There is also an emerging question as to whether, when the markets tumble, the HFTs don't withdraw their trading, depleting market liquidity just when it is needed most.

A few significant anomalies emerge from the large increase in transaction activity, of which HFT is now a major driver. Trading in index funds has also soared, and exchange-traded index funds now account for an astonishing 35 percent of the dollar amount of U.S. equity trading volume. Such trading has increased systemic risk in equities, increased cross-sectional trading volatility, and led to higher correlations among stocks and rising equity risks (measured by higher betas).[1] The benefit of the obvious improvements in liquidity and price discovery created by the current staggering volume of stock trading must be measured against these negative factors. "All that glitters isn't gold."

Mission Aborted

Consider now how these tens of trillions of dollars of stock transaction activity in the *secondary* market each year compare with transaction activity in the *primary* market. While the secondary market can be criticized as being highly speculative, the primary market provides, at least in theory, capitalism with its raison d'être. Providing fresh capital to business—let's call it capital formation—is generally accepted as the principal economic mission of Wall Street. That mission involves allocating investment capital to the most promising industries and companies,

[1]Rodney N. Sullivan and James X. Xiong, "How Index Trading Increases Market Vulnerability." See footnote 16 in Chapter 6.

both those existing businesses that seek to provide better goods and services at increasingly economic prices to consumers and businesses, and innovators of new businesses that seek to do the same, only de novo. The overwhelming consensus among academic economists agrees that this function provides the rationale for our financial system. But the importance of Wall Street to spurring healthy capital formation is also confirmed not only by the system's detractors, but by major market participants and regulatory leaders.

- Among investment bankers, Goldman Sachs's chief executive Lloyd C. Blankfein has worked hard to underline the social benefits of capital formation. While his claim to be doing "God's work" was a throwaway joke, he has correctly argued that the financial industry "helps companies to raise capital, generate wealth, and create jobs."
- Among the critics, hear *New York Times* columnist Jesse Eisinger: "The financial industry has strayed far from being an intermediary between companies that want to raise capital so they can sell people things they want. Instead, it is a machine to enrich itself, fleecing customers and widening income inequality. When it goes off the rails, it impoverishes the rest of us."
- For an independent view, hear Mary Schapiro, Chairman of the Securities and Exchange Commission: "At the end of the day, if the markets aren't serving their true function—which is as a place to raise capital for companies to create jobs, build factories, manufacture products—if the markets are not functioning as a rational way for investors to allocate their capital to those purposes, what's the point of markets?"

But in reality, how large is that capital formation activity? Let's begin with stocks. Total equity IPOs (initial public offerings) providing fresh capital to young companies have averaged $45 billion annually over the past five years, and secondary offerings providing additional equity capital have averaged about $205 billion, bringing total stock issuance to some $250 billion. The annual volume of stock trading averaged $33 *trillion* during that period, some 130 *times* the volume of equity capital provided to businesses. Put another way, that trading activity represents 99.2 percent of what our financial system does; capital formation represents the remaining 0.8 percent. Now, *that* is a sizable imbalance! What is almost universally understood to be Wall Street's mission has been aborted.

The issuance of corporate debt is another function of the economic mission of finance. Over the past decade, new corporate debt offerings averaged about $1.7 trillion annually. But fully $1 trillion of that was accounted for by the now virtually defunct area of asset-backed debt and mortgage-backed debt. Too often these securities were based on fraudulent lending and phony figures that were willingly accepted by our rating agencies, willing coconspirators in handing out AAA ratings to debt securities that would tumble in the recent debacle, their ratings finally slashed. I'm not at all sure that this massive flow of mortgage-backed debt is a tribute to the sacred cow of capital formation.

Futures and Derivatives

This huge wave of speculation in the financial markets is not limited to individual stocks. Trading in derivatives, whose values are derived from the prices of the underlying securities, has also soared. For example, trading in S&P 500-linked futures totaled more than $60 trillion(!) in 2011, five times the S&P 500 Index total market capitalization of $12.5 trillion. We also have credit default swaps, which are essentially bets on whether a corporation can meet the interest payments on its bonds. These credit default swaps alone had a notional value of $33 trillion. Add to this total a slew of other derivatives, whose notional value as 2012 began totaled a cool $708 *trillion*. By contrast, for what it's worth, the aggregate capitalization of the world's stock and bond markets is about $150 trillion, less than one-fourth as much. Is this a great financial system . . . or what!

Much of the trading in derivatives—including stock index futures, credit default swaps, and commodities—reflects risk aversion and hedging. However, a substantial portion—perhaps one-half or more—reflects risk seeking, or rank speculation, another component of the whirling dervish of today's trading activity. Most of this excessive speculation is built on a foundation of sand, hardly a sound basis for our financial well-being. Sooner or later—as the great speculative manias of the past such as

Tulipmania and the South Sea Bubble remind us—speculation will return to its proper and far more modest role in our financial markets. I'm not sure just when or how, but the population of investors will one day come to recognize the self-defeating nature of speculation, whether on Wall Street or in a casino.

I imagine that I'm not the only author who, poring over his manuscript yet one more time, gets a huge lift when he comes across a perceptive essay in a celebrated newspaper that (at least to the author!) endorses the ideas in his book, even the most controversial ones. So it was when I read the article in the March 3, 2012, issue of *The Economist*. You'll note that virtually every idea in the excerpt in Box 1.1 on the next page echoes the conclusions I express in these next few chapters.

The Wall Street Casino

Way back in 1999, I wrote an op-ed for *The New York Times* entitled "The Wall Street Casino." It called attention to the negative impact of the "feverish trading activity in stocks." At the time, daily trading volume averaged 1.5 billion shares, puny by today's standards. In 2010, the *Times* revisited the issue with an editorial with virtually the same title, "Wall Street Casino." It called attention to the even higher levels of speculation that had come to distort our markets and ill-serve our investors.

To understand why speculation is a drain on the resources of investors as a group, one need only understand the tautological nature of the markets: Investors, as a group, inevitably *earn* the gross return of, say, the stock market, but only before the deduction of the costs of financial intermediation are taken into account. If beating the market is a zero-sum game *before* costs, it is a loser's game *after* costs are deducted. How often we forget the power of these "relentless rules of humble arithmetic" (a phrase used in another context by former Supreme Court Justice Louis Brandeis a century ago), when we bet against one another, day after day—inevitably, to no avail—in the stock market.

Over time, the drain of those costs is astonishing. Yet far too few investors seem to understand the impact of that simple arithmetic, which ultimately causes investors to relinquish a huge portion of the long-term returns that our stock market delivers. Even if the cost of financial market

Box 1.1

The Economist of London Speaks

"Short-Changed—The Stock Market Is Not Fit for Purpose,"
by Buttonwood

"The main economic functions of the equity markets are twofold. The first is that savers can participate in economic growth by linking their savings to business profits. The second is to encourage the efficient allocation of capital. These are long-term goals that have virtually nothing to do with the daily fluctuations of the market. The problem is that the regulatory framework has increasingly moved to favor liquidity and trading activity over long-term ownership. . . . The result is an excessive focus on short-term targets. . . .

"Worse still, such frequent reporting has forced bosses to focus on "beating the numbers" at the expense of long-term planning. . . . Performance measures such as earnings per share or return on equity may encourage excessive risk-taking.

"Why haven't shareholders redressed the balance? . . . (Because) most shares are no longer owned by private investors, but by professional fund managers. Those managers are themselves judged on the basis of short-term measures and on their performance relative to a stock market index.

"In short, the current market structure does not seem fit for purpose. How to fix it is not clear. There is clearly no silver bullet. Rewards for long-term shareholders, in the form of tax breaks or better voting rights, may be part of the answer. Smarter rules on executive pay wouldn't hurt. Above all, it would help to remember that the stock market serves a wider goal. It is not supposed to be a sophisticated version of the National Lottery."

activity—transaction costs, advisory fees, sales loads, and administrative costs—totals as little as 2 percent a year, its long-term impact is huge. Over today's likely 60-year investment lifetime for young investors just starting out, for example, an initial investment earning a 7 percent market return would produce an aggregate gain of 5,600 percent. But after those costs, the return would drop to 5 percent and the cumulative gain to 1,700 percent—less than one-third as much.

The reality of the investment business is that as a group, we investors don't get what we pay for, which is the returns earned by our corporations. We get precisely what we *don't* pay for. So, as strange as it sounds, the less we pay as a group, the more we get. And if we pay nothing, (or almost nothing, as in an all-stock-market index fund) we get everything, the market return. There's simply no way 'round these mathematics of the markets. This financial math, of course, is the very same model as the casino math on which the so-called gaming industry relies. The winning clients' good luck is balanced by the losing clients' bad luck. But regardless of winners or losers, the croupiers rake off the house share of every bet. It's not just Las Vegas or Foxwoods or Atlantic City, but it's also our pervasive state lotteries (think Mega Millions and Powerball), except that in these giant lotteries, the croupier's take, relative to the amount wagered, is even higher than in the Wall Street casino and our nation's racetracks and gambling dens.

Calling Wall Street a casino, of course, is not entirely fair. Wall Street is more than that. It provides the liquidity on which long-term investors as well as short-term speculators rely. Wall Street also facilitates the capital formation mentioned earlier, however small relative to today's stock market volumes. But every once in a while, even a market insider acknowledges the similarity. Late in 2010, a senior executive of Wall Street powerhouse Cantor Fitzgerald owned up to the obvious, stating, "I don't see any difference between Las Vegas Boulevard and Wall Street: Over time we can't lose, but there will be games where we take a hit."

This executive is explaining why Cantor Fitzgerald, one of the largest brokers in super-safe (so far!) U.S. government securities, is now running sports bookmaking at a new casino in Las Vegas. "There's big money in . . . moving onto the strip," another Cantor executive added, especially through a new license that allows sports betting, roulette, and slot machines (so far, only in Nevada) on mobile devices. Could Wall Street, where you can now trade stocks on cell phones, be far behind? Indeed, with all the computing power, the technology, the quantification, and the algorithms we have today—and the enormous size of financial gambling relative to casino gaming—Wall Street already is far ahead.

How Speculation Overwhelmed Investment

Today's domination of financial markets by the loser's game of speculation over the winner's game of investment is no accident. It has been fostered by critical changes in the elements of investing. First in my list of causes is the decline of the old ownership society in favor of a new agency society where the tables have been turned. In 1950, individual investors held 92 percent of U.S. stocks and institutional investors held 8 percent. The roles have flipped, with institutions, now holding 70 percent, predominating, and individuals, now holding 30 percent, playing a secondary role. Simply put, these institutional agents now collectively hold firm voting control over Corporate America. (I discuss these agency issues much more fully in Chapter 2.)

Originally managers of pension funds and mutual funds, and later of hedge funds, these new investor/agents were hardly unaware of their own financial interests. As a group—with far too few exceptions—they took advantage of their agency by charging high advisory fees and adopting investment policies that focused on the short-term. In part, they recognized that their clients would judge them based on these terms. Mutual fund managers capitalized on the reality that hot, short-term performance—even though it couldn't last (and didn't)—would enrich them with higher fees. In order to reduce pension contributions and enhance short-term earnings, corporate pension executives projected totally unrealistic high future returns. State and local government officials, pressed by labor unions for higher wages and pensions, not only did the same, but failed to provide financial disclosure that revealed—or even hinted at—the dire long-term financial consequences that are already beginning to emerge.

The Decline in Unit Transaction Costs

It wasn't just the rise in institutional ownership that fueled the rise of speculation. Speculation was also fueled by the dramatic decline in transaction costs. Simply put, trading stocks got a whole lot cheaper. Taxes virtually disappeared as a limiting factor in stock sales. The lion's share of the assets managed by these now-dominant, powerful investment institutions were in accounts managed for tax-deferred investors such as pension plans and thrift plans, and in tax-exempt accounts such as endowment funds. Even for taxable clients, mutual fund managers supervised the assets in very much the same way, simply ignoring the tax impact and passing the tax liability through to largely unsuspecting fund shareholders. So over time, these agents came to ignore income taxes and capital gains taxes, essentially eliminating them as a major frictional cost in executing portfolio transactions, a cost that had helped to deter rapid stock trading in an earlier era.

Next, in a wonderful example of the law of unintended consequences, commissions on stock trading were slashed, virtually removing the trading cost of transactions. Fixed commissions of about 25 cents per share that had pretty much prevailed up until 1974 were eliminated in favor of commissions set in a free market. Wall Street, otherwise a bastion of free-market capitalism, fought the change to competitive rates with vigor (and money), but finally lost. The decimalization of stock prices, begun in 2001, also took its toll as commissions fell to pennies per share as *unit costs* of stock trading were reduced to bare-bones minimums. Nonetheless, with soaring trading volumes, Wall Street's *total commission revenues* appear to have doubled in the past decade, more than making up for the decline in rates.

It may be stating the obvious to note that great bull markets often foster speculative activity. After all, how much measurable harm could even the earlier drag of taxes and commissions inflict on returns when the S&P 500 Index rose more than tenfold from 140 in 1982 to 1,520 at the 2000 high? What's more, when a culture of high-volume trading becomes embedded in the system, even a bear market that took the S&P 500 to a low of 680 in the spring of 2009 couldn't break the trend toward high trading activity. In some respects, the events of the past few years seem actually to have enhanced the rate of speculation.

Hedge Fund Managers and Other Speculators

The development of this culture of speculation was accelerated by a new breed of institutional investor—the hedge fund, which typically turns over its portfolios at a 300–400 percent annual rate. From a single U.S. hedge fund in 1949, the field has burgeoned to some 4,600 hedge funds today, with assets under management of some $2 trillion, albeit down from $2.5 trillion at their peak a few years ago. While some hedge funds have had remarkably good performance, the failure rate, which is the rate that funds that go out of business, is large. Indeed, some estimates suggest that the failure rate is around 20 percent, meaning that each year, one of every five hedge funds goes up in smoke. Including the earlier records of such funds with those of hedge funds that have survived, they seem to perform no better than, well, average.

For example, over the past 10 years the average hedge fund pro-duced an annual return after fees (but before taxes) of 4.6 percent, compared to 6.2 percent for a pioneering, stodgy, low-risk, low-cost conservative balanced mutual fund named Wellington Fund. Since the traditional "2 and 20" management fee structure—2 percent of assets annually, plus the "carry" of 20 percent of realized and unrealized profits—likely consumed as many as 3 percentage points a year of the *gross* returns of the average hedge fund, small wonder that the *net* returns have been, at best, undistinguished. (I write more about Wellington's costs in Chapter 8.)

While hedge funds may have led the speculative wave, many pension funds and mutual funds also moved toward the new, quanti-tatively oriented, high-turnover strategies, as ever more sophisticated computer hardware and software made data almost universally available. Analysts and academics alike massaged the seemingly infinite data on stock prices to the nth degree, often using complex techniques—relative valuations, classes of stock (growth versus value, large versus small, etc.), market momentum, changes in earnings estimates, and many others.

Each of these models was designed to provide *positive Alpha* (excess return over a market benchmark), which came to be seen as the Holy Grail of consistent performance superiority. But too few in the profession asked the existential question: Does that Holy Grail actually exist? No. Positive Alpha does not exist—cannot exist—for investors as a group, who earn zero Alpha before costs, and negative Alpha after costs.

Another great fomenter of this new rapid trading environment was, of course, *money*. Not only big money for hedge fund managers, but big money for brokers and investment bankers, big money for mutual fund managers; and, collectively at least, big money for all those lawyers, marketers, record keepers, accountants, prime brokers, and bankers who are part of the extraordinarily well-paid constituency of our casino society. Inevitably, as noted earlier, every dollar of this big money comes directly out of the pockets of the industry's clients.

In fairness, the rise of speculation also seems to reflect a broader change in our national culture. All across American life, trusted professions—traditionally focused on service to the community—have increasingly taken on the characteristics of businesses—focused on maximizing profits to providers of capital, too often at the expense of the moral values of an earlier age. What's more, a gambling culture, always part of our society, seemed to first strengthen and then ultimately prevail, a diversion from the hard times that so many of our families are going through.

Whether gambling on stocks or in casinos (where the odds are even worse), we have given even the relatively wealthy a means to quickly build their wealth, and low-income families who need it most an opportunity to prosper at last—even though the odds that they will succeed are terribly long. What's more, we Americans like to buy things—in abundance—before we have the cash to pay for them. We focus on today's wants rather than tomorrow's needs. Even our wealthiest citizens never seem to have *enough*. We compare ourselves with our neighbors and, since the realities of life can be so hard to overcome, we look to speculation—even at long odds—to lift us out of the everyday-ness of our lives.

We Can't Say We Weren't Warned

Long ago, the possibility that speculation would come to play a far larger role in finance concerned the legendary investor Benjamin Graham. Way back in 1958, in his address to the New York Society of Financial Analysts, he described what he saw as the coming change in culture as "some contrasting relationships between the present and the past in our underlying attitudes toward investment and speculation in common stocks." Some excerpts from this address follow in Box 1.2.

Box 1.2

The Prescience of Benjamin Graham—1958

"In the past, the speculative elements of a common stock resided almost exclusively in the company itself; they were due to uncertainties, or fluctuating elements, or downright weaknesses in the industry, or the corporation's individual setup. . . . But in recent years a new and major element of speculation has been introduced into the common-stock arena from outside the companies. It comes from the attitude and viewpoint of the stock-buying public and their advisers—chiefly us security analysts. This attitude may be described in a phrase: primary emphasis upon future expectations.

"The concept of future prospects and particularly of continued growth in the future invites the application of formulas out of higher mathematics to establish the present value of the favored issues. But the combination of precise formulas with highly imprecise assumptions can be used to establish, or rather to justify, practically any value one wished, however high.

"Given the three ingredients of (a) optimistic assumptions as to the rate of earnings growth, (b) a sufficiently long projection of this growth into the future, and (c) the miraculous workings of compound interest—lo! The security analyst is supplied with a new kind of philosopher's stone that can produce or justify any desired valuation for a really "good stock."

"Mathematics is ordinarily considered as producing precise and dependable results; but in the stock market the more elaborate and abstruse the mathematics, the more uncertain and speculative are the conclusions we draw therefrom. . . . Whenever calculus is brought in, or higher algebra, you could take it as a warning signal that the operator was trying to substitute theory for experience, and usually also to give to speculation the deceptive guise of investment.

"Have not investors and security analysts eaten of the tree of knowledge of good and evil prospects? By so doing have they not permanently expelled themselves from that Eden where promising common stocks at reasonable prices could be plucked off the bushes?"

Graham's reference to Original Sin reflected his deep concern about quantifying the unquantifiable, and doing so with false precision. When Graham spoke these words in 1958, the consequences of that bite into the apple of quantitative investing were barely visible. But by the late 1990s, this new form of investment behavior had become a dominant force that continues to be a major driver of the speculation that has overwhelmed our financial markets. Eden is nowhere to be seen.

The Wisdom of John Maynard Keynes

Years before Benjamin Graham gave his landmark speech in 1958, we were also warned about excessive speculation by another legendary figure. The great British economist John Maynard Keynes drew a firm distinction between investment and speculation, and did so in words of great clarity and simplicity.

The change in the culture of financial markets—the broad trend toward the dominance of speculation over investment—and in the conduct, values, and ethics of so many market participants has been fostered by the profound change that has taken place in the *nature* of our financial markets. That change, largely unnoticed, reflects two radically different views of what investing is all about, two distinct markets, if you will. One is the *real* market of intrinsic business value. The other is the *expectations* market of momentary stock prices.

It's a curious coincidence that I've been concerned about this sharp dichotomy ever since I first encountered Lord Keynes in my study of economics at Princeton University as an undergraduate student. Really! In my 1951 senior thesis, inspired by a 1949 article in *Fortune* on the then "tiny but contentious" mutual fund industry, I cited a critical distinction made by Lord Keynes. He separated "forecasting the prospective yield of the asset over its whole life"—*enterprise* (what I call *investment*)—from *speculation*—"forecasting the psychology of the markets."

Speculation Will Crowd Out Investment

Keynes was deeply concerned about the societal implications of the growing role of short-term speculation on stock prices. "A conventional valuation [of stocks] which is established [by] the mass psychology of a large number of ignorant individuals," he wrote in 1936, "is liable to change violently as the result of a sudden fluctuation of opinion due to factors which do not really matter much to the prospective yield . . . resulting in unreasoning waves of optimistic and pessimistic sentiment."

Then, prophetically, Lord Keynes predicted that this trend would intensify, as even "expert professionals, possessing judgment and knowledge beyond that of the average private investor, would become concerned, not with making superior long-term forecasts of the probable yield on an investment over its entire life, but with forecasting changes in the conventional valuation a short time ahead of the general public." As a result, Keynes warned, the stock market would become "a battle of wits to anticipate the basis of conventional valuation a few months hence, rather than the prospective yield of an investment over a long term of years."

In my thesis, I cited those very words, and then had the temerity to disagree with the great man. Portfolio managers, in what I predicted—accurately, as it turned out—would become a far larger mutual fund industry, and would "supply the market with a demand for securities that is *steady, sophisticated, enlightened, and analytic* [italics added], a demand that is based essentially on the [intrinsic] performance of a corporation [Keynes's *enterprise*], rather than the public appraisal of the value of a share, that is, its price [Keynes's *speculation*]."

Alas, the steady, sophisticated, enlightened, and analytic demand that I had predicted from our expert professional investors is now only rarely to be seen. Quite the contrary! Our money managers, following Oscar Wilde's definition of the cynic, seem to know "the price of everything but the value of nothing." As the infant fund industry matured, the steady, sophisticated, enlightened, and analytic demand that I had predicted utterly failed to materialize, while speculative demand soared. So, six decades after I wrote those words in my thesis, I must reluctantly concede the obvious: Keynes's sophisticated cynicism was right, and Bogle's callow idealism was wrong. Call it Keynes 1—Bogle 0. But that doesn't mean we should allow that system to prevail forever.

Fixing the Social Contract

Today's dominance of a culture based on short-term speculation instead of long-term investment has major implications that go far beyond the narrow confines of our financial sector. It distorts our markets and ultimately distorts the way our businesses are run. If market participants demand short-term results and predictable earnings in an inevitably unpredictable world, corporations respond accordingly. When they do, there is heavy pressure to reduce the workforce, to cut corners, to rethink expenditures on research and development, and to undertake mergers in order to "make the numbers" (and often to muddy the accounting waters).

When companies are compelled by short-term speculators to earn a return on their capital as it is valued by the price of its stock set by the *expectations* market, rather than the intrinsic value of the capital provided to them by their shareholders in the *real* market, the task of fulfilling the two roles can become nigh impossible. Indeed, any attempts to do so may lead to dire consequences for company employees, for their communities, for the integrity of the products and services they provide, and even for their long-term viability. When a corporation's focus on meeting Wall Street's expectations (even its demands) takes precedence over providing products and services that meet the ever-more-demanding needs of today's customers, the corporation is unlikely to serve our society as it should. Yet that corporation's service to its customers and the broader society is the ultimate goal of free-market capitalism.

Perhaps even more important, we've largely lost the essential link between corporate managers and corporate owners. Ownership has its privileges—one of the most important of which is to ensure that the interests of shareholders are served before the interests of management. But most short-term *renters* of stocks are not particularly interested in assuring that corporate governance is focused on placing the interests of the stockholder first. Even long-term *owners* of stocks have not seemed to care very much about exercising their rights—and indeed their responsibilities—of stock ownership.

The agency society I've described earlier has too often failed to lend itself to significant involvement in corporate governance. Index funds ought to be in the vanguard of serious reforms, for they can't and don't sell stocks of companies whose managements are deemed to have produced inadequate returns on the capital they oversee. Despite the growing importance of index funds, many managers are loath to rock the boat, let alone engage in a more muscular activism, including proxy proposals, director nominations, executive compensation, and vigorous advocacy.

Compensation Issues

Consider executive compensation. While it is now absurdly excessive, it is generally ignored by shareowners. Consider, too, the corporate political contributions, only now subject to even limited disclosure to the funds' owners. Part of the challenge is that our institutional investors too often have a different agenda from that of the fund shareholders and pension beneficiaries they represent. Like the corporate managers they oversee, these money managers are too often inclined to put their own interests first, taking advantage of their agency position. (I discuss both of these subjects—the agents who manage our corporations and the large investment pools, and participation in corporate governance—in more depth in the following two chapters—"The Double-Agency Society and the Happy Conspiracy" and "The Silence of the Funds.")

It is surely one of the great paradoxes of the day that the largest financial rewards in our nation are received by an investment community that *subtracts* value from its clients, with far smaller rewards received by a business community that *adds* value to society. Ultimately, such a system is all too likely to bring social discord to our society and engender a harsh public reaction to today's record disparity between the tiny top echelon of income recipients and the great mass of families at the base. The highest-earning 0.01 percent of U.S. families (150,000 in number), for example, now receives 10 percent of all of the income earned by the remaining 150 million families, three *times* the 3 to 4 percent share that prevailed from 1945 to 1980. It is no secret that about 35,000 of those families have made their fortunes on Wall Street.

Creating Value versus Subtracting Value

In yet another distortion aided and abetted by our financial system, too many of the best and brightest young people in our land, instead of becoming scientists, physicians, educators, or public servants, are attracted by the staggering financial incentives offered in the investment industry. These massive rewards serve to divert vital human resources from other, often more productive and socially useful, pursuits. Even in the field of engineering, "financial" engineering, which is essentially *rent-seeking* in nature, holds sway over "real" engineering—civil, electrical, mechanical, aeronautical, and so on—which is essentially *value-creating*. The long-term consequences of these trends simply cannot be favorable to our nation's wealth, growth, productivity, and global competitiveness.

Finally, the dominance of speculation in our financial affairs shifts our society's focus from the enduring reality of corporate value creation, on which our nation ultimately depends, to the momentary illusion of stock prices. We spend far too much of the roughly $600 billion annual cost of our investment sector on what is essentially gambling. It may be intelligent and informed gambling, but gambling on the notion that the wit and wisdom and algorithms of one firm can capture an enduring advantage over another has been shown over and over again to be a bad gamble. (Evidence supporting the systematic achievement of sustained superiority simply does not exist.) So perhaps we should listen carefully when Lord Adair Turner, chairman of Britain's Financial Services Authority, describes much of what happens in the world's financial centers as "socially useless activity." I have often pointed out much the same thing: "The stock market is a giant distraction from the business of investing."

Once again, I'm not alone in my concern about this obvious dominance of the culture of speculation over the culture of investment in
our financial markets. Indeed, I'm proud to associate my philosophy
with that of legendary financial economist Henry Kaufman, whose
wisdom places him in the top echelon of the worthy mentors of my long
career. In Box 1.3 I present excerpts from his 2001 book *On Money and
Markets: A Wall Street Memoir*. While his words were written a decade-
plus ago, they hit home even more strongly in the years following the
2008 financial crisis that has slammed into our economy, our society, and
our communities, it is high time that we take his wisdom to heart.

Box 1.3

The Timeless Wisdom of Henry Kaufman (2001)

"The United States has not sustained a proper balance between
financial conservatism and financial entrepreneurship—the
fundamental and long-standing tension between two broad
financial groups. At one end of the spectrum are financial
conservatives, who favor preserving the status quo in the marketplace and hold in high esteem the traditional values of
prudence, stability, safety, and soundness. At the opposite end
are financial entrepreneurs—risk takers restlessly searching to
exploit anomalies and imperfections in the market for profitable
advantage. They consider existing laws and regulations to be fair
game, ripe to be tested and challenged.

"The modern quantitative and econometric techniques
developed in the last generation have given investors and portfolio
managers a new sense of confidence in the ability to forecast
financial trends and behaviors. By compiling and analyzing historical data, and by building models that take into account current
variables, econometricians often try to predict the movement of
interest rates, stock prices, inflation, unemployment, and so on.
During times of financial euphoria and investor panic, however,

these techniques become virtually worthless. The reason is fairly simple: The vast majority of models rest on assumptions about normal and rational financial behavior. But during market manias, logical and analytical minds do not prevail. Such markets are driven more by hubris, elation, fear, pessimism, and the like—emotions that the current models do not, and perhaps cannot, compute.

"People in finance are entrusted with an extraordinary responsibility: other people's money. This basic fiduciary duty too often has been forgotten in the high-voltage, high-velocity financial environment that has emerged in recent decades. With the absorbing excitement of the trading floor—which for some becomes a sort of game, an end in itself—the notion of financial trusteeship is frequently lost in the shuffle. In the final analysis, the tilt toward unbridled financial entrepreneurship has exacted economic costs that often far outweigh their economic benefits. Only by improving the balance between entrepreneurial innovation and more traditional values—prudence, stability, safety, soundness—can we improve the ratio of benefits to costs in our economic system.

"Today's financial community is suffering from a bad case of amnesia. Most Wall Streeters are unaware of or have forgotten about the damaging effects of irresponsible behavior in their rush to "innovate" and profit. Business majors at most colleges and universities were once required to take courses in business and financial history, while the history of economics and economic thought was a staple in economics programs. This is no longer the case. In their entrancement with new quantitative methods, most business schools long ago abandoned their historically oriented courses. Anything having to do with the qualitative side of business practice—ethics, business culture, history, and the like—was subordinated or eliminated as being too "soft" and "impractical." Yet only a long historical perspective can help us sort out what is lasting and salient from what is ephemeral and faddish. In finance, as in all human endeavors, history has valuable lessons to teach."

Restoring Balance in Our Investment Sector

Although our financial sector in many ways functions in a different fashion from our productive economy, the two are hardly independent. As the economist Hyman Minsky has pointed out, "Since finance and industrial development are in a symbiotic relationship, financial evolution plays a crucial role in the dynamic patterns of our economy."

So, the dominance of today's speculative orientation requires not only thought but also corrective action. In the effort to restore a sounder balance between investment and speculation in our financial sector, there are many actions that we should consider. While each has much to recommend it, any action must withstand rigorous intellectual analysis of its consequences, and also withstand the resistance of powerful detractors with vested interests in the status quo. So now let's consider some of the possibilities, as well as the benefits to society, if we can better rebalance the two cultures of investors.

Tax Policies and Financial Transactions

Taxes can be brought back into play, replacing some of the frictional costs of investing that served to moderate the speculation that prevailed in an earlier era. Years ago, Warren Buffett suggested a tax on very short-term capital gains realized by both taxable and tax-deferred investors. (He says he was speaking tongue-in-cheek.) Alternatively, taxes on transactions, as suggested by professor James Tobin years ago, should be considered— perhaps in the range of one to five basis points (0.01 percent–0.05 percent of the value of the transaction). It should be paid by both the buyer and the seller of the shares, but not by the market makers. This kind of Pigouvian tax,[2] which is essentially a "sin" tax designed to elicit appropriate behavior, is generally unpopular not only with investment managers, but with economists as well. But it deserves a fair hearing. Less radically, disallowance of the tax deduction for short-term losses is also an idea worth pursuing. Yes, the lower trading volumes that would likely result from tax changes such as these could negatively impact liquidity in

---

[2]After Arthur Cecil Pigou, British economist of the early twentieth century.

our markets, but do we really need today's staggering levels of turnover, quantum amounts above the norms of a half-century ago?

Taxes on earnings from stock trading should also be considered. A century ago, President Theodore Roosevelt distinguished between activities with positive utility that add value to our society and activities with negative utility that subtract value from our society. He referred to speculators as "the men who seek gain, not by genuine work, but by gambling." If trading pieces of paper is akin to gambling (remember the earlier "casino" example), why should trading profits not be subject to *higher* rates? Yet we live in an Alice-in-Wonderland world in which even that hedge fund "carry" mentioned earlier is subject to substantially *lower* rates. Such income is subject only to the minimal taxes applicable to long-term capital gains rather than the higher taxes on ordinary earned income. I can't imagine how our legislators can continue to endorse such an absurd and unfair tax subsidy, one that favors highly paid stock traders over the modestly paid workers who, by the sweat of their brows and the furrows of their brains, provide the valuable products and services that give our nation the living standards that are the envy of the world.

Develop Limits on Leverage, Transparency for Derivatives, and Stricter Punishments for Financial Crimes

We need stronger, smarter, and wiser regulation that is principles-based where possible, and rules-based in all other cases. No, I do not believe that our government should run our financial sector. But I would be willing to accept the cost of its inevitable bureaucratic drag on the system since, after all, most government activity itself is also rent-seeking rather than value-adding. Regulation is needed in order to:

- Establish and enforce sterner limits, as appropriate, on leverage and portfolio quality.
- Bring the opacity of today's derivatives trading into the bright sunlight of transparency and openness, with public reporting of all transactions.

- Develop much stronger rules that would preclude—or at least minimize—obvious malfeasance such as insider trading, conflicts of interest, and the remarkably widespread Ponzi schemes that we've recently witnessed.

Yes, the Dodd-Frank Wall Street Reform and Consumer Protection Act of 2010 attempted to deal with some of these issues. Certainly derivative transparency will be a plus, as will new requirements for banks' capital. But after all the horse trading between Democrats and Republicans—and reformers, bankers, and lobbyists—I fear that its complex, obtuse regulations (some 170 separate rules are still being developed) involved in limiting proprietary trading by banks makes me wish we'd taken the simple step of restoring the separation of *deposit taking* banks from *investment* banks. The Glass-Steagall Act of 1933 worked well until it was gradually eroded and finally repealed in 1999.

We've had too much crime and not enough punishment in our financial sector. I'd like to see far harsher penalties for white-collar criminals who abuse their clients' trust. But, I salute the federal authorities for bringing wire-tapping into play in their prosecutions of insider trading, earning tough victories over highly placed executives who thought they could get away with breaking the law. The jail sentences now being imposed will do more to deter these criminals than any other form of punishment. We also need far better data on most of the issues I've raised in this chapter. Sound regulation can foster such transparency, and the new Dodd-Frank–created Office of Financial Research (OFR) will be a big step. So will the parallel Bureau of Consumer Protection, now at least functioning after an ugly political dogfight.

The Rules of the Game

The rules of the game and the appropriate behavior of its players also must be regulated. However, I hold as a general principle that government should, under nearly all circumstances, keep its hands off the free functioning of the marketplace. I wince when the Federal Reserve states its intention to raise asset prices—including "higher stock prices"—apparently irrespective of the level of underlying intrinsic stock values.

Substantive limits on short selling are another nonstarter for me. The overriding principle should be: *Let the markets clear*, at whatever prices that willing and informed buyers agree to pay to willing and informed (but often better-informed) sellers.

Individual investors need to wake up. Adam Smith—like, they need to look after their own best interests. Of course, that would mean that individual investors must demand much better, clearer, and more pointed disclosures. We need a campaign to educate investors about the hard realities of investing. Investors need to understand not only the magic of compounding long-term returns, but the tyranny of compounding costs; costs that ultimately overwhelm that magic. (I presented the math earlier in this chapter.) Investors need to know about sensible asset allocation and the value of diversification; they need to understand the huge gap that exists between the illusion of *nominal* returns and the reality of *real* (after-inflation) returns; they need to recognize that short-term trading—like casino gambling—is ultimately a loser's game, and they need to understand the demonstrated costs of the behavioral flaws that plague so many market participants. As I suggested earlier— *investments usually perform better than investors*.

Our financial money manager/agents should focus primarily on long-term investment, to act as prudent trustees of the "other people's money" that they oversee. Financial institutions are trustees, they should behave as such. Investment professionals need to do a far better job of due diligence. We need to focus on investment fundamentals. We need to assume the rights and responsibilities of corporate governance. We need to take on an activist role in assuring that the companies whose shares our institutional manager/agents hold and control are run in the interest of the investor/principals whom we are bound to serve as fiduciary agents. A big step in the right direction would be the enactment of a federal standard of fiduciary duty for those who put themselves forth as trustees. This standard would include a long-term investment focus, due diligence in security selection, participation in corporate affairs, reasonable fees and costs, and the elimination of conflicts of interest. (In Chapters 3 and 4, I discuss the subject of fiduciary duty and explain some standards for measuring it.)

Finally—and this may surprise you—we institutional managers need a far deeper sense of caring about our clients' interests to permeate our conduct and values. We need introspection—that rarest of qualities—from today's leaders of our financial sector as well as tomorrow's. We need leaders with integrity and wisdom, leaders with a sense of history; a sense of the conditions, practices, and character of our present financial sector; and a sense of what we want our field to look like in the decades down the road. It all comes down to a better understanding of what has been, what is, and what will be. Is today's system what we would design if we were present at the creation of a new system designed to serve our investors, our communities, and our society at large? If we can do better, isn't it time for those of us who care about the future of the financial profession to stand up and be counted? As it is said, "If I am not for myself, then who will be for me? And if I am only for myself, then what am I? And if not now, when?"

The Goal: Stewardship Capitalism

We must seek a financial sector of a size appropriate to its capital formation responsibilities, to its ability to provide liquidity for long-term investors as well as speculators, and to its responsibility for our nation's 150 million individual investors. We must seek an investment sector in which a culture of stewardship and longer-term thinking dominates a culture of speculation, short-term trading, salesmanship, and marketing, however necessary they may be in moderate doses. We must seek a culture of financial trusteeship and fiduciary duty that should play the *starring role* in the long saga of investment, with entrepreneurial innovation and speculation playing only a *supporting role*—the exact opposite of the way the system works today. In this new and better-balanced culture, our financial sector should do a far better job of earning sound returns for our investors at competitive costs, all the while assuming reasonable risks. It is the responsibility of our financial system to deliver to our nation's families—who are ultimately the providers of all of the capital investment in our economy—their fair share of whatever returns our corporate businesses are able to generate over an investment lifetime.

In the course we choose, there's a lot at stake for today's beleaguered system of free market capitalism. Lord Keynes got it right with the warning with which I began this chapter: *When enterprise becomes the bubble on a whirlpool of speculation . . . [and] when the stock market takes on the attitude of a casino, the job [of capitalism] is likely to be ill-done.* No matter how each of us may feel about the issues raised in this chapter, that's the one thing that none of us can afford to have happen. For free market capitalism is the best system ever devised for the allocation of economic resources, risks, and rewards. In Chapter 2, I discuss how its proper functioning was so substantially diminished during the recent era.

Chapter 2

The Double-Agency Society and the Happy Conspiracy

In the short run, the stock market is a *voting* machine; in the long run it is a *weighing* machine.
—*Benjamin Graham,* Security Analysis (*1934)*

I described the pervasive bullishness of the moment as the result of the "happy conspiracy" among corporate managers, CEOs and CFOs, directors, auditors, lawyers, Wall Street investment bankers, sell side security analysts, buy side portfolio managers, and indeed investors themselves—individual and institutional alike.
—*John C. Bogle,* The Battle for the
Soul of Capitalism (*2005)*

The "double-agency society" is, I suspect, a phrase that most readers have not encountered before in this context. But it has become a critical factor in the corporate/financial structure of our nation. The first agency society developed in our business culture two centuries ago. Beginning with the Industrial Revolution, the

ownership of corporations shifted from founding families and entrepreneurs to public shareholders. But corporate managers—agents,
entrusted to place the interests of shareholders first—far too often took
advantage of their agency, placing their own interests in the pre-eminent
position over the interests of their principals.

The second agency society, unprecedented in history, began to
develop with the rise of our financial corporations a half-century ago.
Giant aggregations of capital began to be accumulated by pension funds,
mutual funds, and other managers of investment capital. Today, these
agents have become by far the dominant owners of U.S. corporations.
But, like their corporate agent cousins, they also succumbed too often to
placing their own interests ahead of their principals—those mutual fund
shareholders and pension beneficiaries (and others)—to whom they owe
a fiduciary duty.

Together, these two sets of agents came to an apparent, if tacit,
understanding that the principal focus of corporate accomplishment is
"creating shareholder value." That's a fine goal, of course, but their
shared definition of value focused on the short-term, evanescent,
emotion-driven price of the stock, rather than the long-term, solid,
reality-driven intrinsic value of the corporation.

It is the interlocking interests of both sets of agents—aligned in this
focus on the expectation market rather than the intrinsic value of the
corporation in the real market—that I describe as "the happy conspiracy." Happy for the agents, to be sure. But because our financial markets
gradually became dominated by "short-termism," unhappy for the
investors they serve. This change in the financial environment has been
the major force in the change from a financial culture predominantly
based on the wisdom of long-term investment to a culture now driven
largely by the folly of short-term speculation.

The Development of the Double-Agency Society

We begin this chapter with a brief sweep over the history that has
brought us to this point, in which an unhealthy symbiotic relationship
has developed among market participants. The interests of the bottom
owner/principals have too often been given short shrift to the interests

of their two agents: the corporate manager/agents of our giant corporations, and money manager/agents in the new and unprecedented *double-agency society* of the recent era.

The nature of this largely tacit conspiracy is not complex, and its web is wide. It includes the managers of our giant corporations—their CEOs and CFOs, directors, auditors, and lawyers—and Wall Street—investment bankers, sell-side analysts, buy-side research departments and the managers of our giant investment institutions. Their shared goal: to increase the price of a firm's stock, the better to please "the Street," to raise the value of its currency for acquisitions, to enhance the profits executives realize when they exercise their stock options, to entice employees to own stock in its thrift plan, and to make the shareholders happy.

How to accomplish this objective? Project high long-term earnings growth, offer regular guidance to the financial community as to your short-term progress, and, whether by fair means or foul, *never* fall short of the expectations you've established. Ultimately, these ambitious goals are doomed to failure for our corporations as a group. Yes, some firms will dazzle us with their performance (think Apple computer; so far so good). But ultimately our corporations as a group are destined to grow at roughly the pace of our nation's GDP. That growth rate has averaged 6 percent per year in nominal terms, and 3 percent per year after adjustment for inflation. In the so-called "new normal" economy that many experts expect, the growth rates are expected to fall to 5 percent nominal, 2 percent real. Focusing on long-term forces is the soundest basis for true investing; focusing on short-term forces—as we do today—is speculation.

Ever since the rise of what we might call modern-day capitalism—beginning with the Industrial Revolution—the owners of large corporations have entrusted their supervision and direction to professional managers. These agents have been expected to honor their fiduciary duty to place the interests of their shareholders before their own interests. While this system worked fairly well—at least most of the time, with most of the managers, and with most of the shareholders—its traditional values were gradually eroded by the same temptations that have challenged agent/principal relationships since the beginning of time: the natural temptation for agents to enrich themselves at the expense of their principals.

To protect against such conflicts of interest, English common law had developed, centuries earlier, the concept of fiduciary duty—the duty of the *agents* entrusted with the care of the property of others to protect the interests of their *principals*, the owners of these assets. But while this concept may seem simple and obvious, its actual implementation was too often honored more in the breach than in the observance. Indeed, in 1776, Adam Smith eloquently described— in his *The Wealth of Nations*—the challenges that existed even in that far simpler era:

> . . . the managers of other people's money (rarely) watch over it with the same anxious vigilance with which . . . they watch over their own. . . . Like the stewards of a rich man, they very easily give themselves a dispensation. Negligence and profusion therefore must always prevail.[1]

Examining the Conflict

Some 150 years later in 1932, Columbia University professors Adolph A. Berle and Gardiner C. Means set forth a thesis that echoed the observations of the great Adam Smith. In their classic book *The Modern Corporation and Private Property*, Berle and Means described the increasingly dominant role of large publicly held corporations in the United States. Their principal conclusions:

- The position of ownership has changed from that of an active to that of a passive agent. The owner now holds a piece of paper representing a set of rights and expectations with respect to an enterprise, but [he] has little control. The owner is practically powerless to affect the underlying property through his own efforts.
- The spiritual values that formerly went with ownership have been separated from it. Physical property capable of being shaped by its

---

[1]In those days, *profusion* was defined as a "lavish or wasteful expenditure or excess bestowal of money, substance, etc., squandering, waste." *Oxford English Dictionary*, 2nd ed., vol. XII (1989) 584.

owner could bring to him direct satisfaction apart from the income it yielded in more concrete form.

- The value of an individual's wealth is determined on the one hand by the actions of the individuals in command of the enterprise—individuals over whom the typical owner has no control—and on the other hand, by the actions of others in a sensitive and often capricious market. The value is thus subject to the vagaries and manipulations characteristic of the marketplace.
- Individual wealth has become extremely liquid through the organized markets, convertible into other forms of wealth at a moment's notice.
- Finally, in the corporate system, the "owner" of industrial wealth is left with a mere symbol of ownership while the power, the responsibility, and the substance that had been an integral part of ownership in the past has been transferred to a separate group in whose hands lies control.

Berle and Means had cogently identified a problem that would come to plague modern capitalism. For a time the system worked with reasonable effectiveness, since individual corporate shareholders still had both the legal rights and voting rights to protect their own interests. As ownership was gradually diffused into far smaller shareholdings, however, effective shareholder power declined, even as the latent power of those voting rights remained intact.

Agency Costs and Managerial Behavior

In 1976, another pair of wise academics—Harvard Business School's Michael C. Jensen and University of Rochester's William H. Meckling—added another brilliant insight on corporate behavior. "America has a principal/agent problem," as *The Economist* explained their seminal paper. "Agents (i.e., managers) were feathering their own nests rather than the interests of their principals (shareholders)." In "Theory of the Firm: Managerial Behavior, Agency Costs, and Ownership Structure," Jensen and Meckling set forth "a theory of (1) property rights, (2) agency, and (3) finance (as they relate to) the ownership structure of the firm."

The business organization, they argued, consists of a series of "individual property rights that determine how costs and rewards will be allocated among its participants." The paper continues:

> We define agency relationship as a contract under which one or more persons (the principals) engage another person (the agent) to perform some service on their behalf which involves delegating some decision-making authority to the agent. If both parties to the relationship (seek to further their own ends), there is good reason to believe that the agent will not always act in the best interests of the principal. The *principal* can limit divergences from his interest by establishing appropriate incentives for the *agent* and by incurring monitoring costs designed to limit the aberrant activities of the agent. . . . *However, it is generally impossible for the principal . . . to ensure that the agent will make optimal decisions from the principal's viewpoint.*
>
> Since the relationship between the stockholders and the managers of a corporation fits precisely the definition of a pure agency relationship, it should come as no surprise to discover that the issues associated with the separation of ownership and control in the modern diffused-ownership corporation are intimately associated with the general problem of agency. The problem of inducing an "agent" to behave as if he were maximizing the welfare of the "principal" is quite general. *It exists in all organizations at every level of management in firms, in universities, in mutual companies, in cooperatives, in governmental authorities and bureaus, (and) in unions. . . .*

It is impossible to deny the logic of the Jensen-Meckling thesis that posits that managers rarely maximize the interests of the shareholders they are duty-bound to serve, and instead mainly look out for themselves. More important, its truth has been confirmed, over and over again, by actual experience in the functioning of our giant corporate and investment institutions.

Leo Strine, now chancellor of the Delaware Court of Chancery, nicely articulated this reality in his comprehensive 2007 essay in *The Journal of Corporation Law*, excerpts from which are included in Box 2.1.

Box 2.1

"Toward Common Sense and Common Ground?"

Excerpts from an Essay by Chancellor Leo Strine

"Most ordinary Americans have little choice but to invest in the market. They are in essence "forced capitalists" who invest primarily for two purposes, both of which are long-term in focus: to send their children to college and to provide for themselves in retirement. This class of investors has no interest in quarter-to-quarter earnings fluctuations or gimmicks that deliver quick bursts of cash at the expense of sustainable growth. These investors want corporations to focus on fundamentally sound policies that generate durable earnings through the sale of high-quality products and services.

"For powerful reasons, this class of investors invests in the market primarily through intermediaries. It is these intermediaries, and not the forced capitalists, who determine how the capital of these investors is put to work and how the mountain of shares owned for their benefit is used to influence the management of public corporations. Given the directional momentum of public policy in the United States and Europe, the inflow of funds from forced capitalists to these intermediaries is likely to continue to increase. . . .

"[But] the standard play for these institutional investors is to encourage the public company to deliver some form of immediate value to its stockholders, through increased dividends or, even better from a hedge fund's perspective, a hefty stock buy-back program. Often, the target must take on greater leverage or decrease its capital expenditures to fund these initiatives. The impact of such initiatives upon short-term and long-term investors can be very different, as the benefits are immediate and the risks come to roost down the road. . . .

(Continued)

"American corporate law scholarship since the new Deal has been preoccupied with addressing the agency costs that arise from the separation of ownership and control exemplified by public corporations. The laboratory rats for this aspect of social science continue to be operating corporations that make money by selling products and services. . . .

"As a normative matter, it is often argued that the stockholders, as the residual claimants of the corporation, are the group best able to keep management honest and focused on increasing the value of the corporation. Therefore, the more tools and the more opportunities stockholders have to influence corporate policies, the better. Restrictions on takeover defenses are not enough; there must be the opportunity to unseat directors without even nominating opposing candidates. Unseating directors is not enough; stockholders need to be able to adopt specific policies that management must implement. . . .

"As much as corporate law scholars fetishize the agency costs that flow from the separation of ownership and control in operating companies, they have been amazingly quiet about the "*separation of ownership from ownership.*" What I mean by this is that the equity of public corporations is often owned, not by the end-user investors, but by another form of agency, a mutual fund, or other institutional investor. It is these intermediaries who vote corporate stock and apply pressure to public company operating boards. . . .

"It would be passing strange if corporate law scholars truly believed that professional money managers would, as a class, be less likely to exploit their agency than the managers of corporations that make products and deliver services. Nonetheless, the corporate law scholarship of the last 25 years obsesses over the agency costs of operating company boards, particularly in the mergers and acquisitions context. Little of it considers that the "empowerment" of stockholders does not empower end-user investors so much as it empowers intermediaries.

"Ironically, the influence [of academia] remains directed at the management of operating corporations, precisely when the traditional Berle-Means paradigm has fundamentally changed in favor of stockholders. No longer are the equity holders of public corporations diffuse and weak. Instead, the equity holders of public corporations represent a new and powerful form of agency, which presents its own risks to both individual investors and more generally to the best interests of our nation. (Our legal and academic community) is ignoring the dangers of this new form of agency."

SOURCE: *The Journal of Corporation Law* 33, no. 1 (October 2007).

Essentially, this respected and blunt-speaking jurist is demanding that the legal community at long last turn its attention to the agency costs involved in what he felicitously terms "the separation of ownership from ownership," and to the tendency of corporate managers and money managers alike to exploit their agency positions. Chancellor Strine's common sense warning about individual investors' declining power has yet to attract the public attention it deserves, nor even to spawn a host of positive (or for that matter negative) responses. Meanwhile, the ability of shareholders to exercise control over the corporations whose shares they held has exploded into massive potential power.

The Ownership Revolution

What Chancellor Strine is telling us, simply put, is that we're in the midst of an ownership revolution, and we'd best recognize it and control its consequences. Beginning in the 1950s, this ownership revolution consisted of a gradual shift from corporate ownership overwhelmingly dominated by *individual* investors to ownership overwhelmingly dominated by *institutional* investors. It started with the rise of corporate pension funds investing ever-larger proportions of their assets in common stocks, later joined by pension funds of state and local governments and agencies. The federal government jumped on the bandwagon in 1986. Its Thrift Savings Plan, the defined-contribution pension fund created for federal employees, with over $300 billion in assets, is now the largest pension plan in the nation.

During the 1980s, this "institutionalization" of equity ownership was greatly accelerated by the rise of the mutual investment fund. The first "open-end" mutual fund, Massachusetts Investors Trust (MIT), was formed in 1924. But the Great Depression virtually stopped the emerging industry in its tracks. The stock market crash revealed the self-dealing, conflicts of interest, and inadequate disclosure that punctuated the actions of fund managers. The Investment Company Act of 1940 helped clear the air by reforming much of the industry's over-reaching and abusive practices. Most of those problems were manifested by often highly leveraged "closed-end" funds, rather than the "open-end" funds we know as mutual funds today.[2]

While most of the closed-end funds failed to survive the crash and its aftermath, virtually all of the open-end funds survived; and even grew. After World War II ended, the mutual fund industry began its rise to national prominence. Its primary offering to individual investors was a diversified package of stocks (sometimes with a modest bond position), professional management supervision, daily liquidity, and investor convenience. The industry's steady growth was interrupted by a sharp bear market in stocks in 1973–1974 and its aftermath. But when a great bull market began in 1982 and continued into early 2000, the industry's growth rapidly accelerated. While another bear market—a 50 percent market decline into 2003—again slowed the industry's growth, it quickly recovered. When another, even worse, crash took place in 2008–2009, growth came to a virtual standstill.

---

[2]Open-end (mutual) funds continuously offer shares for purchase and redemption, providing the daily liquidity required for each share to be linked to its current net asset (market) value. Closed-end funds, by contrast, offer a fixed number of shares that are traded among investors, usually at a premium or discount to net asset value.

Assets of equity funds and equity-focused balanced mutual funds had grown from $1 billion in 1945 to $54 billion in 1972. Then the growth turned to decline, with industry assets dropping to $36 billion by 1981. But when stock prices, as measured by the S&P 500 Index (including dividends), leaped by an amazing 200-fold through early 2000, equity fund assets again exploded, growing to $4 *trillion*. Despite the bear market debacles of 2000–2003 and 2007–2009, assets of equity-oriented mutual funds continued to grow, albeit at a far more modest rate, and reached $6.3 trillion in early 2012. (It belabors the obvious to note that the industry's growth is highly correlated with the performance of the stock market. It's equally obvious that such a correlation is counterproductive to the returns actually earned by fund investors.)

This "institutionalization" of equity ownership—the combined holdings of private pension funds, public pension funds, mutual funds, and, to a lesser extent, insurance companies and endowment funds— fully justifies my description of "a revolution in equity ownership." In 1945, institutions held only 8 percent of all U.S. equities; today our financial institutions hold fully 70 percent of U.S. stocks—an all-time high (see Exhibit 2.1). Accordingly, individual ownership tumbled from 92 percent to 30 percent during the same period.

Exhibit 2.1 The Revolution in Equity Ownership. Percentage of Market Value of U.S. Stocks Held by Institutional Investors

SOURCE: Federal Reserve Bank Flow of Funds Report.

Changing Leadership

The pattern of institutional ownership has changed in highly significant ways. At the outset, private defined benefit (DB) pension plans were the dominant factor in retirement plans. Their ownership share reached a peak of 16 percent of all stocks in 1980. But DB plans currently represent just 6 percent of equity ownership, gradually replaced by defined contribution (DC) plans. Defined contribution plans held a share of zero in 1980; they now hold 13 percent of all stocks. Government plans, late to the game, now own 10 percent.

The importance of pension plans has dwindled from a high of 30 percent in the early 1990s to today's 22 percent ownership share, only slightly larger than the 19 percent share in 1980. Along the way, the primary driver of the ownership revolution became mutual funds. The industry's 3 percent share of stock ownership in 1950 grew to 5 percent a decade later, to 8 percent by 1990, to 22 percent in 2000, and to 32 percent currently. Now holding more than $4 trillion of domestic equities, mutual funds are by far the largest holder of U.S. stocks in our nation (see Exhibit 2.2).

Today, this ownership revolution is reflected in institutions holding $10.8 trillion of the $15 trillion total market value of U.S. equities. Our newly empowered institutions now hold 60 to 75 percent of the shares of virtually every U.S. publicly held corporation, giving them a firm grip on control over Corporate America.

Renters and Owners

With far too few exceptions, however, these powerful new institutional agents act less like owners of stocks than renters. They turn their portfolios over with abandon, trading (obviously) largely with one another, clearly engaging in a zero-sum game that enriches only Wall Street and ill-serves their principals. The average equity mutual fund turned over its portfolio at a 17 percent rate in the 1950s and 25 percent in the 1960s. But by 1985, turnover had leaped to 100 percent, and has

Exhibit 2.2 The Rise of America's Money Managers: Institutional Equity Ownership

Total Equity Assets	1950	1960	1970	1980	1990	2000	2011
Private defined benefit	$0	$16,545	$67,087	$232,046	$344,036*	$1,248,035*	$818,832*
Defined contribution	0	0	0	0	277,390*	1,546,273*	1,993,564*
State and local government	29	600	10,100	44,300	284,569	1,298,683	1,527,792
Federal government	0	0	0	0	340	56,576	124,109
Total retirement plans	$29	$17,145	$77,187	$276,346	$890,812	$3,325,841	$3,366,113
Mutual funds	$4,497	$19,770	$43,982	$47,356	$249,429	$3,328,983	$4,936,165
Insurance companies	4,690	12,437	27,771	78,573	161,869	1,083,259	1,558,973
Endowments	1,273	5,993	17,959	47,840	148,209	843,370	1,057,589
Other	3,510	10,579	30,649	76,125	179,981	695,618	714,639
Total	$13,999	$65,924	$197,548	$526,240	$1,630,300	$9,277,071	$11,633,479
Share of Total Equity Market							
Private defined benefit	0%	4%	8%	16%	10%*	8%*	5%*
Defined contribution	0	0	0	0	8*	10*	12*
State and local government	0	0	1	3	9	8	9
Federal government	0	0	0	0	0	0	1
Total retirement plans	0%	4%	9%	19%	27%	21%	20%
Mutual funds	3%	5%	5%	3%	7%	21%	30%
Insurance companies	3	3	3	5	5	7	9
Endowments	1	1	2	3	4	5	6
Other	2	3	4	5	5	4	4
Total	10%	16%	24%	36%	49%	59%	70%

Notes: *From 1990 on, private defined benefit and defined contribution include holdings of equity mutual funds. The totals exclude this duplication.

Endowment assets estimated based on 2000 reported figures.

SOURCE: Federal Reserve Flow of Funds report, Third Quarter 2011.

remained around that astonishingly high level ever since. Put another way, in 1950, the average holding for a stock in a mutual fund portfolio was 5.9 years; in 2011, it was barely one year.[3]

Such an average is a simple but inexact way to evaluate mutual fund turnover, so let's look at the turnover for equity funds as a group, weighted by assets. In 2011, equity holdings of actively managed stock funds averaged $3.8 trillion, while purchases of portfolio stocks totaled $2.69 trillion, and sales totaled another $2.70 trillion.[4] Taking the lesser of the two figures (to account for portfolio transactions necessitated by capital flow into or out of the fund) as a percentage of assets yields a turnover rate of 71 percent. The reality of transaction costs, however, suggests that we should pay more attention to total trading volume— including *both* purchases *and* sales—an incredible $5.4 trillion in total transactions, not far from one-and-a-half times the $3.8 trillion of equity fund assets of the group.

However high the levels of mutual fund trading in stocks have soared relative to traditional norms, they pale by comparison to the trading volumes of hedge funds, to say nothing of the levels of trading in exotic securities such as interest rate swaps, collateralized debt obligations, derivatives such as futures on commodities, stock indexes, stocks, and even bets on whether a given company will go into bankruptcy (credit default swaps). The aggregate nominal value of these instruments, as I noted in Chapter 1, now exceeds $700 trillion. Yes, what we have come to describe as speculation has clearly come to play the starring role in our nation's huge financial market colossus, with investment taking only a supporting role, if not a cameo role.

---

[3]The conventional industry metric sets the average holding period for a fund as the turnover rate divided by 100. Thus, a 100 percent turnover rate equates to a one-year average holding period; a 20 percent turnover rate equates to a five-year average holding period, and so on.

[4]Including only *actively managed* equity funds. *Passively managed* market index funds (now accounting for fully 28 percent of equity fund assets) generally have turnover rates that run in the range of 7 percent per year.

The Creation of Corporate Value

As I mentioned at the start of this chapter, the focus of our two sets of powerful agents has seemingly united on the quest to enhance the economic value of the corporation. So, how could this investment goal have fostered the rise of the rampant speculation that plagues our financial markets today? It's a compelling story, and one that depends on how we define corporate value. As a long-time independent director of the Mead Corporation (now MeadWestvaco), the Fortune 500 paper-maker, I have some firsthand experience in this area. Here is how the Mead Board stated its goal:

> The mission of the Board is to achieve long-term economic value for the shareholders. The Board believes that the Corporation should rank in the top third of peer companies in the creation of economic value . . . which is created by earning returns over full cycles which are higher than the cost of capital, usually reflected in total return to shareholders.

In Mead's case, total return was measured by Return on Total Capital, with the ROTC then compared with the average ROTC of both its peers and Corporate America in the aggregate. In addition to serving as the benchmark for the evaluation of corporate success by the Board, this joint measurement serves as the basis for Mead's incentive compensation system.

The mission of the corporate board at MeadWestvaco, then, is to create additional economic value, measured by achieving an ROTC that exceeds the firm's cost of capital. If such a firm cannot earn the cost of capital for its shareholders, so the essential logic goes, why should they entrust the board with their own capital? As *Fortune* magazine puts it: "The true cost of equity is what your shareholders could be getting in price appreciation and dividends if they invested instead in a portfolio about as risky as yours." While we know that in the *short run* stock prices are affected by both the company's reported quarterly earnings and the market's evanescent expectations, we also know that the return on the firm's capital—the dividends that the company distributes, and the earnings growth that it achieves—ultimately determines 100 percent of shareholder value in the long term.

Time Horizons and the Sources of Investment Return

So how do we define "shareholder value" for the business corporation? How do we measure that value, and over what period? In particular, should it be the short-term, even momentary, price of the stock? Or should it be the long-term accretion of the firm's intrinsic value? Truth told, in the long run it makes little if any difference. For the long-term return on a corporation's shares in the stock market is almost entirely determined by its investment fundamentals. For example, dividend yields and the real, after-inflation earnings growth of U.S. corporations have aggregated just short of 7 percent over the past 150 years (4.5 percent yield, 2.5 percent real earnings growth) almost precisely equal to the real return of 7 percent in stock prices. *Over the long haul, investment fundamentals, not market valuations, are the piper that calls the tune.*

Over the *short run*, however, the fundamentals are often overwhelmed by the deafening noise of speculation—the price at which the stock market values each dollar of earnings. This noise can be surprisingly persistent. As shown in Exhibit 2.3, on a one-year basis the gap between annual *investment* returns on stocks (dividends plus earnings) and their *market* returns (swings in valuation measured by changing price-earnings ratios) can be staggering, exceeding fully 10 percentage points in annual returns in 85 of the 125 one-year periods since 1872, and 5 percentage points in 105 of the periods. On a 10-year rolling basis,

Exhibit 2.3   Differences between Investment Returns and Market Returns over 125 Years of Market History

Holding Period	Greater than 2% +/−	Greater than 5% +/−	Greater than 10% +/−
1 Year	94%	84%	68%
10 Years	62	27	3
25 Years	23	0	0

Note: A 5 percent gap, for example, would mean that if the fundamental business return were 10 percent, the market return might be more than 15 percent or less than 5 percent.

the gap shrinks considerably, exceeding 10 percent only three times, but exceeding 5 percentage points in 30 periods, and more than 2 percent in 72 periods. Over 25 years, however, the gap shrinks radically, never exceeding 4 percentage points and exceeding 2 percentage points in only 25 periods.

Looking at the annual returns generated in the U.S. stock market during the past four decades clearly illustrates the wide variations that take place, even during decade-long periods. As shown in Exhibit 2.4, during the 1970s the *fundamentals* of investment, measured by earnings growth and dividend yields on the S&P 500 Index, provided a return of 13.4 percent per year, and the total stock market return was but 5.9 percent annually. (The *reduction* in valuation of −7.5 percent per year reflected a drop in the earnings ratio from 15.8 to 7.3 times.)

During the 1980s, by contrast, the fundamental return of 9.6 percent came hand-in-hand with an annual valuation increase of 7.7 percent, as P/E ratios more than doubled, from 7.3 to 15.2 times, bringing the total annual return to 17.3 percent. Incredibly—and bereft of historic precedent—the same sort of scenario continued during the 1990s. That two-decade-long steady, almost-clockwork-like rise in

Exhibit 2.4   Stock Returns: A Tin Decade, Two Golden Decades, Then Another Tin Decade

	Annual Rate of Return				
	1970s	1980s	1990s	2000s	1970–2010
Earnings Growth	9.9%	4.4%	7.4%	0.8%	5.5%
Initial Dividend Yield	+3.5	+5.2	+3.2	+1.2	+3.5
Investment Return	13.4%	9.6%	10.6%	2.0%	9.0%
Speculative Return*	−7.5	+7.7	+7.2	−3.2	+0.3
Market Return	5.9%	17.3%	17.8%	−1.2%	9.3%
P/E Ratio—Start	15.8X	7.3X	15.2X	30.6X	15.8X
End	7.3	15.2	30.6	22.0	22.0

*Annualized impact of change in P/E ratio.
SOURCE: Robert Shiller, www.econ.yale.edu/~shiller/data.htm.

valuations couldn't continue. And it didn't. During the first decade of the 2000s, the P/E took a mammoth 30 percent drop from 30.6 to 22.0—reducing market returns by −3.2 percent per year, and leading to a negative total return on stocks of −1.2 percent per year, one of the two poorest decades for stock returns in the past 150 years. (That shouldn't surprise anyone. Over time, reversion to the mean (RTM) in stock valuation has always finally asserted itself. I'll talk about the RTM principle in depth in Chapter 9.)

We know—we *know*—that in the long run, market returns represent the triumph of investment fundamentals—earnings and dividends—over speculation in the market's valuation of these returns. Yet during the recent era, it is speculation that has been in the driver's seat. We continue to ignore Benjamin Graham's profound wisdom, cited at the outset: "In the short run, the stock market is a voting machine; in the long run it is a weighing machine."

However, the trend toward the crowding out of "weighing" in the financial markets by "voting" would not have amused Graham. Nor would it have surprised the worldly wise Lord Keynes. I reiterate his concerns here: The powerful role of speculation in the markets is based on ". . . the conventional valuation of stocks based on the mass psychology of a large number of ignorant individuals." Unable to offset the mass opinion, he predicted, even professional investors would try to "foresee changes in the public valuation." How right he was!

Keynes's conclusion has been reaffirmed—and then some! As expert professional investors—managers of pension funds and mutual funds alike—have come to dominate the financial markets during the past four decades, they have largely replaced those earlier "ignorant individuals" in the investment marketplace. Rather than endeavoring to place appropriate values on business enterprises, however, these financial pros are, in a real sense, focusing their professional careers on attempting to foresee changes in the public valuation of stocks. In the long run, of course, precious few will succeed in doing so. Nonetheless, not only our investment agents but our corporate agents find this short-term focus on the expectations of the stock market—rather than the real market of intrinsic value—as one more way to further their own ends.

"Short-Termism" and Managed Earnings

It was only a matter of time until what became known as "short-termism" entered the public dialogue. It is largely short-termism that has given us a world of managed earnings. While it is corporate executives who do the managing, they do so with at least the tacit approval of corporate directors and auditors, and with the enthusiastic endorsement of institutional investors with short-term time horizons, even speculators and arbitrageurs, rather than in response to the demands of long-term investors. Like it or not, corporate strategy and financial accounting alike focus on meeting the earnings expectations of "the Street" quarter after quarter.

The desideratum is steady earnings growth—manage it to at least the 12 percent level if you can—and at all costs avoid falling short of the earnings expectations at which the corporation has hinted, or whispered, or "ballparked" before the year began. If all else fails, obscure the real results by merging, raising assumptions for future returns on the pension fund, taking a big one-time write-off, or accelerating the booking of orders for goods. All of this creative financial engineering apparently serves to inflate stock prices, to enrich managers, and to deliver to institutional investors what they want.

But if the stock market is to be the arbiter of value, it will do its job best, in my judgment, if it sets its valuations based on punctiliously accurate corporate financial reporting and a focus on the long-term prospects of the corporations it values. However, the market's direction seems quite the opposite, and there is much room for improvement. For while the accounting practices of America's corporations may well be the envy of the world, our nation's financial environment has become permeated with the concept of managed earnings.

The accepted idea is to smooth reported earnings, often by "guiding" security analysts to establish earnings expectations for the year, and then, each quarter, reporting earnings that "meet expectations," or, better yet, "exceed expectations." Failure to meet expectations may be preceded by lower "whisper earnings," which must, in turn, be met. It is an illusory world that ignores the normal ups and downs of business revenues and expenses, a world in which "negative earnings surprises" are to be avoided at all costs.

Former Securities and Exchange Commission (SEC) Chairman Arthur Levitt's warnings in a 2007 speech to Wall Street were, in retrospect, prescient. He expressed his deep concern that earnings management had gone too far. He cited abuses in huge restructuring charges, creative acquisition accounting, "cookie jar" reserves to be drawn down when necessary, excessive "immaterial" items, and premature recognition of revenue. He added that "almost everyone in the financial community shares responsibility (with corporate management) for fostering this climate." His words clearly reflect the perverse nature of the happy conspiracy.

Closely tied to all of this creative financial accounting is the stock market's focus on short-term events—aberrations rather than long-term valuations. The most fundamental tenet of investing, in my view, is *owning businesses and holding them*, for the long term, even "forever," which is said to be Warren Buffett's favorite holding period. But today the vast majority of trading involves precisely doing the opposite, *buying pieces of paper and trading them back and forth*, with one another and with alacrity.

As I have noted, playing such games in the stock market casino increases the proportion of the market's returns that is arrogated by the croupiers, and reduces the residual proportion of the market's returns that remains for the gamblers. Where, indeed, are the customers' yachts, or, in today's coin of the realm, the customers' jets? In such an environment, it would seem obvious that the successful strategy is to buy stocks and hold them, and never again enter the casino.

A distinguished commentator has expressed these problems far better than I can, so in Box 2.2 I present a summary of the problems and a range of solutions from Professor Alfred Rappaport, whose 2011 book, *Saving Capitalism from Short-Termism: How to Build Long-Term Value and Take Back Our Financial Future* (McGraw-Hill) sets forth his strong convictions.

Professor Rappaport's analysis and conclusions were by no means the first on the vital subject of short-termism and managed earnings. A few years earlier, in 2006, as these issues of our failed ownership society began to heat up, the Business Roundtable Institute for Corporate Ethics, sponsored by the Chartered Financial Analyst (CFA) Institute Centre for

Box 2.2

Excerpts from *Saving Capitalism from Short-Termism: How to Build Long-Term Value and Take Back Our Financial Future*

By Alfred Rappaport

"Too many corporate managers are obsessed with quarterly earnings and the current stock price. Likewise, too many investment managers, fearing that poor short-term performance will cause fund withdrawals, focus excessively on quarterly performance relative to their benchmark and competing funds. These behaviors are not hard to understand. People do what they are rewarded for doing. Incentives matter.

"Short-termism, the obsession with short-term results irrespective of the long-term implications, was a prime factor in the recent global financial crisis. If we as a society do not address it, not only will short-termism exacerbate future crises, but it will jeopardize the dominance of the free-market system.

The Problems
- "The obsession with short-term performance seriously compromises the potential of companies, the economy, and the savings that individuals need to accumulate for retirement. Our economy has evolved from the era of entrepreneurial capitalism, when owners managed and managers owned, to today's agency capitalism, where corporate and investment managers responsible for other people's money dominate public companies and the financial markets.
- "Outsized short-term financial incentives drove homebuyers, appraisers, mortgage lenders, credit rating agencies, investment banks, and institutional investors to take

(Continued)

reckless, value-destroying risks that helped fuel the financial meltdown in 2007–2009. Each party acted in its own self-interest by responding to the incentives that it faced. The essential problem is that the corporate and investment communities have failed to adapt their business practices, and in particular their compensation practices, to an economy in which professional managers who are responsible for other people's money dominate.

- "The ubiquitous maxim, 'We manage to maximize shareholder value,' is at odds with the way public companies actually operate. Managing for shareholder value means focusing on cash flow, not earnings; it means managing for the long term, not the short term; and, importantly, it means that managers must take risk into account. Instead, many managers seem obsessed with Wall Street's quarterly earnings expectations game and the short-term share price, thereby compromising long-term shareholder value.

- "Quarterly performance measurement of fund managers encourages them to prefer the safety of performing acceptably close to their benchmark index over maximizing long-run shareholder returns. Short-term relative performance measurement not only encourages a short-term point of view, but also induces fund managers to follow the herd even when they are convinced that stocks are mispriced, thereby exacerbating price bubbles and crashes.

"Incentive compensation plans for CEOs, operating unit managers, and front line employees should encourage each to focus on creating long-term value as the governing objective of the company.

"Senior management and the board should be committed to making the case that the benefits of pursuing long-term value outweigh the risk of poor short-term share price performance. Since corporate financial reporting has fallen short in achieving its principal objective of supplying capital providers and other financial statement users with information that is useful for estimating the magnitude, timing, and riskiness of future cash flows, we need an overhaul of corporate financial reporting with a new corporate performance statement that overcomes major shortcomings of the income statement by separating observable facts (historical cash flows) from uncertain estimates of future cash flows (accruals).

"Because active management is considerably costlier than passive management, actively managed funds must underperform index funds in the aggregate. Since only a small fraction of funds will be able to beat their benchmark indexes over a sustained period, actively managed equity funds will have to make meaningful changes if they are to continue to attract investment dollars in the future. One promising possibility is a move from fees based on the market value of assets managed (fees paid irrespective of relative fund results) to performance fees that align the interests of managers with those of long-term fund shareholders."

Financial Market Integrity, took up the task in a 20-page white paper entitled "Breaking the Short-Term Cycle." And in 2009, the Aspen Institute published "Overcoming Short-Termism: A Call for a More Responsible Approach to Investment and Business Management."

Both of these excellent public policy reports sought to encourage patient capital, discourage investor "churning," and generally reinforce long-term investing, enlisting natural market forces and establishing incentives for market actors to modify their respective behaviors. The reports demanded a clearly defined and rigorously enforced enhanced fiduciary duty standard to better align the interests of investors and financial intermediaries, and structural changes designed to base the compensation of long-term oriented fund managers on the long-term performance of the funds they manage.

Both groups also urged coordination of targeted tax incentives such as significantly increasing the tax differential between long-term and short-term holding periods and implementing an excise tax (including its application to tax-exempt entities) in ways that are designed to discourage excessive share trading and encourage long-term share ownership, and both groups identified the need to reform earnings guidance practices, as well as the advisability of meeting financial targets through aggressive accounting techniques.

Still earlier, in 2003, the Commission on Private Enterprise and Public Trust, a group of leading professional investors, corporate chieftains, and managers of public pension funds organized by the Conference Board and sponsored by the Pew Foundation, laid out its analysis of the problems created not only by the short-term time horizons of investors, but the failure of corporate governance to face the range of challenges before our corporate system, and made a series of recommendations to restore the trust in our corporate system that had been undermined by the conduct of corporate managers and money managers. The Conference Board Commission was a response to the collapse of some of our nation's largest corporations—including Enron, WorldCom, Quest Communications, Tyco International, and HealthSouth—along with the failure of Arthur Andersen, one of the "Big Five" accounting firms, and deserved public airing and discussion. Like its "sister" reports, the Commission urged firms to enhance communications with shareholders, especially transparent and comprehensive financial reporting.

With respect to governance issues, the Conference Board Commission urged greater proxy access for long-term investors, enhancing shareholder participation rights, adopting minimum holding periods to establish full voting rights, and establishing standards for ownership levels necessary for director nominations (for example, aggregate holdings of 5 percent of shares outstanding, held for at least three years). Shareholders, they urged, should have the right to approve plans for equity-based compensation and other compensation arrangements. Finally, the Commission agreed to encourage corporations to establish long-term performance incentives that support and reinforce the corporation's long-term strategic goals set by the board, and whose award is linked to achievement of specific strategic goals. Yes, private enterprise depends on public trust.[5]

The Failure of the Gatekeepers

How, one might ask, could these kinds of transgressions against the culture of long-term investing not only exist, but continue—even proliferate—in our society of free and competitive markets? While they all transpired under the very noses of our political and professional institutions designed to serve as the gatekeepers of Corporate America and Investment America, far too rarely did any of these gatekeepers rise up and sound the alarm.

During the recent era, our financial sector has played an ever-increasing role in the corporate sector, with roots that are widespread and, in many cases, mutually reinforcing the happy conspiracy that has been one focus of this chapter. With the substantial displacement of a once-dominant culture of long-term investment by a culture of short-term speculation, short-termism has plagued us with adverse consequences, and the outcome was never in doubt.

When our corporate manager/agents and our institutional investment manager/agents alike come to focus on ephemeral stock prices rather than intrinsic stock values, nearly all of those gatekeeper institutions that we trusted to watch over the public interest seem either to have ignored the potential consequences, or even to have abetted the damaging actions that followed. Not only corporate cultures but government cultures were involved, and self-interest and economic forces were never far from shaping the shared culture surrounding what I have

---

[5]Full disclosure: I served as a participant in all three of these studies. First, I was a commissioner on the Conference Board study, ably co-chaired by former Secretary of Commerce Peter G. Peterson, and including former Federal Reserve Chairman Paul Volcker, Intel founder Andrew Grove, and Johnson & Johnson CEO Ralph Larsen. I was also a participant on the CFA panel, and a member of the Aspen Institute Coalition. I was honored by the opportunity both to express my own views and to learn from the views of the other members of these three "Blue-Ribbon" groups, and I wholly endorse the reports that were issued.

described as the "corporate/investment complex." Let's briefly look at the role that our major gatekeepers—10 in all—have played in abetting the new culture of speculation, particularly in the period leading up to the Great Crash of 2007–2009 and its aftermath.

1. Congress

Congress, asleep at the switch during the 1990–2000 period, ignored the growing problems or even made them worse; for example, by repealing the Glass-Steagall Act, and by allowing stock option costs to be omitted from firms' expense statements. Then, alarmed by the shocking scandals that came to light in 2001 at some of the nation's largest corporations, our elected officials stepped up to the plate with the Sarbanes-Oxley Act of 2004. While much maligned by industry, what is commonly known as SOX required the implementation of many prudent and reasonable reforms.

But Congress added fuel to the fire that was about to blaze in the mortgage-securities scandal by pushing our government-sponsored lenders, Fannie Mae and Freddie Mac, too far. Congress demanded that these government-sponsored (but publicly owned) enterprises (GSEs) increase their commitment to the undeniably worthy social objective of home ownership, but ignored the equally undeniably baneful economic consequences. Private firms such as Countrywide and Washington Mutual, already having issued billions of dollars in mortgages to unqualified borrowers, added to the potential losses. The inevitable crash in home prices followed.

Following the collapse of the real estate market, the abuse of complex financial derivatives, and the failure of some of America's largest financial firms—and the subsequent government bailout—Congress again acted, passing the Dodd-Frank Wall Street Reform and Consumer Protection Act of 2010. As usual, it was looking back instead of forward. With so many implementation rules still pending, the ultimate effectiveness of this blunderbuss of an Act remains to be seen. My own view is that the Act, while it is well-motivated, contains many flaws that will come back to haunt us. Yes, the Volcker Rule is now a necessity, but bringing back the Glass-Steagall Act—which in 1933 separated deposit banking and investment banking, but was repealed by

Congress in 1999—would have been far simpler and more effective. And, yes, I approve of the idea of the new Consumer Financial Protection Bureau (CFPB), but the bitter frost of Washington politics is almost certain to spoil its implementation. The box score for Congress: just one hit; many errors.

2. The Judiciary

While our nation's judicial system does its important work largely with integrity and without fear or favor, in recent years we have witnessed serious failures to make decisions based on common sense and a full understanding of the facts. As I note in Chapter 3, I'm appalled by the U.S. Supreme Court's decision in the 2011 *Citizens United* case that not only allows, but even seems to encourage, political contributions by corporations and other groups, often without disclosure. (In that chapter, I also describe my attempt to allow corporate shareholders to decide on whether to allow such contributions.) One year after that judicial decision, we have already seen the effect that profligate expenditures on political campaigns made by billionaires has had on hard-fought primary elections. One can only imagine the "hate advertising" (which, alas, seems to work best) to which we'll be subjected in the coming general election. The Court also failed the test of serving the interests of mutual funds in the setting of advisory fees by fund managers. Justice Alito, writing for the majority in *Jones v. Harris Associates*, couldn't seem to figure out the critical difference between advisory *fees* and advisory *fee rates*.[6]

The lower courts have also let us down. The Second Circuit Court of Appeals refused to allow the SEC to do its job of protecting the rights of investors, frustrating the Commission's attempts to allow corporate shareholders their right of access to proxy statements, usually on the basis that the federally mandated requirement of a "cost-benefit" analysis had not been adequately met. Noble as that goal may be, the Court couldn't seem to understand that while the *costs* of most federal regulations

---

[6]In my Amicus Curiae brief on *Jones v. Harris Associates* that I submitted to the Supreme Court in 2009, I hammered at this distinction as hard as I could. But my impassioned plea was apparently not even considered in Justice Alito's opinion for the majority.

are tangible and easily can be counted, the major *benefits* may be largely intangible and can't be counted. How, for example, could one place even a rough value on shareholder rights and corporate democracy?

An op-ed essay by Danish author and academic Bjorn Lomborg, published in *The Wall Street Journal* in April 2012, nicely captured the dichotomy. "Economists haven't enjoyed much popularity since the financial crisis, with their profession painted as recklessly focused on flimsy mathematical models over common sense. . . . Cost-benefit analysis can seem cold—a hard-nosed, money-focused, GDP-is-God approach. But a world of scarce and competing resources requires it, and *proper cost-benefit analysis encompasses much more than simple economic costs.*" [Italics added.]

3. The Securities and Exchange Commission

The SEC too often failed to live up to its purpose: the protection of the interests of investors. Failure to rectify the, at best, misleading financial disclosures of many of our largest corporations, rarely seemed to catch the SEC's usually watchful eye. And the failure to uncover the vast Madoff "Ponzi scheme" fraud, involving $60 billion worth of investors' assets, gave the Commission's critics the opportunity they sought to deprive it of the resources necessary to do its job. Chairmen Arthur Levitt and William Donaldson both served surely, wisely, and with distinction at the SEC's helm during their terms in office (1993–2000 and 2001–2005, respectively), but the records of their successors were mixed at best. It's early in the term of present chairman Mary Schapiro, but my impression is that she has the right values and a powerful dedication to investor protection. Certainly, her principled stand aimed at protecting money-market fund shareholders from another "run on the bank" confirms my assessment.

Some of the Commission's most important initiatives—in mutual fund regulation, corporate governance, and proxy-access—have unfortunately been rejected on technical grounds by the courts. We can blame Congress for part of this problem. As noted earlier, the demand that all new federal regulation be justified by a comprehensive cost-benefit analysis is a nice enough idea. But to use another example, how would one measure the benefits of a federal standard of fiduciary duty for money managers? As a result, the cost-benefit requirement has been used by opponents of reform to stifle regulatory action, a gambit that has so far succeeded in our courts.

4. *The Federal Reserve Board*

Behind the housing bubble lay the extremely easy money policies fostered by then-Federal-Reserve-Chairman Alan Greenspan that made borrowing cheap for speculators and tolerated excessive debt and leverage in our financial system. But perhaps equally significant was that the Fed almost totally ignored the highly risky lending activities of the banks and commercial lenders exemplified by the firms I cited above, severing the essential link between borrower and lender. Chairman Greenspan simply swept aside warnings from his fellow board members about this growing mortgage scandal, to our society's ultimate regret.

To his credit, in his testimony before Congress in October 2008, Chairman Greenspan admitted his mistake. He acknowledged that the crisis had been prompted by "a once-in-a-century credit tsunami," which had arisen from the collapse of a "whole intellectual edifice." "Those of us who have looked to the self-interest of lending institutions to protect shareholders' equity—myself especially—are in a state of shocked disbelief," he said. This failure of self-interest to provide self-regulation was, he said, "a flaw in the model that I perceived as the critical functioning structure that defines how the world works." As *New Yorker* writer John Lanchester observed, "That's a hell of a big thing to find a flaw in."

5. *The Rating Agencies*

By giving AAA ratings to the plethora of issuance of new mortgage-backed debt obligations, these federally empowered rating agencies converted high-risk and leveraged speculations into acceptable investments for lenders, eager to put their capital to work at generous rates. Why these lenders and their investment staffs accepted the ratings uncritically is another story. Both Standard & Poor's and Moody's, the two major rating agencies, were, of course, paid large sums, typically

$300,000 to $500,000, but as high as $1,000,000 per issue, by the issuers to provide these "investment grade" ratings. This is an obvious potential conflict of interest, especially when top ratings were often awarded only after the ratings services worked directly with the issuers to resolve or correct any impediments that stood in the way of earning the coveted "triple A" ratings required to sell these flawed securities to supposedly well-informed institutional investors. The influence of the ratings agencies is so deeply imbedded in our regulations and in our financial marketplace that neither our Congress nor our regulators have yet found any means of significantly mitigating the central role that they have played in our market system.

6. Public Accountants

Our CPAs were surely supporting actors in the happy conspiracy between our two sets of agents—corporate managers and investment managers alike—both of which gradually turned their focus to short-term earnings goals. Our CPAs too often acted as partners of managements. Yet they were supposed to act as independent attesters to the financial soundness of a company's balance sheet and profit and loss statement.

It's easy to see why a company would want to take advantage of the many holes in GAAP (Generally Accepted Accounting Principles) in order to enhance reported corporate earnings. For decades our public accountants, for example, saw no problem in providing management consulting services—a high revenue and high margin activity—while supposedly providing independent attestation services to the firm. This obvious conflict of interest belies the principle of independence. At the same time, they were defending the rationalizations justifying why stock options should not be counted as a corporate expense. To Chairman Levitt's credit—despite heavy opposition in Congress—he finally won the option expense battle and was also able to bar public accountants from providing both auditing services and consulting services to the same client.

In my service on Chairman Levitt's Independence Standards Board, I worked with three other members and the CEOs of four of the nation's largest accounting firms. When the accountants put forth the reasons why their independence would assure the integrity of their attestations, they cited, over and over again, "reputation risk"—that to do other than act with independence would fatally damage their reputations. I couldn't help wondering, however, whether their real reputation risk wasn't instead coming to be known as tough, unyielding in their positions, and demanding punctilious compliance with both the spirit and letter of GAAP. Would they still retain their clients? Would they attract new clients? Alas, the issue was never debated.

7. The Financial Press

With a few wonderful exceptions, journalists and business-page editors failed to adequately consider the smoke that was forming and would culminate in the financial firestorm of 2008–2009. Perhaps it would have required too much tedious digging. Perhaps the machinations were simply too complicated. Perhaps our financial engineers were clever enough to hide what they were cooking up. Less understandable, however, is the fixation of financial journalism on the momentary movements of the stock market, in which every sudden rise or fall is treated as a newsworthy event, even though the trading activity merely reflects the transfer of stock ownership from one investor to another. Why didn't the media focus on the broad trends and cross-currents taking place in our financial sector rather than regularly reporting—quarter after quarter—on "the best" mutual funds in short-term (or even longer-term) past performance? (There were some journalists who raised the warning flag over and over again—I'm thinking of Gretchen Morgenson and Floyd Norris of *The New York Times*, Jonathan Clements and Jason Zweig of *The Wall Street Journal*, and a handful of others. But too few of their colleagues saluted when they raised the warning flag.)

8. Security Analysts

One might think that the professional security analysts of our giant financial institutions would have been the principal line of defense against the accounting scandals that we have witnessed over the past decade. After all, these trained investment professionals usually have direct access to the chief executive officers and chief financial officers of the firms that they evaluate. But our *sell-side* analysts (i.e., advice givers representing brokerage firms) largely failed to notice, or at least to report, the financial shenanigans that were taking place on the books of the companies whose stocks they were covering. Conflicts of interest were rife, especially when the firms employing them—for huge compensation—were engaged in public offerings of the very companies for whose stock coverage they held responsibility. A negative appraisal of a stock meant not only the risk of losing *that* piece of profitable underwriting business; it was the risk of losing the business of *all* potential underwritings.

In a settlement with New York attorney general Eliot Spitzer for what they did (and what they failed to do), the firms employing these conflicted Wall Street sell-side analysts were finally fined $1.2 billion. Sad to say, however, while the *buy-side* analysts employed by our giant institutional money managers had no comparable conflict of interest, they too seemed oblivious of the aberrations that were taking place in the reporting of corporate earnings. Or perhaps it was in their own career interest to go along with the system of "earnings guidance."

It's hard to find more than a handful of stock analysts who, usually to the detriment of their careers, took on the flawed system and examined Wall Street's failures. One who did was long-time bank analyst Mike Mayo, who did his best to explain why Wall Street couldn't handle the truth. As a result, he became an *Exile on Wall Street*, the title of his 2011 book. Here are some of Mayo's perceptive (and blunt) words:

> Analysts are supposed to be a check on the financial system— people who can wade through a company's financials and tell investors what's really going on. There are about 5,000 so-called sell-side analysts, watchdogs over U.S. companies. Unfortunately, some are little more than cheerleaders—afraid of rocking the boat at their firms, afraid of alienating the companies they cover and drawing the wrath of their superiors. The proportion of sell ratings on Wall Street remains under 5 percent even today, despite the fact that any first-year MBA student can tell you that 95 percent of the stocks cannot be winners.
>
> Over the years, I have pointed out certain problems in the banking sector—things like excessive risk, outsized compensation for bankers, more aggressive lending—and as a result been

yelled at, conspicuously ignored, threatened with legal action and mocked by banking executives, all with the intent of persuading me to soften my stance. What we need is a better version of capitalism. That version starts with accounting: Let banks operate with a lot of latitude, but make sure outsiders can see the numbers (the real numbers). It also includes bankruptcy: Let those who stand to gain from the risks they take—lenders, borrowers and bank executives—also remain accountable for mistakes. . . . Doing it involves a culture change to ensure that analysts can act with sufficient intellectual curiosity and independence to critically analyze public companies that control so much of our economy.

9. The Directors

One might have expected that both directors of business corporations and directors of mutual fund corporations would have acted to prevent the corporate scandals (Enron, for example) and mutual fund scandals (time-zone trading, for example). But if there were directors who stood up for the interests of the shareholders whom they were duty-bound to serve, I haven't heard of them. The giant Wall Street investment banking firms that blew up (or would have, without the bailouts we taxpayers so generously provided) were heavily populated with directors with some of the most impeccable credentials one can imagine. (Here, I won't name names.)

But they were either misinformed or uninformed by the seamy financial shenanigans that were going on right under their noses. I know of no explanation but that these directors failed to consider the fiduciary duty that they owed to the shareholders who elected them. Even before the recent financial crisis fell upon us, Warren Buffett noted that even "intelligent and decent directors have failed miserably," calling them "tail-wagging puppy dogs" who meekly follow recommendations by compensation consultants.

Buffett is even more critical of mutual fund directors. Here, he expands his metaphor from "puppy-dogs" to "lap-dogs," who were expected to be "Dobermans" but turned out to be "cocker spaniels." His criticism is right on the mark. Where were the fund directors who oversaw the mutual funds that participated in the market timing scandals uncovered by New York Attorney General Eliot Spitzer in 2003? Did they even read the annual reports of the funds that they directed, which clearly showed the astonishing level of purchases and liquidations of fund shares? (Sometimes the annual transaction activity in fund shares was even larger than the total assets of the funds themselves!) Why didn't they pursue legal action against their fund managers who had participated in these conspiracies to defraud the long-term fund shareholders whom they were duty bound to protect? Why did they renew their management contracts for the funds that had engaged in this (again) happy conspiracy? Quoting Buffett yet again, "Like directors throughout Corporate America, these fiduciaries must decide whether their job is to work for owners or for managers."

10. Stock Owners

Stock owners should be the ultimate gatekeepers. The very futures of the corporations whose shares they own are at stake. So they should care, and care deeply, about the various transgressions that I've described in this chapter. The greatest mystery of all is how and why the institutional investors who own—and ultimately hold absolute control over—virtually all of our nation's public corporations decided to ignore—or perhaps failed to understand—what so many corporations were doing to foster unrealistic short-term earnings (the voting machine) rather than real long-term values (the weighing machine). What were these owners thinking? How could they endorse so many corporate managers and directors engaged in the financial engineering of the firm's earnings by voting for them year after year? Did they even care that the corporations that they controlled were too often operated with the interests of their managers taking precedence over the interests of their shareholders? What about using their rights and responsibilities of ownership to demand corporate governance in the interest of the shareholders these institutional managers represent?

That is a subject unto itself. In the next chapter, I examine why our absentee institutional owner/agents largely failed to adequately look after the interests of their principals, predominately as a result of this potential driving force of the happy conspiracy and the short-termism that has come to characterize the culture in our double-agency society. I'll also set forth a variety of recommendations to help restore our broken system of capitalism to its traditional culture.

Conclusion

Amid the pervasive failures among these 10 sets of gatekeepers—charged with the responsibility of guarding corporate integrity in America—the failure of institutional money managers is the most inexplicable. After all, these managers have the greatest stake in the outcome, the greatest opportunity to measure up to their responsibility, and the greatest power to bring about reform. As I wrote in an earlier book, "somebody's gotta keep an eye on these corporate and financial geniuses." While our other gatekeepers have hardly filled that role with distinction, and most fund shareholders can't possibly do it by themselves, fund managers, with their vast research and analytical capabilities and extensive proxy voting experience, must fill the gap. After remaining silent on governance issues for too many years, it's time for these giant institutional investors of mutual funds and pension funds to break that silence, and to take a stand on the side of their clients.

Chapter 3

The Silence of the Funds

Why Mutual Funds Must Speak Out on the
Governance of Our Nation's Corporations

The good shepherd lays down his life for the sheep. He who is a hired hand and not a shepherd, who does not own the sheep, sees the wolf coming and leaves the sheep and flees, and the wolf snatches them and scatters them. He flees because he is a hired hand and cares nothing for the sheep.

—*John 10:11-13*

There are only two kinds of clients we can't afford to offend: actual and potential.

—*Anonymous money manager*

My 1951 thesis on the mutual fund industry also explored the role of mutual funds in corporate governance. In those ancient days, funds were quite hesitant to make their votes count. The common refrain was, "If you don't like the management, sell the stock." I was, however, able to find a number of examples of fund activism. The most notable was the Montgomery Ward case of 1949, in which mutual funds joined in the effort to remove Chairman Sewell L. Avery from his job. Avery was a controversial character—a few years earlier, in 1944, a pair of soldiers removed him from his office while he was seated in his desk chair, a moment that was immortalized in a famous photo. The negative votes cast by the funds were based on his notorious reluctance to spend money on future growth, fearing a postwar depression that would never come to pass.

My thesis reflected my then, as now, idealism. I predicted that it was only a matter of time until mutual funds exercised their duties as corporate citizens:

> *. . . basing their investments on enterprise rather than speculation . . .* and exerting influence on corporate policy, often in a decisive manner, and in the best interest of investment company shareholders. Since they possess not only a greater knowledge of finance and management than the average stockholder, but also the financial means to make their influence effective, the mutual funds seem destined to fulfill this crucial segment of their economic role.

My words echoed the position of the Securities and Exchange Commission. In its 1940 report to Congress, the SEC called on funds to serve ". . . the useful role of representatives of the great number of inarticulate and ineffective individual investors in industrial corporations in which investment companies are also interested." In 1951, when I cited those words in my thesis, mutual funds owned less than 3 percent of the shares of U.S. corporations, and I expected their voice would strengthen in tandem with their muscle.

Alas, I was wrong. So was the SEC. Now, more than 60 years later, mutual funds have become the largest investors in U.S. stocks, owning fully 30 percent of all shares. Mutual fund managers, who typically provide investment management services to pension plans and other institutions, control more than 60 percent. Together these institutional money managers are by far the most potent force in Corporate America, and their power is highly concentrated—the largest 25 managers alone own $6 trillion of U.S. equities, about three-quarters of the institutional total.[1] But the strong voice I expected to hear is barely a whisper. Switching metaphors and putting a reverse twist on the saying that "the spirit is willing, but the flesh is weak," the mutual fund flesh is strong, but the spirit is unwilling. The silence of the funds is deafening.

As far as I can tell, while the managers of most large fund groups carefully review and consider corporate proxies, they overwhelmingly endorse, with few major exceptions, the proposals of corporate management. When they vote, they usually do just as they are asked; they support management's recommendations. This practice is a far cry, not only from activism and advocacy, but from the very process of corporate governance. *Most mutual funds have failed to live up to their responsibilities of corporate citizenship.*

Thanks to Congress and the SEC, there has been halting movement to give stock owners some access to participation in corporate proxies. In the 2012 "proxy season" (usually the spring), a wide range of proposals by shareholders are appearing on a variety of issues, including the issues of executive pay and corporate political contributions. Increasingly, the proposals are included in corporate proxies. Now the financial institutions that hold absolute control over Corporate America will have to stand up and be counted, unless, of course, they choose to abstain.

Why Mutual Funds Are Passive Participants in Corporate Governance

The reasons for this passivity by institutional investors are not hard to fathom. First, as other chapters of this book discuss, funds are often essentially short-term holders of stocks, moving away from investment

---

[1]There is no longer a significant distinction between mutual fund managers and pension fund managers. With only a single exception, all 25 of the largest investment institutions in the United States manage both mutual funds *and* pension funds. Mutual funds account for about 40 percent of the $6 trillion of total assets under the management of these 25 giants, with the remaining 60 percent managed for pension funds and other separately managed client accounts. But since only the proxy voting of mutual funds is now fully disclosed, I had no choice but to limit the focus in this chapter to them. But consider this chapter as a critique of managers of both mutual funds and pension funds.

and toward speculation. We've moved, as I've often said, from an "own-a-stock" industry to a "rent-a-stock" industry. Simply put, renters all too rarely handle their property with the same care as they would if they were owners.[2] As the late Columbia Law School Professor Louis Lowenstein has said, fund managers "exhibit a persistent emphasis on momentary stock prices. The subtleties and nuances of a particular business utterly escape them." Pure and simple, most mutual fund managers, while they seem to care about corporate governance, shun active participation in the proxy voting process.

A second obstacle to mutual fund activism is the commercial nature of the mutual fund business. We've become primarily a marketing business rather than a management business, a business in which salesmanship has come to overwhelm stewardship. When a fund manager takes a position on controversial proxy issues, it generates unwanted publicity. Better, it seems, to keep a low profile and avoid the risk. Perhaps even more significantly, our giant investment managers seek giant corporate clients, for managing their retirement plans is where the big money is . . . and where the big profits lie for the managers.

Since the mid-1990s, corporate 401(k) thrift plans have been among the driving forces in generating new mutual fund assets. Corporate pension funds—absent the need for all of that complex and costly sub-accounting—are also considered plums by institutional money managers. Given the drive to attract corporate clients, the reluctance of fund managers to risk the opprobrium of potential clients by leaping enthusiastically into the controversial areas of corporate governance is discouraging, but hardly astonishing. One manager hit the nail on the head with this (perhaps apocryphal) comment: "There are only two kinds of clients we can't afford to offend: actual and potential."

A third obstacle to activism, or so it has been alleged by the fund industry, is that corporate activism would be expensive for the funds to undertake. In a sense, it would be. Yet TIAA-CREF, whose investment portfolio totals some $500 billion, is unique in this industry in taking on the responsibilities of corporate activism. Several years ago, it spent an amount said to exceed $2 million per year on the implementation

---

[2]As former Treasury Secretary Lawrence Summers plaintively asked, "When was the last time someone washed a rental car?"

of its splendid—and productive—corporate governance program.[3] This expenditure, however, would amount to but 0.003 percent (3/1,000ths of 1 percent) of its present invested assets. But the benefits generated for TIAA-CREF's academic community participants are said to have been well worth the modest costs.

While small fund managers could hardly spend the resources necessary for a broad-gauge program, they could at least engage their security analysts in some kind of serious review of the governance of their major corporate holdings. And there is nothing that prevents fund managers from banding together and joining forces. Given the fund industry's now—$6.3 trillion worth of stock holdings, an industry-wide governance effort that entailed just 1/1,000 of 1 percent of expenses (relative to fund assets) would produce an annual budget of $60 million for an active corporate governance program—far in excess of what such a program would require.

Even that huge sum of money, however, would be but a drop in the bucket relative to today's roughly $100 *billion* that funds spend each year on administrative, investment management, marketing, and operating costs. I tried to form such a coalition—"The Federation of Long-Term Investors"—in 2002. My effort was applauded by Warren Buffett, who offered to support the effort if other large fund managers joined the effort. Alas, my proposal failed abjectly to attract a single one of the 10 largest mutual fund groups, and the proposed federation never got under way.[4]

A fourth and final obstacle might be described as the "people-who-live-in-glass-houses" syndrome. The mutual fund governance system itself has come under severe and well-deserved criticism. The problem is that it has enabled external managers, paid under contract, to essentially control the affairs of the mutual fund industry that they work for. These

---

[3]It may be significant that TIAA-CREF does not manage retirement plans for corporations, and therefore has no such clients to offend.

[4]Importantly, such a federation would have represented the participation of some 60 percent of mutual fund equity holdings, and would have largely responded to the "free-riding" issue. That is, the concern that if a fund owning 1 percent of the shares of a corporation spent its resources to make a proxy proposal that was implemented, the benefits would be shared by the shareholders of the other 99 percent who contributed nothing to the effort.

firms with relatively small capitalization (say, $1 billion) actually control the huge capital of the giant mutual funds (say, $100 billion) that they contract to serve.

How can that happen? Largely because the manager holds the nexus of control over the funds, usually solely responsible for as much as 100 percent of the administrative, accounting, shareholder record-keeping, legal, investment management, and marketing and distribution services required to run the mutual fund complex. The manager usually provides the funds' officers, and plays an influential role in selecting the funds' directors. Yes, the funds' manager typically does all of those things, and the fund itself is little more than a corporate shell.[5]

Where else in Corporate America is there a parallel to the control of a series of giant publicly held corporations (the mutual funds themselves) by a relatively small outside firm (the management company)—with its own separate group of shareholders—whose principal business is providing those giant corporations with all of the services required to conduct their affairs? As far as I can tell, *nowhere* else in the corporate world does such a perverse and counterintuitive structure exist. Looking at this peculiar fund structure a few steps removed, it's hard to imagine why it exists. But it is easier to understand than to accept the reluctance of fund managers to become corporate activists, daring to throw stones from their own glass houses at the managements of the corporations whose shares the funds own.

One fund executive who dared to throw stones—at corporate directors in general—is the CEO of Fidelity Management Company. In 1994, in an extremely rare public speech, Edward C. Johnson, III, CEO of Fidelity Management Company and CEO of each of the now—280 mutual funds managed by Fidelity, demanded that corporations (without naming them) put their owners first. The excerpts in Box 3.1 are from that speech. He is speaking about the responsibilities of the directors of the corporations in which the Fidelity fund owns shares.

Mr. Johnson was calling on corporate directors to challenge their CEOs, and if necessary, get rid of underperforming managers. Similarly,

---

[5]Janus Capital Group, for example, manages some $89 billion in mutual fund assets, but itself has a market capitalization of only $1.6 billion, a ratio of more than 55 to 1.

Box 3.1

"Physician, Heal Thyself"

Excerpts from Comments by Edward C. Johnson III

"We want directors who will mind the store for us, making sure management's doing a good job. . . . Their final responsibility is to the shareholders. Too often they represent their own interests or the Chief Executive Officer's. . . . [Managers must be] the best available. If not, [the Board] has to fire, rehire, and pay new managers . . . diligently spotting issues where the interests of managers and shareholders may conflict and then taking the initiative to deal with them. . . . [When the chairman sets the directors' pay], he can influence their loyalty. . . . When it comes to an issue where shareholders' interests diverge from management's, which way will this person vote? . . . We should have intelligent national laws that spell out directors' accountability to shareholders. . . . [We must] ensure better boardrooms—boardrooms that are responsible to shareholder interests and not passive rubber stamps for the chairman's agenda."

---

one would expect mutual fund directors also to challenge their own CEOs and replace failed managers. So it is ironic that these totally appropriate demands were directed to the directors of the giant corporations that make up the Fortune 500. Mr. Johnson seemed to ignore the obvious fact that his demands should also have been directed to independent directors of mutual funds, specifically including the independent directors of the Fidelity funds.

Yet those directors have *never* fired Fidelity Management from its position as manager of any Fidelity fund, nor—even when a fund's performance turned miserable—*ever* hired a new firm as manager. The failure of Magellan Fund, once by far the industry's largest fund, is a case in point. Its once outstanding early investment performance faded away in the early 1990s, replaced by mediocrity ever since. Fund shareholders left in droves, leading to a drop of almost 90 percent in its assets—from $103 billion to $15 billion. Yet Fidelity's lucrative contract to run the fund continues.

Further, so far as we know, Johnson has never lobbied Congress to pass intelligent national laws that spell out directors' accountability to shareholders . . . boardrooms that are responsible to shareholder interests." "Passive rubber stamps" continue to dominate the roles both of corporate directors and of mutual fund directors, even though, as a legal matter, their responsibilities are identical. Neither group should be allowed to shirk the solemn responsibilities that Johnson appropriately urged on them back in 1994. But he has yet to break the long silence that began when his speech ended.

The Picture Begins to Change

Mutual funds have been the epitome of nonactivism in the governance of the corporations in their portfolios. This silence has been the dominant standard of conduct ever since the beginning of the fund industry's history in 1924. Up until the 1980s, however, the industry had limited resources, fund voting power was but a tiny fraction of what it is today, and the issues presented to shareholders were rare. It's no wonder the industry was timid. (The Montgomery Ward case described earlier was a rare exception.)

But corporate policy issues that rightfully concerned many fund managers gradually began to loom large. Beginning in the mid-1980s, societal issues came to the fore; for example, apartheid in the Republic of South Africa. Many institutional shareholders—especially university endowment funds—demanded that corporations doing business in South Africa shut down their operations and pull out. Other so-called "corporate responsibility" issues also arose in that era, notably regarding munitions makers, tobacco manufacturers, and protection of the environment. Mutual funds, like other shareholders, had to take a stand, pro or con, or abstain. But we have no way to know which course they chose, for at the time there was no requirement that their proxy votes be disclosed.

By the mid-1990s, more substantive issues arose that affected corporate performance: executive compensation, including option issuance;

corporate restructuring; dividend policy; staggered board terms for corporate directors; and antitakeover defenses such as "poison pills" and the like. These issues were far more likely to be raised by relatively small investors with little clout (such as religious organizations and labor unions) than by the major mutual funds and pension funds that had the power to wield the big stick and ultimately impose their will on the corporations involved. Did they vote their proxies for or against these resolutions? We just don't know. For there remained a giant information gap on how or even whether institutional investors voted the proxies they controlled. Were they indeed serving the interests of the fund shareholders and pension beneficiaries whom they were duty bound to serve? Again, we had no way of knowing.

Reporting Proxy Votes

Finally, the Securities and Exchange Commission decided to shine the spotlight of full disclosure on the proxy voting practices of mutual funds. The Commission, however, took no position on voting by pension funds, labor unions, endowment funds, trust companies, and insurance companies—perhaps because only their mandate to regulate mutual funds was beyond challenge or perhaps because of the ascendance of mutual funds as the dominant ownership institution. In any event, in September 2002, the SEC released a proposal that would require mutual funds to report their voting decisions, company by company, to their shareowners. Given that there were tens of millions of fund shareowners, this was essentially the public at large. (Today, access to information on proxy votes by funds is generally available on the website of each fund complex, and from the SEC.)

In my opinion, the SEC position was conceptually correct—agents have a duty to report to their principals, for heaven's sake. It was also the right direction for public policy to take in serving the interests of fund shareholders and in serving the national interest. I hoped—and expected—that proxy vote disclosure would force funds to reexamine their heretofore passive approach to governance in favor of a more active approach. The single overriding goal: *to force our giant publicly held business corporations to place the interests of their own stockholders first, ahead of the interests of their managers.*

Soon after it was issued, I applauded the SEC proposal. My op-ed piece in *The New York Times* on December 14, 2002 explained the logic of my support. It did not take long for the opponents of the proposal to respond. Just two months later, on February 14, 2003, in an op-ed in *The Wall Street Journal*, John Brennan, my successor as CEO of Vanguard, and Edward C. Johnson, III, CEO of Fidelity, spoke out in opposition. Excerpts from both op-eds are presented in Box 3.2.

Box 3.2

The Great Debate on Proxy Voting Disclosure

FOR: The Author Supports Disclosure.

Op-ed in *The New York Times* (December 14, 2002)
Mutual Fund Secrecy

When, 27 years ago, I founded what is now the world's second largest mutual fund organization, I did my best to create a company that would live up to the ideal enshrined in the preamble to the Investment Company Act of 1940: that mutual funds should be managed in the interest of their shareholders rather than in the interest of their managers. Now the industry I helped to create is squandering an opportunity to show the public that this ideal still matters.

Most of the country's largest mutual fund companies oppose a new rule proposed by the Securities and Exchange Commission that would require mutual funds to tell the public how they voted their shares in corporate proxy elections. (Today) I cast my lot in opposition to the industry that I've been part of for my entire career.

In the mutual fund director's world, the fund's officers and managers are agents for their principals, the fund shareholders. It is management's responsibility to act solely on their behalf. It would thus seem self-evident that mutual fund shareholders should have the right to know how the shares of the corporations the funds own in their portfolios are voted. Such shareholders are partial owners of these stocks, and to deny them that information would stand on its head the common understanding of the principal-agency relationship.

Given that relationship, the fiduciary principle underlying the SEC's proposal seems beyond controversy. Nonetheless, when funds are required to report their votes, some business difficulties may arise. Votes against management, for example, may make it harder for fund managers to get information from a corporation or to win the right to advise its pension plan. Controversial votes may draw unwanted publicity.

By their long forbearance and lassitude on corporate governance issues, mutual funds bear no small share of the responsibility for the failures in corporate governance and accounting oversight that were among the major forces creating the stock market bubble of the late 1990s, and the (50 percent) bear market that followed.[6] If the owners of our corporations don't care about governance, who else is there to assume that responsibility?

The first step toward greater accountability is for mutual fund agents to disclose how they vote the shares they own on behalf of their shareholder principals. The time has long since come for funds to cease their passivity as corporate owners and to assume the important responsibilities of corporate citizenship.

AGAINST: Vanguard and Fidelity CEOs Oppose Disclosure.

Op-ed in *The Wall Street Journal* (February 14, 2003)
No Disclosure: The Feeling Is Mutual
The Securities and Exchange Commission is considering a proposal to require mutual funds to disclose how they vote the proxies of the corporations whose stock they hold. While it seems a well-intended effort to restore investor confidence in

(Continued)

---

[6]The same causal relationship would apply again in the financial crisis of 2007–2008, and the even worse bear market that followed.

Corporate America and promote accountability, the proposal's unintended consequences could undermine the best interests of 95 million mutual-fund shareholders in the U.S. The threat is so severe that we, the leaders of the fund industry's two largest competitors, come together now, for the first time ever, to speak out publicly against it.

Our fiduciary duty (to our mutual fund stockholders) brings our two companies together to oppose the SEC's disclosure proposal. If the SEC's proposed rule (to require disclosure of votes) goes into effect, one—and only one—group of investors will be singled out to lose this right: mutual funds. Pension funds, insurance companies, foundations, bank-trust departments and other investors would retain their rights of confidentiality. The effect would be to make mutual funds the prime pressure point for veiled threats from every activist group with a political or social ax to grind with Corporate America.

Disclosing the individual proxy votes of the hundreds of securities owned by the typical mutual fund is neither practical nor useful. . . . Instead of all the regulation, why not simply enhance the proxy oversight role of mutual-fund boards? Ensure that they hold their companies to clearly established proxy voting guidelines. Let them see that fund managers' votes are consistent with the company's guidelines—subject to SEC examination.

On January 23, 2003, the SEC approved the proxy disclosure requirement by a unanimous vote. (A senior Commission official told me that my *New York Times* op-ed had played an important role in their decision.) As a result, ever since 2004, funds have had to disclose their proxy votes, without, as far as I know, veiled threats or mass protests from *any* "activist group with a political or social ax to grind."

Mobilizing Institutional Investors

The requirement that mutual funds disclose their proxy votes to their owners has created a new and powerful motivation for funds to exercise their rights as corporate citizens. We ought to require similar disclosure on the part of *all* fiduciaries to their constituencies, including traditional corporate pension funds; pension funds of federal, state, and local governments; trust companies and insurance companies; and endowment funds. With 100 million fund shareholders, of course, this disclosure is equivalent to public disclosure. But with rights come responsibilities, and we need to develop standards so that *all* of those with trusteeship responsibilities—including those of university endowment funds, where political and economic judgments have been known to overshadow other factors in voting—will also be held to high standards of fiduciary duty.

With voting disclosure providing the motivation to do what's right, institutional investors should be given the tools to do what's right, with clear access to the corporate proxy statement. Corporations, however, allow such access only grudgingly. A 2003 SEC proposal to facilitate access only left the door ajar. This complex proposal would have allowed large shareholders to nominate one to three directors depending on the board's size, but only after certain triggering events take place; namely a 5 percent combined ownership position for at least three years. The Commission, I thought, should have gone further, and opened that door wide enough to permit much greater freedom of collective investor action. But at least its proposal would give institutional investors a seat at the table, so to speak, by potentially playing a role in the selection of directors for corporate boards.

When the SEC issued that proposal in 2003 to facilitate access to corporate proxy proposals, it asked for comments. But I saw not one single response by a large institutional manager demanding even more access. Indeed, rather than seeking greater access, institutional investors seemed to seek even less. Some commentators sought to make a weak access proposal even weaker, suggesting even higher ownership thresholds. Nowhere did I see a hue and cry to encourage—or even allow—fiduciaries to behave as active owners.

As far as I could determine, most of the industry's biggest guns—Dreyfus, Fidelity, Janus, MFS, Putnam, Vanguard—didn't even respond to the SEC proposal. Neither did Citibank, Goldman Sachs, Merrill Lynch, nor Morgan Stanley respond, despite their control of giant fund empires. And other institutions—Schwab, Prudential, Northern Trust, and JPMorgan Chase, all with large institutional investment and mutual fund units—actually opposed the SEC's modest thrust toward corporate democracy.[7] If we are to return to true owners' capitalism, Investment America apparently will have to be dragged kicking and screaming into the fray.

In the face of such opposition by corporations, and the demonstrated lack of interest by their institutional owners, the SEC proposal was ultimately dropped. (When the corporations are organized and determined to win and the managers are unorganized and don't care, such an outcome is less than astonishing!) Since then, sad to say, we've actually moved backward. For in 2006, the U.S. Court for the Second Circuit ruled essentially that the proposed limits on proxy access were illegal, requiring the SEC to amend its proposal to virtually eliminate proxy access by shareholders. The Commission subsequently abandoned its effort for reform.

In a new proposal in 2009, the Commission tried again, formally adopting new rules for granting access by shareholders in 2010. But the Business Roundtable and the U.S. Chamber of Commerce went to court in opposition, and the D.C. Circuit Court struck down the new rule, stating that the SEC "acted arbitrarily and capriciously for having failed once again adequately to assess the economic effects of a new rule."

The court's decision was based on the Congressional requirement for a "cost-benefit" analysis of any new regulation. As noted earlier, the costs of a new rule can be easily measured in tangible dollar terms and the benefits are often largely intangible. How does one measure the potential shareholder value added by the active participation of stockholders in the governance of the corporations whose shares they own? One can only agree that the federal government, as the court said, should "tailor regulations to impose the least burdens on society," as its statement reads, and should "achieve the common good . . . ensuring that benefits outweigh costs." But when that noble principle is ignored in the quest for mathematical purity in its implementation, it is our

---

[7]It is significant that except for Fidelity and Vanguard, each of these corporations were either publicly held or owned by public corporations. In effect, they could be affected by the proposal in one way as the owners and another way as the owned—an obvious conflict.

society that is the loser. In any event, the SEC chose not to appeal the court's wrong-headed ruling, and there the matter rests today.

The Rights and Responsibilities of Ownership

The judiciary has failed to give the owners of stocks—and the agents of those owners—the full power to execute all of the rights that would seem implicit in such ownership. Yet there is still much that our institutional money managers can do. The first task is to demand that these financial intermediaries that dominate Investment America put the interests of those they serve as their first and overriding priority. We must strengthen the traditional fiduciary law, now only loosely administered by the states in which corporations are chartered. We ought to impose a federal statute of fiduciary duty, as well as consider whether federal chartering of corporations—something that was debated at the Constitutional Convention in 1787—would be wise.

All those years ago, James Madison argued that the new federal government should be authorized to charter corporations. But as author Roger Lowenstein describes it, "federal charters smacked of royal perquisites, [so] it was left to the states to write the rules. Delaware, through its utter permissiveness, became the corporate residence of choice, much as the Cayman Islands is a paper domicile for secrecy-minded bankers. To this day, more than half of America's largest companies are incorporated in its second-smallest state. Delaware laws are so lax they don't even require publishing an annual report."

Acting Like Owners

What is essential, finally, is that the last-line owners—the investors themselves—demand high standards of trusteeship from those who represent their ownership interests. In mutual funds, those 100 million direct owners have no individual power, but awesome collective power. These fund investors need to understand what investing and trusteeship are all about, and, by voting with their feet, gradually gravitate to fund organizations that are serious about putting their interests first.

In retirement plans, while the contributors to the thrift plans and the beneficiaries of pension plans presently have no mechanism for bringing about the same result, they surely deserve some formal legal voice. They could establish standards of conduct for the trustees of the assets that have been set aside to fund their retirements. State law is clear that retirement plan fiduciaries have the traditional duties of loyalty and prudence. Now we need a federal statute that goes even further, one that codifies that the agents of those institutions entrusted with the responsibilities for managing other people's money have a fiduciary duty to the principals whom they serve. Such a duty would be broad and far-reaching. It would include:

1. A requirement that all fiduciaries must act solely in the long-term interests of their beneficiaries.
2. An affirmation by government that an effective shareholder presence in all public companies is in the national interest.
3. A demand that all institutional money managers should be accountable for the compulsory exercise of their votes, in the sole interest of their shareholders.
4. A recognition of the right of shareholders to nominate directors and make proxy proposals, subject to appropriate limits.
5. A demand that any ownership structure of managers that entails conflicts of interest be eliminated.

That five-point list is not my own. Rather, I'm citing—with enthusiasm—the ideas of Robert A. G. Monks, author, founder of International Shareholder Services (ISS), cofounder of The Corporate Library, and former federal government official with responsibility for the U.S. pension system. The title of Monk's monograph—*Capitalism Without Owners Will Fail*—(with Allen Sykes) is no overstatement. Corporate managers must be focused on creating long-term value for their *owners* rather than focusing on short-term stock prices for their *renters*. Monks speaks with a passion and intensity that few others can equal. Box 3.3. presents excerpts from his 2011 essay, "Capture."

The fact is that, yes, *capitalism without owners will fail*. Only if managers are focused on creating long-term value for their *owners* rather than on short-term stock prices for the *renters* of their stock can Corporate

Box 3.3

Capture

By Robert A. G. Monks

"American corporations today are like the great European monarchies of yore: They have the power to control the rules under which they function and to direct the allocation of public resources. This is not a prediction of what's to come; this is a simple statement of the present state of affairs. Corporations have effectively captured the United States: its judiciary, its political system, and its national wealth, without assuming any of the responsibilities of domination. Evidence is everywhere.

- *"The 'smoking gun' is CEO pay.* Compensation is an expression of concentrated power—of enterprise power concentrated in the chief executive officer and of national power concentrated in corporations. Median U.S. CEO pay for 2010 was up 35 percent in the midst of a lingering recession.
- *"Retirement risk has been transferred to employees.* During the same period that CEOs were doubling their own compensation, the 'best' CEOs of the 'best' companies abrogated the century-old commitment by employers to provide pensions to their workers. IBM has been the corporate leader in abolishing a 'real' pension system for its employees, eliminating its on-going defined benefit plans to save IBM as much as $3 billion through the next few years . . . (and) provide it with a more predictable cost structure. . . . CEOs are enriched, while all other corporate constituencies, including government, are left with liabilities.
- *"The financial power of American corporations now controls every stage of politics—legislative, executive, and ultimately judicial.* With its January 2010 decision in the *Citizens United* case, the

(Continued)

Supreme Court removed all legal restraints on the extent of corporate financial involvement in politics, a grotesque decision that can have only one effect: maximizing corporate—*not national*—value.

- "*Capture has been further implemented through the extensive lobbying power of corporations.* Abraham Lincoln's warning about 'corporations enthroned' and Dwight Eisenhower's about the 'unwarranted influence by the military/industrial complex' have been fully realized in our own time.

- "*Capture has placed the most powerful CEOs above the reach of the law and beyond its effective enforcement.* Extensive evidence of Wall Street's critical involvement in the financial crisis notwithstanding, not a single senior Wall Street executive has lost his job, and pay levels have been rigorously maintained even when TARP payments had to be refinanced in order to remove any possible restrictions.

- "Finally, capture has been perpetuated through the removal of property 'offshore,' where it is neither regulated nor taxed. The social contract between Americans and their corporations was supposed to go roughly as follows: In exchange for limited liability and other privileges, corporations were to be held to a set of obligations that legitimatized the powers they were given. But modern corporations have assumed the right to relocate to different jurisdictions, almost at will, irrespective of where they really do business, and thus avoid the constraints of those obligations.

"Government cannot and will not hold corporations to account. That much is now obvious. Indeed, the dawning realization of this truth is what has informed the Occupy movement, but *only the owners of corporations can create the accountability that will ultimately unwind the knot of government capture.*

"The essence of the problem is quite straightforward: a failed system of corporate governance. So is the cause: the unwillingness of trustee owners of America's corporations to assert their responsibility, legal duty, *and* civic obligation to monitor and oversee the corporations they invest in. Fiduciary institutions own more than 70 percent of the outstanding shares of Corporate America and thus bear at least 70 percent of the responsibility for present circumstances as well as 70 percent of the onus for saving the system itself.

"Now, men and women of conscience need to reoccupy the boardrooms of America's corporations. The boardroom is where the takeover began, and it's where capture can finally be undone and a government of, by, and for the *people*, not the *corporations*, restored to the land."

America be the prime engine of the nation's growth and prosperity and a major source of innovation and experimentation. To the extent that corporate managers sit unchecked in the driver's seat, feathering their own nests at the expense of their own stock shareholders, and rent-a-stock shareholders focus solely on momentary, ephemeral prices, capitalism cannot flourish.

The giant institutions of Investment America are obviously hesitant to take the lead in accomplishing these goals. But who else can lead the effort? These money managers not only hold more than 70 percent of all shares, but they have the staffs to pore over corporate financial statements and proxies; the professional expertise to evaluate CEO performance, pay, and perquisites; and (now that full disclosure of all proxy votes by mutual funds is mandatory), they have the incentive to vote in the manner that their beneficiaries have every right to expect. As they move away from today's culture of short-term speculation and return to their traditional focus on long-term investing, these institutional owners must fight for the access to the levers of control over the corporations they own. These are powerful levers that are both appropriate for their ownership position and a reflection of their willingness to accept both the rights and responsibilities of corporate citizenship.

Accomplishing these goals forces us to consider some ideas about corporate democracy that are rarely mentioned. What about allowing longer-term owners greater voting rights? Or even requiring a specific holding period (say, three years) before shares can be voted? What about a premium dividend payment on a new class of stock available only to those same long-term owners? Surely a little imagination could provide even more encouragement to owners of stocks who care about good governance vis-à-vis renters of stocks who don't seem to care.

"The Proof of the Pudding"

So far, however, our money managers seem far more inclined to shun those rights and responsibilities than to embrace them. If "the proof of the pudding is in the eating," the SEC regulation that required mutual funds to report their proxy votes seems to have had no more than a modest positive influence on mutual fund voting practices. So far, I've seen no academic articles whatsoever that have examined mutual fund proxy voting patterns. But an exhaustive analysis of fund voting practices has been undertaken by the giant American Federation of State, County, and Municipal Employees (AFSCME) and produced annually over the past five years.[8]

The union's report for the year ended June 30, 2011, focused on the differences between the voting profiles for funds that are the dominant providers of retirement plan services to corporate retirement plans, a $4 trillion business for the fund industry. The AFSCME data showed that the four largest providers (Fidelity, Vanguard, American Funds, and BlackRock) "exhibited the most corporate-management-friendly voting patterns," generally supporting director's elections, approving management proposals, and opposing shareholder proposals. To reach that conclusion, AFSCME examined the votes cast by the 26 largest

---

[8]Critics of the work of this labor union group describe its work as biased. But the data appear to be accurate, and the critics have not attempted to rebut its central conclusion about the general passivity of fund proxy voting. Further, whatever bias may exist would hardly seem to influence the relative ranking of these 26 managers.

mutual fund managers, ascertaining how often they supported three broad types of proposals:

1. *Selection of specific directors* of S&P 500 companies where 30 percent or more of shares were withheld from or voted against one or more directors for reasons related to concern over executive pay and where proxy advisory services specifically recommended voting against the selected directors.

2. *Company management proposals* affirming compensation-related proxy proposals made by company management, such as equity compensation plans, bonus plan performance criteria, management advisory vote on executive compensation, or "Say on Pay" proposals and option issuance.

3. *Shareholder proposals* relating largely to limiting executive compensation.

The report ranked the voting practices of these 26 fund families from the most supportive of efforts to tie executive pay to company performance (and in turn, to shareholder value) to the least supportive of those efforts (see Exhibit 3.1). AFSCME chose categories of shareholder proposals on executive pay that the union believed to be most likely to enhance shareholder value. They dubbed the fund families that most consistently supported measures to rein-in pay the "Pay Constrainers" and those that voted least often for such measures the "Pay Enablers," with the lowest scores going to them. The data for 2011 were roughly consistent with the data for the prior year. Here's what the study found:

The four largest defined contribution (DC) retirement plan managers were Fidelity, Vanguard, BlackRock, and American Funds, which together supervised nearly one-half of all DC plan assets held in funds that were reviewed in the report. The other 22 fund families controlled the remainder. Plan assets supervised by all 26 families totaled $3.1 trillion.

- The largest plan providers exhibited the most management-friendly voting patterns on the shareholder proposals and director-voting categories.
- While these firms apparently do apply a higher level of scrutiny to management proposals than the majority of fund families, they

Exhibit 3.1 How the 26 Largest Defined Contribution Managers Voted

Manager	Defined Contribution Money Managed 2011 (thousands)	Director Support	Votes for Manager Compensation Proposals	Votes for Shareholder Compensation Proposals	AFSCME Rank
Fidelity	$493,000,000	65%	67%	4%	24
Vanguard	362,000,000	94	90	2	26
BlackRock	324,000,000	86	91	15	20
American Funds	232,000,000	86	70	4	25
LargestFour Managers	$1,411,000,000	83%	80%	6%	–
Remaining 22 Managers*	$1,692,000,000	50	80	56	–
Total: Largest 26 Managers	$3,103,000,000	55%	80%	48%	–

*Voting data are for the 5th through 26th major DC providers.

rank among the bottom five fund managers in favoring shareholder proposals.

Unfair as such a broad generalization may be, their singling-out of Vanguard as the least shareholder-friendly manager—the firm ranked #26 on the list of 26—hardly gladdens my heart. But the AFSCME numbers, however interpreted, are not inconsistent with the data used by Vanguard in its public report: 94 percent in favor of directors; 89 percent in favor of management proposals; 13 percent in favor of shareholder proposals.

I do not presume to know how Fidelity or BlackRock or American Funds would respond to the question of whether their fiduciary duty to vote proxies in the interests of mutual fund shareholders is compromised by the managers' desire for more revenue and profits, or simply reflects their competitive instincts to prevail in that huge marketplace. Vanguard management flatly denies any such connection. In the firm's policy statement describing its Proxy Voting Policies, Vanguard states, in effect, that the actual number of votes cast is less relevant than the "significant amount of time spent in engaging—whether in writing, conference calls, or face-to-face meetings—with management and board members of portfolio companies regarding potential governance and compensation issues. . . . In some cases, company officials acknowledged our concerns and pledged responsive actions . . . (if not) we voted against."

I take at face value Vanguard's statement, and have no information that would contradict its position. But what surprised me—and, I confess, disappointed me—was that the two index fund providers among the "Big Four"—Vanguard and BlackRock—were both notably passive in their voting policies. After all, if an index fund isn't happy with a corporation's management, it *can't* sell the stock. So logic would suggest that it should work to change the management. In a 2010 *Wall Street Journal* op-ed, John Brennan, former Vanguard CEO, seemed to agree that index funds should be active in their voting decisions: "As one of the largest index providers in the world, Vanguard hardly takes a passive approach to corporate governance. As permanent shareholders of a corporation, [we have] a shared interest in maximizing long-term value and in meeting short-term goals." Yet Dimensional Fund Advisors—also a major index manager (but one with a relatively small $15 billion in defined contribution plan assets under management) ranked #1 in shareholder activism in the ACFSME study, supporting a remarkable 99% of shareholder proposals.

While the voting data and the policy statement are not necessarily inconsistent, the issue is whether the giant managers of defined contribution plans are honoring their responsibility to serve the interests of their own shareholders rather than protecting their dominant position in serving the retirement plans of Corporate America—and protecting their ability to attract more business from other corporations. You'll recall the idea that money managers want to offend neither actual nor potential clients; that is, *all* of the large corporations with either defined contribution plans or defined benefit plans or both.

Only time will tell if Vanguard and the other large institutional money managers—whether they manage retirement plans or not—will take a higher profile in their activism in the governance of our nation's publicly held corporations. Perhaps they will decide to have more discussions with management; perhaps they will support more aggressive shareholder-friendly proxy votes; perhaps one day they will even make their own proxy proposals that demand increased management focus on shareholder interests of all kinds.

So far, however, most proxy proposals have come from individuals and small institutions. Few, if any, have been made by these giants. The variety and number of shareholder proposals is substantial. In recent years, proposals have increasingly focused on environmental and social issues, and demand for "proxy access" to elect directors is growing. In 2012, two of the major thrusts are "say on pay" proposals and corporate political contributions, both of which are worthy of special discussion.

Executive Compensation

In the case of executive compensation, our giant institutional manager/ agents seem particularly reluctant to take on this issue. By failing to do so, they must assume at least partial responsibility for the extraordinarily high salaries, bonuses, deferred compensation, stock options, and other compensation to corporate CEOs and their highest-ranking fellow officers. Compensation has simply flown "off the wheels" in the recent era, and the numbers, it seems to me, have gotten totally out of hand.

How high are these compensation levels and wealth levels for CEOs? We can thank *The New York Times* for its annual survey of the

Exhibit 3.2   Corporate Executive Compensation, 2011

Name and Company	2011 Salary (in millions)
Timothy D. Cook, Apple	$378.0
Lawrence J. Ellison, Oracle	77.6
Ronald B. Johnson, J. C. Penney	53.3
Philippe P. Dauman, Viacom	43.1
David M. Cote, Honeywell	35.3
Stephen I. Chazen, Occidental Petroleum	31.7
Robert A. Iger, Walt Disney	31.4
Clarence P. Cazalot Jr., Marathon Oil	29.9
Alan R. Mulally, Ford Motor	29.5
Rupert Murdoch, News Corp.	29.4
Gregory Q. Brown, Motorola Solutions	29.3
Samuel J. Palmisano, IBM	24.2
William C. Weldon, Johnson & Johnson	23.4
Lowell C. McAdam, Verizon	23.0
Louis R. Chênevert, United Technologies	22.9

SOURCE: Company Reports.

compensation of chief executives of 200 companies with at least $5 billion of revenue, published in April 2012. Exhibit 3.2 shows a list of the 15 highest paid CEOs.

The next 15 CEOs all received compensation in the $18–$22 million range, and the lowest among the top 50 received $11 million. The median compensation for the 100 highest paid CEOs was $14.4 million, 320 times the average American salary of $45,230. Ironically, if CEOs are able to increase profits by holding the lid on the compensation of their workers, they win and their millions of employees who produce what the company makes and sells are the losers.

That 320/1 ratio of the compensation of CEOs relative to the average worker's pay in 2011 compares with a ratio of just 42/1 in 1980. Over that 30-year span, CEO compensation measured in nominal dollars rose nearly 16 times over that of the average worker, while the compensation of the average worker slightly more than doubled. Measured in real 1980 dollars, CEO compensation rose at a rate of 6.5 percent annually, increasing by more than 560 percent in real terms during the period. In comparison, the compensation of the average worker increased by only 0.7 percent per year, leading to an insignificant cumulative increase (compounded over 30 years, an increase of only 14 percent) in family living standards. I find this change shocking, and virtually inexplicable.

The rationale of today's ratio is that these executives had "created wealth" for their shareholders. But were CEOs actually creating value commensurate with this huge increase in compensation? Certainly the average CEO was not. During the past 24 years, corporations had *projected* their earnings growth at an average annual rate of 11.5 percent. But they actually *delivered* growth of 6 percent per year—only half of their goal, and even less than the 6.2 percent nominal growth rate of the economy. In real terms, profits grew at an annual rate of just 2.9 percent, compared to 3.1 percent for our nation's economy, as represented by the Gross Domestic Product. How that somewhat dispiriting lag can drive average CEO compensation to a cool $9.8 million in 2004, and then to $11.4 in 2010, is one of the great anomalies of the age.

Much of the corporate executive compensation and wealth has been created by the "heads I win, tails you lose" nature of stock options. The share dilution by these options is often kept within seemingly reasonable limits, within 2 percent to 3 percent of shares outstanding each year, often offset by the repurchase of a number of shares equal to those issued to executives. But limited attention seems to be paid to *cumulative* dilution over the years, which comes to staggering levels—perhaps as much as 25 percent or more over a decade. However, I have been unable to find a single governance study or academic paper on the overpowering significance of such dilution over time.

Another explanation given for soaring CEO compensation is that it merely reflects the enormous (and increasingly public), compensation paid to star athletes, entertainment personalities, and movie stars. Such comparisons are irrelevant and absurd. These celebrities are essentially paid by their fans, or the owners of teams or networks, out of their own pockets. But CEOs are paid by directors, not out of their own pockets but with other people's money.[9] Corporate directors are the agents of

---

[9]When CEO compensation exceeds federal standards, one is subject to a tax surcharge. The corporation often then "grosses-up" the compensation to make the executives whole. Isn't it grand to be indemnified for one's taxes! As I've often noted, it's amazing how cheap something is if you can buy it with other people's money.

the shareholders, but whether they are acting in shareholders' best interests is another matter. This agency problem—yet *another* agency problem—permeates corporate governance, and bears a major responsibility for the rise in CEO compensation.

How Did It Happen?

It is easy to identify the major causes of the soaring benefits to America's corporate chieftains, and the distressing dichotomy between their compensation and the compensation of those whom they employ. To begin with, when CEOs engage in downsizing (sorry, we're supposed to call it "right-sizing"), and are under pressure to meet the earnings guidance they give to Wall Street, placing stringent limits on workers' compensation acts to reduce costs and increase profits. It benefits management with higher salaries and bonuses.

But it is these workers who commit their lives to the company day after day, and who create and produce the products and services that are every company's bread and butter, who are almost always the victims. The steps to be taken are no secret. They include: reducing staff, laying-off higher-paid or older employees (without appearing to have done so), curtailing wage increases, cutting research and development costs, and slashing retirement plan benefits. Consider the virtual demise of the defined-benefit pension plan that once dominated the corporate retirement system, which I discuss in Chapter 7.

Leave aside for the moment that such steps are designed to increase corporate earnings, to meet Wall Street's expectations, and to increase the firm's stock price. And usually downsizing does just that, at least in the short run. But the jury is still out as to whether these near-term efficiencies and these failures to invest adequately for the future eventually erode the company's prospects for long-term growth. Once again, the central issue posed is a manifestation of the basic issue of this book—the harm done when a culture of short-term speculation focused on the price of a *stock* overwhelms a culture of long-term investment focused on the intrinsic value of a *corporation*.

Further, the enormous existing structure of corporate stock option plans for senior management is almost all about evanescent prices, with little relevance to durable intrinsic values. This dichotomy can easily persist in the short run. But in the long run, price and value must be virtually identical. Warren Buffett got it just right: "When the price of Berkshire Hathaway stock temporarily overperforms or underperforms the business, a limited number of shareholders—either sellers or buyers—receive outsized benefits at the expense of those they trade with. [But] over time, the aggregate gains made by Berkshire shareholders must of necessity match the business gains of the company."

The Ratchet Effect

The rise of the executive compensation consultant is also heavily responsible for our flawed system of CEO compensation. First, consider what those in the business of recommending executive compensation must do to stay in business: lots of good analysis, yes; handsome presentations, yes; persuasiveness, of course. But above all, *never recommend lower pay or tougher standards for CEO compensation.* Not if you want to be in business for long. To make matters worse, the well-known methodology of consultants—grouping CEOs into peer groups measured in quartiles—inevitably leads to a ratchet effect.

Here's how it works: When a board finds that its own CEO's pay reposes in the fourth quartile, it is all too likely to raise his or her compensation to bring it into, say, the second quartile. (Directors rarely seem to jump it all the way to the first quartile.) This leap, of course, drops another CEO into the fourth quartile. Eventually, he'll be moved to a higher quartile, too. And so the cycle repeats, onward and upward over the years, almost always with the encouragement of an ostensibly impartial overseer retained by the board of directors, who is at least tacitly endorsed by the CEO. So the so-called "free market" that sets CEO compensation doesn't exist. Rather it is a controlled market that is essentially created by compensation consultants.[10]

Such a methodology is fundamentally flawed, and has the obvious effect: The figures in these compensation grids almost always go up for

---

[10]There ought to be a word for such a perverse market anomaly. Not a monopoly, not an oligopoly, but perhaps "consultopoly" would do the job.

the *group*, and almost never go down. Again, Warren Buffett pointedly describes the typical consulting firm by naming it, tongue-in-cheek, "Ratchet, Ratchet, and Bingo." This name calls attention to the lottery that executives cannot lose when they receive stock options: Stock up, exercise the option; stock down, forget it. Until we pay CEOs on the basis of *corporate performance* rather than on the basis of *corporate peer groups*, CEO pay will, almost inevitably, continue on its upward path.[11]

I must add that one reason that our very highly paid institutional managers have basically been inert in challenging the astounding compensation of our also very highly paid corporate managers may well be that these money managers themselves are so highly paid.[12] Finally, most of these large money management firms are in fact owned and controlled by *other* publicly held corporations. ("If the CEO of the parent of my money manager is up there at the top, how can I vote against similar compensation for one of the corporations in my portfolio?") The obvious conflict involved in this circular ownership pattern in which one hand washes the other ought to hold a high priority among the emerging issues of the coming decade.

What's to Be Done?

What's to be done? First, CEO compensation should be based on the building of long-term and enduring intrinsic value, which is as real as it is imprecise. (Now there's a paradox!) Yes, stock prices correlate nicely

---

[11]An idea for improvement: Require that the quartiles into which CEOs fall are consistent with the quartiles in which the success of their firms is measured. (Performance would be measured not by stock price performance, but by return on the firm's total capital.) Perhaps such a comparison would help to halt the perpetual motion machine that executive compensation has become.

[12]CEOs of fund managers aren't exactly impoverished. Data are available only from publicly owned fund managers, and they show that in 2011 T. Rowe Price's CEO James A. C. Kennedy was paid, $7.9 million; BlackRock CEO Laurence D. Fink, $21.9 million; Franklin Resources CEO Gregory E. Johnson, $9.9 million; Federated CEO J. Christopher Donahue, $4.6 million. These compensation figures, however, ignore the value accumulated in the stock of the management company: Kennedy $200 million; Fink $310 million; Johnson family $9 billion; Donahue family $140 million.

with business results, but only over the very long run. In the short term, the correlation seems random at best. Simply put, stock prices are a flawed measure of corporate performance. Using Lord Keynes's classic formulation, the level of stock prices involves both *enterprise*—the yield on an investment over the long term—and *speculation*—betting on the psychology of the market. I argued for the ultimate validity of the triumph of enterprise 60 years ago. Today, I continue to opt for the preeminence of enterprise.

During the 1980s and 1990s, for example, earnings of the corporations in the S&P 500 grew at about 5.9 percent a year, well below their growth rate of 7.7 percent during the previous two decades. Yet stocks performed well during that period, simply because the price-earnings multiple on the S&P 500 soared from 8 times to 32 times, adding about 7.5 percent per year of speculative return to stock prices. Obviously, this outcome was a nonrecurring event that, compounded, dwarfed the actual earnings growth rate. That is, high stock performance generated by higher stock market valuations led to high pay. Short-term emotions-based market madness played a critical role in the "lottery effect" that underlies stock options. It suggests, at the absolute minimum, that options prices should be adjusted to reflect changes in the general level of stock prices, as measured by, say, the S&P 500 Index.

Basing compensation on increasing the intrinsic value of a business would be a far better way of rewarding executives for durable long-term performance. For example, CEO compensation might be based on corporate earnings growth—or even better, corporate cash flow, which is far more difficult to manipulate—and dividend growth. Return on total corporate capital (not only equity capital)—both relative to the company's peers, and relative to corporations as a group, say, the S&P 500. Such returns should be measured only over an extended period of time, but *only after deducting the corporation's cost of capital.*

Consider the Cost of Capital

Yet this return on capital is a concept rarely, if ever, considered in compensation plans. But it must not be ignored. The corporation should set a sort of "hurdle rate" that takes into account the firm's cost of capital.

Even if it is set at a relatively modest annual rate—say, 8 percent—executives should be paid *only* for returns in excess of that rate. If a corporation has, say, $1 billion of capital, it ought to earn at least an 8 percent return, or $80 million. Until that target is reached, no bonuses and no options. Compensation should be paid only on profits in excess of that return on corporate capital. Of course, these standards are challenging, but meeting tough competitive standards is what real business success is all about.

It is now obvious that CEO compensation should have a contingent component, and a durable one. Incentive pay should be spread out over an extended period of years, and stock options should be phased in as well. For example, say, 50 percent of options should be exercisable on the first exercise date, with 10 percent exercisable annually over the subsequent five years. The acquired holdings would be mandated to be held for a significant time, perhaps until the executive leaves the firm. There should also be "claw-back" provisions for returning incentive compensation to the company if earnings are restated. (I had understood that Section 304 of the Sarbanes-Oxley Act provided effective claw-back provisions for equity-based executive compensation when restatements occur. However, such claw-backs are limited to restatements resulting from "misconduct," and the SEC has yet to pursue a single case.)

Slight Progress on Reform

One important step is now being taken. Significantly, it is not at the behest of our institutional money managers, but by Congress. The Dodd-Frank Wall Street Reform and Consumer Protection Act of 2010 provides a mandate for all public corporations to allow nonbinding shareholder votes on executive compensation. Its implementation costs will be relatively modest, and it will force institutional shareholders to consider compensation issues with greater care—a nice step forward. Anything that draws the institutional owners who now control Corporate America into acting as responsible corporate citizens should benefit our society at large.

Yet even though the first proxy season allowing the so-called say-on-pay votes at all public companies took place in the spring of 2011, little seems to have changed. Later that year, in July, *The Wall Street Journal* reported that shareholders rejected their firms' executive compensation plans at only 39 of 2,532 companies. (Proxy advisor Institutional Shareholder Services had recommended votes against executive pay for 298 firms.) Some 71 percent of companies received at least 90 percent of shareholder votes in favor of their executive compensation practices.

Why such an overwhelming agreement? There were two apparent reasons. One, many companies enhanced disclosure in their compensation discussion and analysis statements, providing a clearer view of their compensation philosophy and the metrics used to make compensation decisions, giving shareholders a better understanding of the issues. Two, many companies engaged in dialogue with their largest shareholders to understand the factors institutional shareholders use to evaluate executive compensation, and presumably persuaded them of their fairness.

But it's not at all clear that "say-on-pay" will slow the rise of executive compensation. Robert A. G. Monks was quoted as saying "say-on-pay is at best a diversion and at worst a deception. You only have the appearance of reform, and it's a cruel hoax." Lynn Turner, former Chief Accountant of the SEC, noted the conflict of interests that mutual funds have as they try to attract corporate 401(k) clients, saying that the big fund companies "won't vote against management proposals on compensation unless they're really bad."[13] Interestingly, the giant California State Teachers Retirement Systems (CalSTRS), which faces no comparable conflict of interest, voted against management compensation fully 23 percent of the time.

Corporate Political Contributions

Another major emerging issue on corporate governance relates to political contributions. Particularly in the face of the Supreme Court's decision in

---

[13]On April 18, 2012, Citigroup shareholders voted to reject the management's pay package proposal, a stinging rebuke that was the first such vote to reject the compensation plan at a once-near-failed financial giant. Some 55 percent of shareholders voted against the nonbinding plan.

the landmark 2011 *Citizens United* case that opened the door to virtually unlimited political contributions by our corporations, this issue may well be the "hot issue" of the 2012 proxy season. So far, the political contribution question is in the process of being resolved by voluntary corporate disclosure of such contributions, a result of enlightened self-interest by corporate managers and the demand by some institutional investors to make such disclosure mandatory.

Mere disclosure, however, may not be enough. Investors should be raising the issue of *whether any contributions whatsoever* should be allowed without the approval of shareholders. Unlike the executive compensation issue, where the standards were established by the SEC early in 2011, the Commission has as yet made no attempt to establish appropriate and uniform standards for voting on disclosure of political contributions. I believe that the SEC must promptly do exactly that.[14]

In November 2011, a coalition of asset managers and investment professionals representing over $690 billion in assets wrote to the SEC to express their strong support for the proposition that the SEC promulgate rules requiring corporate political transparency. (However, not a single major mutual fund manager joined in this plea.) Since there are significant gaps in the type of spending that is required to be disclosed, they asked the SEC for clear rules on full disclosure by all public companies on their political expenditures. The Council for Institutional Investors seconded the motion:

> Shareowners have a right to know whether and how their company uses its resources for political purposes. Yet the existing regulatory framework creates barriers to this information. Disclosure is either dispersed among several regulatory authorities or entirely absent in cases where political spending is channeled through independent organizations exempt from naming donors.

---

[14]At least one Commissioner agrees with me. Luis Aguilar, in a speech in February 2012, stated that "while some companies are voluntarily providing disclosure, many others are not . . . and the disclosure that is provided is not uniform, and may not be adequate. It is important that shareholders are not left in the dark while this money is paid without their knowledge or consent. The Commission should (set standards for) uniform and consistent disclosure."

As one state treasurer added: "It is troubling that many companies are funding political campaigns without their shareholders' consent or even knowledge."

While I applaud the principles of full disclosure, I believe that more than mere disclosure is required. In the wake of the *Citizens United* case, the institutional investor community has an obligation to act even more forcefully, insisting that, before we even consider appropriate standards for disclosure, shareholders should have the right to decide whether they should allow corporations *to make any political contributions whatsoever*. It is the shareholders, after all, who *own* the company, and they have the right to decide company policy on political spending. On May 14, 2011, in an op-ed in *The New York Times*, I urged that institutional investors should propose that the proxy statement of each company in which they invest contain a resolution like this one:

> RESOLVED: That the corporation shall make no political contributions without the approval of the holders of at least 75 percent of its shares outstanding.

Because of the inevitably wide range of political views that characterize any shareholder base, such a "supermajority" requirement is appropriate. As it happens, 75 percent is halfway between a simple majority and a standard under earlier Delaware corporate law that required a unanimous shareholder vote to ratify a gift of corporate assets other than for charitable purposes. Surely at least some political contributions are "a gift of corporate assets." (I am not suggesting, of course, that each political contribution be approved by shareholders, but that shareholders must approve a policy of making such contributions.)

For all its faults, the *Citizens United* ruling upheld the disclosure requirements of the campaign financing law. I had hoped that full disclosure might limit corporate contributions. But in fact, corporations are now able to exploit provisions in the law that enable nonprofit groups to make lavish political contributions without any disclosure. This shocking loophole has made it easier than ever for mountains of cash—spent on lobbying, attack ads, and advocacy ads that are theoretically uncoordinated with a candidate's own campaign—to subvert our political system, and indeed the national interest. Action to limit contributions at the corporate level is therefore urgent.

"The Procedures of Corporate Democracy"

Indeed, the Supreme Court itself put the onus on shareholders to control corporate political giving. In his opinion for the majority in *Citizens United*, Justice Anthony M. Kennedy predicated the First Amendment right of free speech on the ability of shareholders to ensure that corporate speech, as it were, reflects their views, rather than diverting corporate assets for the benefit of executives. He suggested that any abuse could be corrected by shareholders "through the procedures of corporate democracy."

Well, corporate democracy is on the way. The critical battle over political spending by corporations has been joined. For the first time, the financial institutions—not only mutual funds, but pension funds and other large institutional investors—that now hold absolute control over Corporate America will have to stand up and be counted. The ballots on mandatory disclosure of corporate political contributions and on shareholder approval of corporate contributions are appearing on the 2012 proxies of many companies. They have passed SEC review, so now our powerful institutional money managers will have to vote yes or no.

It seems logical to me that, if and when institutional investors vote against corporate political contributions, they will have to forswear such contributions by their own firms. Entering the fray "with clean hands" would seem mandatory.[15] Once again, however, given that a huge portion of our largest money management firms are either publicly held or controlled by publicly held financial conglomerates, these clean hands will take a lot of scrubbing. Will these agents put the interests of their principals first? Or will their own interests come first? We shall see.

Since 2004, the SEC has mandated that our nation's mutual fund agents break their silence and disclose to their principals how they have voted. But in terms of being active participants in corporate governance, the silence of nearly all mutual funds remains. The same silence also emanates from pension funds and their managers. With critical issues like executive compensation and political contributions now in the spotlight,

---

[15]That will not happen easily. Fidelity, one of the largest mutual fund managers recently disclosed a total of more than $5 million in political contributions from its organization during 2011.

Box 3.4
"Even One Person Can Make a Difference"

Way back in the late 1970s, I placed an epigram—"Even One Person Can Make a Difference"—on the newly created Vanguard Award for Excellence, presented quarterly to our crewmembers who have gone above and beyond the call of duty in service to our fund shareholders and to their colleagues. Now, decades later, I'm again reminded of how even a single human being—no matter what his or her line of work—can make a difference in the world. Early in 2012, I again witnessed the truth of that tenet. I saw one person succeed, against all odds, in having the resolution that I cited earlier placed on the corporate agenda, a resolution that would require a 75 percent approval by shareholders before the corporation could make *any* political contributions whatsoever.

I've known James Mackie as a friend and neighbor for many years. But I was surprised, not only that he had read my *New York Times* op-ed ("The Supreme Court Has Had Its Say. Now Let Shareholders Decide"), but had also decided to, well, make it happen. He has a number of modest holdings in individual stocks, and he took it upon himself—all alone and without counsel—to send the proposal to a select group of those corporations and request they submit it to their shareholders in their 2012 proxy statements.

The hurdles were high; the process was tortuous; the corporations were hardly eager to include the proposal in their proxy material. But Jim finally got one done. Johnson & Johnson, one of America's most prominent and successful medical companies, agreed to include in its proxy the resolution—to "let the shareholders decide" on allowing political contributions by the firm. The vote took place at the J&J annual meeting on April 26, 2012.

J&J opposed the adoption of the proposal on the grounds that it could restrict the ability of the company to contribute in "support of those whose policy positions are supportive of the legitimate business interests of the company and its shareholders." With this opposition, the contribution resolution received only a small minority of shareholder votes. But fund managers will have to go on record with their own votes—a small victory for shareholder democracy, but an important one.

For me, the lesson of the Mackie proposal is far broader. First, since it has been accepted by J&J under SEC rules, it's easy to imagine that many other investors will present it to many other companies. With the precedent set, it should spread widely. But second, and even more important, it shows that it is possible for even one shareholder, with limited resources and limited experience, to move the world in a better direction. If Jim Mackie can do it, why can't our giant institutional investors, with their infinite resources and long experience, do the same?

it is high time for fund managers to stand up and be counted on the controversial issues of the day. They also must break their long silence and actually make their own proposals, demanding that they be placed in corporate proxies. I see these steps toward greater activism in corporate governance by our giant investor/agents who represent the shareholder/principals, as essential to sound long-term investing, to our system of modern capitalism, and to the national interest. The mutual fund industry should be in the, well, vanguard of this movement. I discuss its evolution in the chapter that follows.

Chapter 4

The "Mutual" Fund Culture—Stewardship Gives Way to Salesmanship

Managers of other people's money rarely watch over it with the same anxious vigilance with which . . . they watch over their own.

—Adam Smith

The clash of the cultures in finance is well illustrated by one specific example: the mutual fund industry. As I mentioned earlier, I recently celebrated my sixtieth anniversary in this field, and I've witnessed this cultural change firsthand. The fund industry of 2012 has a totally different culture than the culture that dominated the field all those years ago. Once characterized primarily by a focus on long-term investment, today the fund industry seems focused largely on short-term speculation. While I'm not pleased with the change, please understand: *I love the mutual fund industry*. But I have a lover's quarrel with the industry to which my long career has been dedicated. I simply want us to live up to our highest potential to fulfill our fiduciary duty to fund investors.

An Industry Changes

The Stunning Growth in Mutual Fund Assets

There are many reasons for the change in the industry's culture. First was the remarkable growth of the industry's equity funds. Their assets leaped from just $2.5 billion when I joined the industry in 1951 to $5.9 *trillion* today, a remarkable 14 percent annual growth rate. When a small industry—dare I say a cottage industry?—becomes something like a mastodon, almost everything changes. "Big business," as hard experience teaches us, represents not just a difference in degree from small business—simply more numbers to the left of the decimal point—but a difference in kind.

For more than a half-century, equity funds were the industry's backbone. But growth was spasmodic, with large cash inflows pouring in from investors when stock market conditions were strong; but low cash inflows, and often outflows, when the market faced tough times. Equity fund assets topped $56 billion in 1972, and then fell to $31 billion in 1974, soaring to $4 trillion in the long bull market that followed through 1999. In the subsequent bear market, assets then tumbled to $2.6 trillion, only to leap to $6 trillion in 2006, when yet another bear market halted the growth. Today, equity fund assets remain at the $6 trillion level. This sensitivity of equity fund cash flows to stock market trends—investors are buyers near the market highs and sellers near the lows—is obviously counterproductive for the returns earned by fund investors.

After the 1972–1974 bear market, bond funds began to assert themselves. As the financial markets changed, so did investors' needs, and income became a high priority. (The dividend yield on stocks had been higher than the interest rates on bonds for nearly a century, from the 1870s through 1959. Then the yield advantage enjoyed by stocks vanished, never—so far—to return. But in early 2012 stock yields and bond interest rates are once again getting close to one another.) With less than $1 billion of assets during the 1950s, bond funds grew slowly during the 1960s and 1970s. But by 1987, bond fund assets had soared to $250 billion, actually exceeding the $175 billion total for equity funds. While bond funds then retreated to a less significant role, their assets gradually grew to $500 billion by 1992. Today, following years of generous interest rates and the introduction of municipal bond funds in the late 1970s, combined assets of tax-free and taxable bond funds total $3 trillion, 25 percent of the fund industry's total assets.

As the dominance of equity funds waned, money market funds, the fund industry's great innovation of the mid-1970s, quickly became the industry's most powerful engine of growth. In 1984, money fund assets of $235 billion were *three times* equity fund assets. Their growth didn't let up until 2008, when money fund assets reached $3.8 trillion. With the failure of a giant money fund in 2008, followed by challenges to the money fund structure by federal regulators, assets retreated to $2.6 trillion, now 21 percent of the mutual fund industry total. With the rise of bond funds and money market funds, nearly all of the large fund managers—which for a half-century had primarily operated as professional investment managers of a single equity fund or a handful of equity funds—became business managers offering a wide range of investment options, financial department stores that focused heavily on administration and marketing.

The Sea Change in Investment Operations

Second, during the industry's long history, we have witnessed a sea change in the operations of fund investment management firms. The *modus operandi* of managers, once dominated by investment committees with a long-term focus and a conservative culture of prudent investment, gradually gave way to portfolio managers, often operating with a short-term focus and a more speculative culture of aggressive investing. This change from a committee to an individual approach has helped foster the leap in the portfolio turnover of the average fund from the 15–20 percent range of the 1950s and early 1960s to the 85–100 percent range of the past four decades. In other words, the average holding period for a given stock in a fund's portfolio has tumbled from six years to a single year, or even much less. While many fund managers were once investors, now most managers seem to be speculators.

The new culture of ever-higher trading activity in stocks was embraced by a preponderance of investors of all types. These traders, of course, were simply swapping shares with one another. More speculative investment strategies began to emerge, with a focus on short-term performance. The old industry model of blue-chip stocks in market-like portfolios—and commensurately market-like performance (before costs, of course!)—evolved into a new model. The relative volatility of individual funds increased, measured in the modern era by "Beta," the volatility of a fund's asset value relative to the stock market as a whole. This increase in riskiness is easily measured. The volatility of equity fund returns increased sharply, from an average of 0.84 (16 percent less return than the market) in the 1950s to 1.11 (11 percent more volatile) in the past decade. That's a 30 percent increase in the relative volatility of the average fund. As shown in Exhibit 4.1, in the early era no equity funds had volatility above 1.11; in the modern era 38 percent of equity funds exceed that level.

This shift toward higher volatility began during the Go-Go Years of the late 1960s, when "hot" managers were treated like Hollywood stars and marketed in the same fashion. It has largely continued ever since. The creation of index funds was a rare and notable exception. By definition, an index fund has the market Beta of 1.00. But as the inevitable reversion to the mean in fund performance came into play, these aggressive manager stars proved more akin to comets, speculators who too often seemed to follow the crowd, focused on changes in short-term corporate earnings expectations, stock price momentum, and other quantitative measures. Too often, they forgot about prudence, due diligence, research, balance sheet analysis, and other traditional notions of intrinsic value and long-term investing. Then, most burn out.

Exhibit 4.1   A Dramatic Increase in Relative Volatility of Equity Mutual Funds

	1950−1956	2008−2011[*]	Difference
Total Number of Funds	56	5,091	
Relative Volatility			
Over 1.11	0%	38%	+38%
0.95−1.11	34	38	+4
0.85−0.94	30	10	−20
0.70−0.84	36	6	−30
Below 0.70	0	9	+9

[*]Sample of largest 200 funds.
SOURCE: Wiesenberger; Strategic Insight.

The manager culture changed. With all the publicity focused on the success of the stars and the accompanying publicity about "the best" funds for the year or even the quarter, along with the huge fees and compensation paid to fund management companies and the huge compensation paid to the fund portfolio managers of the "hot" funds, of course the manager culture changed even more. But even a short-term failing in performance became a career risk, so it became best to be agile and flexible, and watch over the portfolio "in real time." As equity fund assets soared, more aggressive funds proliferated, and deliberate decision making was no longer the watchword. As managers tried to earn their keep through feverish trading activity, portfolio turnover leaped upward, never mind that it seemed to improve fund performance only randomly, and because of advisory fees and trading costs couldn't work for all managers as a group. For each winner there is a loser.

I recall a study I did some years ago on the subsequent returns earned by the stocks held in fund portfolios on the first day of each year compared to the actual returns the funds delivered during the subsequent year. When the year ended, the static portfolios had won the contest 52 percent of the time; the portfolios actively run by the managers won 48 percent of the time. Still, it surely would be a career risk for a portfolio manager to walk out of the office right after New Year's Day and tell his boss, "That's the portfolio I'll hold all year. See you after Christmas."[1]

The Rise of "Product Proliferation"

The third major factor that changed the mutual fund culture was product proliferation, a trend that seems endemic to rapidly growing industries. It began to take hold in the fund industry in the Go-Go Years, but soared as the great bull market of 1982–2000 created ever-higher investment expectations. The number of funds exploded. When I entered the industry in 1951, there were but 125 mutual funds. (Only about 50—all equity funds—were large enough to have their returns reported in the annual Wiesenberger *Investment Companies* manual,

---

[1]One is reminded of Pascal's observation that "all of men's miseries derive from the inability to sit quietly in a room."

issued each year from 1938 until 1995.) Today, the total number of
equity funds comes to a staggering 5,091. Add to that another 2,262
bond funds and 595 money market funds, and there now are 7,948
traditional mutual funds, plus another 1,446 exchange-traded index
funds. It remains to be seen whether this huge increase in investment
options—ranging from the simple and prudent to the complex and
absurd—will serve the interest of fund investors. I have my doubts,
and so far the facts seem to back me up. The good news is that many of
the new funds were bond funds and money market funds, which for
decades have provided generous premium yields over stocks and also
over traditional bank savings accounts, where yields were constrained
by federal government regulation until 1980. Today, of course, these
generous yields have disappeared. But these new "fixed-income" funds
provided more stable portfolio values and offered access to sectors of
the financial market not previously available to most families. The bad
news is that in the equity fund sector of the industry, the massive proliferation of so many untested strategies (and often untested managers)
resulted in confusion for investors. The rise of such proliferation and the
seemingly infinite choices available seemed to imply that achieving
earnings on investment returns that exceeded those of the stodgy stock
market were easy. Just pick the right fund or manager. But how could
investors or their advisers possibly know in advance which funds or
managers would win?

Born to Die

In summary, during its modern era, almost everything changed in
the culture of the mutual fund industry. Enormous growth led to the
expansion of the small profession into a giant business. The transition
from investment decisions by groups to individual managers encouraged
the move from long-term focus to short-term. The competitive culture
of security analysts and portfolio managers became even more competitive, with more and more measurement standards, for shorter and
shorter time periods. Inevitably, this cultural change led to a focus on
stock prices over intrinsic values. The paradoxical result: The proliferation of fund "products" was followed by the subsequent demise of
astonishing numbers of them.

The ongoing waves of faddish fund creation are easy to identify. For example, in the Go-Go Years of the late 1960s, some 350 new equity funds—largely highly volatile and risky "performance" funds—were formed, more than doubling the number of funds from 240 in 1965 to 535 in 1972. With the ensuing collapse of that bubble and the subsequent 50 percent decline in the overall stock market, only seven or eight new funds were formed during each year in the decade that followed. In the next marketing bubble—the rise of the Information Age, beginning in the late 1990s—funds focusing on Internet and high-tech stocks led the way. The fund industry responded just as one would expect a marketing business to respond. We created an astonishing total of 3,800(!) new equity funds, mostly aggressive growth funds focused on technology and the so-called new economy. Although some 1,200 funds went out of business during this period, the equity fund population still more than doubled, from 2,100 funds at the start of 1996 to 4,700 in 2001.

After each wave of creation, of course, investment reality quickly intruded on speculative illusion. Many of the new creations failed. The large number of fund failures that followed the boom virtually matched the earlier creation rates. Back in the 1960s, about 1 percent of funds disappeared each year, about 10 percent over that early decade. When the frothy decade of the 1990s turned into the dispiriting decade of the 2000s, the equity fund failure rate leaped to an average of almost 6 percent each year. Some 55 percent of the funds in existence at the start of that decade had vanished by its conclusion. Assuming (as I do) that the failure rate persists until the present decade ends, some 2,500 of today's 4,600 equity funds will no longer exist—an average death rate of almost one fund on every business day for the next 10 years. While the mutual fund industry proudly posits that its mutual funds are designed for *long-term* investors, how can one invest for the *long term* in funds that may exist only in the *short term*?

This wide range of profound changes was the reflection of a fundamental change in the very nature of the mutual fund industry. An industry that had been dominated by a professional culture for decades had evolved into an industry with a business culture. From its original and primary focus on prudent investment management, the fund industry had moved to a new focus on aggressive product marketing. The focus on *stewardship* was overwhelmed by *salesmanship*.

Costs and Performance

Fund Costs Soar

Despite the industry's quantum growth, the costs incurred by fund investors grew rapidly. The expense ratio of the average equity fund, weighted by fund assets, rose from 0.50 percent of assets on the tiny $5 billion asset base of 1960, to 0.99 percent for the giant $6 trillion equity fund sector as 2012 began—a stunning increase of almost 100 percent. In dollar terms, the cost of investing in equity mutual funds rose an astonishing 17 percent annually, from $5 million in 1951 to $60 *billion* in 2011. It is clear that relatively little of that increase found its way into manager's investment activities; rather most of the increase reflects soaring marketing costs, expenditures on improved shareholder services, and profits to the firms that manage the funds. Rather than sharing the economies of scale with fund owners, fund managers have arrogated these profits to themselves. (When we talk *money* rather than *basis points* measured in hundredths of 1 percent, we get a far better picture of the staggering profit in fund management.)

Owning a mutual fund management company has often proved rewarding beyond the dreams of avarice—owning mutual funds, far less so. Back in 1967, Paul Samuelson hit the proverbial nail on the head when he told a Congressional hearing that, "there was only one place to make money in the mutual fund business—as there is only one place for a temperate man to be in a saloon—behind the bar and not in front of it . . . so I invested in a management company." When he decided that public ownership of management companies would be not only a boon for the managers who worked behind the bar, as it were, but also a bane for the fund owners who enjoyed their libations in front of the bar, he was wiser than he could have imagined.[2]

---

[2]A personal note: In 1994, interested in keeping informed about the activities of Vanguard rival T. Rowe Price, I purchased 100 shares of its management company for $4,189. This year my dividend alone will total $4,325, and my investment is presently worth $208,960. Yes, managing mutual funds is a great business for the managers and their owners.

Costs and Returns

The role of fund costs in shaping fund returns is no longer arguable. Academic study after academic study has proved the point. In 2010, Morningstar, the respected provider of fund analysis services, conceded that fund costs were a more significant factor in predicting fund performance than its own sophisticated rating system. The combination of fund expense ratios, the costs of portfolio transactions, and the sales loads that so many funds still impose create a huge charge against the returns earned by fund shareholders. But do those costs enhance returns to shareholders? It's simply not possible. Since fund managers, in essence *are* the market, how could they—as a group—beat the market? (Or, for that matter, lose to it?) But when they *are* the market, the gross returns of investors must match those of the market, but net returns after fund expenses must inevitably fall short. So let's look at the appreciation of an initial investment of $10,000 15 years ago in equity funds, compared to the returns earned by the stock market itself, here measured by the S&P 500 Index. During that long period, as shown in Exhibit 4.2, the cumulative wealth gains created on an initial investment of $10,000 in the unmanaged 500 Index exceeded the average comparable actively managed equity fund— an enhancement in wealth of more than 50 percent.

I've limited this comparison with the S&P 500 Index to large-cap funds, simply because that is the group most reflective of the large-cap nature of the S&P 500 Index, and of the total stock market itself. (Some 85 percent of the market's capitalization is accounted for by the

Exhibit 4.2   Returns of Large-Cap Equity Mutual Funds: $10,000 Invested over 15 Years (1997−2011)

Large Cap Category	Annual Return	Investment Gain From Original $10,000 Investment
Core Funds	3.9%	$7,750
Growth Funds	3.7	7,250
Value Funds	4.6	9,630
Average	4.1%	$8,270
S&P 500 Index	5.4%	$12,010

SOURCE: Morningstar, adjusted for survivorship bias. As such, these returns are substantially lower than those displayed in Exhibits 4.3 and 4.4, which include survivorship bias.

S&P Index.) For the record, however, in this particular 15-year period, mid- and small-cap funds, on balance, happened to outpace their large-cap cousins, with annual returns averaging slightly above 6 percent.

The spread in return averaging 1.3 percent per year is a crude reflection of what we know about fund expenses. If we assume an average annual expense ratio of 1.0 percent and average turnover costs of 0.4 percent for a total fund cost of 1.4 percent (excluding sales loads), it's clear that this explanation is well within the rule of reason, crudely explaining the 1.3 percent performance gap. Note especially the com-pounding effect of these seemingly small differences in return.[3]

It is now clear that both the new structure and the new culture of the fund industry has ill-served the interests of equity fund investors. The waves of creation of new mutual funds—too often of the "hot" variety—are designed to meet the momentary perceived demands of the mar-ketplace. Or they meet the perceived demands of multiple market*places*—not only individuals, but institutions, distributors, financial advisers, and brokers as well. The concept of investing for a lifetime and focusing largely on asset allocation and diversification has gotten lost in the noise of short-term, even daily and sometimes minute-by-minute movements of the volatile stock market. I can only restate my warning that "the stock market is a giant distraction from the business of investing."

The Cost of Unfortunate Investor Choices

The product proliferation fostered by these spates of marketing creativity—so often followed by the disappearance of the funds that fail to meet durable investment needs, fail to provide market-competitive performance—all played a role. The eruption of "choice" encouraged investors of all but a handful of managers to become their own worst enemies. Market-following and performance-chasing behavior became a prevalent practice,

---

[3]In proposing that Vanguard create the first index mutual fund, I compared the annual returns of equity mutual funds with the S&P 500. Then, the annual return averaged 11.3 percent for the index over the preceding three decades, compared to 9.7 percent for the funds, a gap of 1.6 percentage points (see Chapter 6). However, I failed to adjust the index return for estimated expenses of 0.3 percent. Result: an identical advantage of 1.3 percentage points for the S&P 500 in the longer, earlier period. That identity in spread, in my view, is more than coincidental.

Exhibit 4.3   Fund Returns versus Investor Returns Over 15 Years (1997−2011)

Category	Average Annual Return			Cumulative Return		
	Funds*	Investors	Investor Lead/Lag	Funds	Investors	Investor Lead/Lag
Large-Cap	5.4%	3.9%	−1.6%	127.9%	94.4%	−33.5%
Mid-Cap	7.5	4.7	−2.8	208.7	119.5	−89.2
Small-Cap	7.4	5.3	−2.1	214.2	141.3	−72.9
International	5.6	3.4	−2.2	141.4	85.9	−55.5
Average	6.5%	4.3%	−2.2%	173.1%	110.3%	−62.8%

*These returns have *not* been adjusted for survivor bias. Therefore, they are significantly overstated relative to the returns presented in Exhibit 4.2.[4]
SOURCE: Morningstar.

at a huge cost to the returns that investors would have earned simply by "staying the course." Exhibit 4.3 shows the difference between the returns reported by the funds themselves ("time-weighted" returns) compared to the return actually earned by their investors ("dollar-weighted" returns).

But if we had been able to take into account survivor bias, the huge gaps presented in the chart would grow far larger. This bias simply reflects "the survival of the fittest," by which we mean that we include in the comparisons only funds that were able to survive for the full 15-year period. Generally, better performers survive, poorer ones do not. So the fund returns strongly overstate the reality. At first glance it might seem that the typical 2.2 percentage point annual gap between actual investor returns and the returns reported by the funds (dragged down by their costs), is small, but the gap gets far larger over time, costing investors an average of almost two-thirds(!) of their potential capital during the past 15 years.

To make matters worse, speculation by managers was soon emulated by fund investors. Investors used to redeem their shares at an annual rate of 8 percent of assets per year. Now they redeem at a 30 percent rate. Result: The holding period for fund shares by their shareholders shrank

[4]I'm not sure that this 2.2 percentage point differential adequately captures the full lag. If we consider those active funds with the largest capital flows, six of the largest 18 earned investor returns that lagged reported returns by 3 percent to 4.5 percent per year. (For funds with little or no capital flows, the two returns would be identical.)

from an average of 12 years when I joined the industry in 1951 to only about three years currently. This foolish trend reflects the readiness of fund investors to impulsively jump around from one fund to another, in a futile effort to time the market all by themselves.

The creation of innovative—and typically more volatile—equity funds has proved to be a strong negative to the returns earned by investors, too many of whom jumped at the opportunity to find the Holy Grail of superior performance, which turned out to be nonexistent. The more volatile the fund returns, the more the investor fell short of the returns the fund actually earned. As shown in Exhibit 4.4, the gap between reported returns and investor returns was just 0.8 percentage points for the funds in the least volatile quintile—quite bad enough—but grew to fully 3.0 percentage points in the most volatile quintile, on average a staggering cumulative 15-year loss of some 82 percent of the potential return an investor could earn by simply buying and holding the fund.

"The Good Old Days"

How different it was in the industry's early days! I'm one of the rare persons, if not the only one, alive today to have observed firsthand the sea change in the industry's business model. At the industry's outset in 1924, most fund management companies engaged *solely* in portfolio

Exhibit 4.4   Investor Returns Erode as Volatility Increases Over 15 Years (1997–2011); Equity Mutual Fund Returns

Quintile	Risk (Standard Deviation)	Average Annual Return			Cumulative Return		
		Funds	Investors	Investor Lead/Lag	Funds	Investors	Investor Lead/Lag
1 Lowest	15.2%	6.3%	5.5%	−0.8%	159.4%	136.2%	−23.2%
2	17.6	5.7	4.2	−1.5	142.9	103.5	−39.4
3 Middle	19.5	5.8	4.0	−1.8	146.6	96.1	−50.4
4	21.8	6.8	3.8	−2.9	186.8	99.4	−87.4
5 Highest	28.2	7.0	4.0	−3.0	205.1	122.4	−82.7

Average annual returns of equity funds, separated into quintiles by standard deviation, not adjusted for survivorship bias.

SOURCE: Morningstar.

supervision, research, and, yes, management. They did *not* engage in marketing or in the distribution of fund shares. For good reason, they held the marketing of fund shares at arm's length, retaining independent, separately owned and separately operated distributors handling that function. The first mutual fund, Massachusetts Investors Trust (MIT), relied on a totally separate wholesale distributor from its inception in 1924 until 1969, nearly a half-century later.

The second mutual fund, State Street Investment Corporation, essentially followed the MIT model until 1989. A separate, independently owned distribution corporation also handled the marketing function for today's giant American Funds group from its inception in 1933 until 1974, when the management company and the marketing company were merged and became one. Has that changed the firm's focus? Obviously. Twelve years ago, even as the assets of the American Funds rose into the hundreds of billions of dollars, the head of its distribution unit assured investors that the firm would *never* close any of its funds, nor limit additional purchases. That giant asset size makes portfolio management even more challenging, narrows investment choice, and reduces transaction flexibility all seems to have been ignored, or at least disregarded.[5]

But asset gathering gradually became the name of the game. Competition for cash flow, asset size, and earnings growth drove ambitious fund executives to make their marks, eager to test their mettle on the fields of combat for the Great God Market Share. The marketing drive especially infected management companies owned by financial conglomerates in which public shareholders demand that managers "increase the bottom line," but even firms under private ownership were hardly exempt from this drive. Remarkably, as mutual fund assets soared, expenses soared even higher, with managers arrogating to themselves the enormous economies of scale in investment management.

---

[5]My own view is that fund managers should look to their enlightened self-interest and close funds before they become too big to deliver the returns they seek. That is why in 1985 Vanguard closed its Windsor Fund (then the largest equity fund in the field) and its small-cap-oriented Explorer Fund. I explained our decision—almost unheard of in the fund industry—with this simple analogy: "We didn't want to kill the goose that laid the golden egg."

But when gathering assets becomes the name of the game, marketing and investment go hand in hand. Hot performance produces lots of sales. (No surprise there!) Sales incentives to brokers rise. The soaring volume of trading activity by mutual funds is used to grease the wheels of distribution. "Pay to play" provides enormous trading commissions to brokers who sell the fund's shares—costs that are paid by the *funds* even as all the benefits go to the *managers*—and generate even more sales. And advertising, which is funded by the fund shareholders through the management fees that they pay, becomes both more strident and more pervasive. For example, advertisements highlight short-term returns, but, of course, only when they are superior. In recent years, fund managers have been spending an estimated $250 million annually on advertising in various media. (The "mother's milk" of brokerage costs on portfolio turnover, however, fed the aggressive sales effort.)

In May 2010, fund manager and distributor Ameriprise Financial announced its forthcoming acquisition of Columbia Funds, and presented the manager's rationale for the merger. A clearer example of how funds are managed in the interests of the giant conglomerates that control them rather than in the interests of the fund shareholders that they have a duty to serve would be hard to find. Excerpts from the Ameriprise management letter and my commentary are presented in Box 4.1.

The Conglomeratization of the Mutual Fund Industry

As I reflect on the change in the mutual fund culture, I now turn to another change, perhaps the most important of all: the perverse metamorphosis from private ownership of fund management companies to public ownership. Many fund management companies, originally owned by their founders and investment executives, made public offerings of their shares (IPOs), opening the door to substantial ownership by public investors. But it was not long until giant financial conglomerates, eager to acquire the profit streams of the management companies in a burgeoning mutual fund industry, moved in. The clash in which short-term speculation attained dominance over long-term investment played a role in this change, as firms with "hot" managers with high returns (and assuming high risks) became

Box 4.1

Ameriprise: An Example That Makes the Point

There can be, I think, little room for debate about the change in the fund industry's culture and character. It can be well summed up in a single recent example that encompasses not only the drive to make the management company more profitable, but also the trafficking in management company stocks that the Securities and Exchange Commission tried—but failed—to prevent in 1958. The example also bluntly explains the rationale behind a giant mutual fund manager's decision to acquire an almost equally large rival. The acquirer was Ameriprise Financial, which traces its roots back to 1894 and entered the fund field in 1940. The firm was acquired by American Express in 1984, only to be spun off in a public offering, after which the American Express funds were rebranded as RiverSource funds in 2005. Another management company, Seligman, was acquired along the way.

Then, on May 3, 2010, Ameriprise completed the acquisition of Columbia Management from Bank of America for approximately $1 billion in cash, adding the Ameriprise fund assets of $462 billion to the Columbia fund assets of $190 billion and creating a $652 billion colossus.[6] Proudly announcing the acquisition, the chief of Ameriprise was surprisingly candid about the motivation for the merger, which was that the "acquisition transforms our asset

(Continued)

---

[6]The Columbia funds, originally formed in 1964, were themselves the result of a rampant acquisition spree, controlled at one time or another by bank-holding companies including Fleet Boston, NationsBank, and Bank of America. Along the way, mutual fund managers Colonial, Stein Roe and Farnham, Wanger, Crabbe Hudson, Newport Pacific, U.S. Trust Advisers, and Marsico were acquired. (Marsico was repurchased by its founder in 2007.) Before its acquisition by Ameriprise, Columbia was courted by fund managers BlackRock, Franklin Resources, and Federated. The SEC's early concern about "trafficking" in management company stocks turned out to have been both prescient and wise.

management capabilities and provides a platform to accelerate our growth [in assets under management]. It enhances our scale, broadens our distribution and strengthens our [fund] lineup . . . [and] allows us [Ameriprise] to capture essential expense synergies that will drive improved returns [in our asset management business] and [profit] margins [for Ameriprise] over time."

The acquisition announcement said nothing about what's in the merger for the shareholders of the funds now run by Columbia, the name adopted for the entire group. (Gone is RiverSource.) But a lengthy paragraph in the announcement does include a claim by the head of Ameriprise's asset management business that "we now offer clients strong-performing funds in every style category." That statement seems to be true: Shortly after the acquisition, 31 Columbia funds were rated as earning four or five stars, the top two of the five rating categories under Morningstar's rating system. But the allegation conceals more than it reveals. Fully 59 Columbia funds—nearly twice as many—carried the *lowest* ratings (1 star or 2 stars). The remaining 75 funds garnered an "average" 3-star rating. The official statement by the fund's management company simply ignored this overall mediocrity (at best). The mutual funds and their shareholders, of course, had no way to speak for themselves, and only the sound of silence emerged from their supposedly independent directors.

immensely profitable. The industry's astonishing growth made the temptation to acquire fund managers irresistible. The early acquirers proved to be smart. The mutual fund industry would become the nation's largest holder of financial assets, and the largest owner of common stocks in the land. Add to those major changes the clash between management and marketing, almost never resolved in favor of management, and what results is the inevitable clash between the interests of fund shareholders and management company owners.[7]

---

[7]While the conglomerates dominated this trend, it was privately-held Fidelity that first introduced the techniques of modern marketing to the fund industry.

It was public ownership that fundamentally changed the industry's course. This baneful development was fostered by an unfortunate district court decision in California in 1958 that overruled the SEC position that such transfers were a sale of fiduciary office and hence a violation of fiduciary duty. On appeal, the U.S. Supreme Court decided to let that decision stand. This seminal event—today long forgotten—changed the rules of the game. It opened the theretofore closed floodgates of public ownership to the huge rewards of entrepreneurship by fund managers, inevitably at the expense of fund shareholders.

Through the 1950s, as I recall, every single one of the industry's then perhaps 35 notable management companies was managed by a partnership or by a corporation owned largely by investment professionals. But within a decade after the court's decision, scores of the large mutual fund management companies would go public, selling their shares (but usually retaining voting control). It was only a matter of time until U.S. and international financial conglomerates acquired most of these new publicly owned firms and most of the privately owned firms as well. These firms, obviously (one could even concede appropriately), are in business to earn a high return on *their* capital, even at the expense of the return on the capital entrusted to them by fund investors.

The Conglomerates Dominate the Fund Industry

The dimension of that change has been extraordinary. Today, among the 50 largest mutual fund complexes, 41 are publicly held, including 33 held by conglomerates. Only eight remain private. The only other ownership form is a single *mutual* mutual fund structure, in which the fund management company is owned by the fund shareholders. I describe this one truly mutual fund complex—The Vanguard Group—further on, but only after discussing the fundamental differences between these two organizational structures in Box 4.2. All of the public fund management companies have external owners, and thus a second master to serve. None can be said to be "mutual" in structure or in spirit. Hence, the quotation marks around my use of the word "mutual" in the title of this chapter.[8]

---

[8]The distinction that mutual funds are not "mutual" was (as far as I know) first made in 1956 in a landmark speech entitled "The 'Mutual' Fund," by then-SEC Chairman Manuel F. Cohen. I quoted from Chairman Cohen's candid and prescient remarks extensively in Chapter 13 of my 2011 book *Don't Count On It!*

"Conglomeratization" has been perhaps the least recognized of all the changes that have taken place in the mutual fund industry. Financial conglomerates, now owning fully two-thirds of the major fund management companies, are the major force in the fund industry. But I must note that while outside owners—conglomerates plus firms with public shareholders—dominate the industry in terms of number of firms (41 of 50), the three largest fund complexes—Vanguard, Fidelity, and American Funds—all remain privately held or mutual. The aggregate assets managed by these three firms alone total $4 trillion, or nearly 40 percent of the $10.3 trillion of fund assets managed by the 50 largest firms. Two other giants—BlackRock and Pacific Investment Management Company (PIMCO)—constitute the other members of today's "Big Five," with another $1.2 trillion of assets. Publicly-owned Blackrock is largely an index-oriented firm specializing in ETFs, while PIMCO, a subsidiary of Germany's Allianz AG, still boasts legendary bond manager William Gross. While their strategies are miles apart, both are worthy competitors to "the Big Three," albeit with more costly mutual funds.

"Trafficking" in Management Contracts

While the growth of the private firms has been entirely from within, many of the public firms have grown by acquisition, a pattern hardly unfamiliar to the business behemoths of Corporate America. In my earlier discussion of the Ameriprise funds, for example, I noted that the new firm is largely the result of acquiring fully 12 previously independent fund managers. Consider too that BlackRock obtained substantially all of its asset base from its acquisition of Barclays Global Investors in 2009 and Merrill Lynch Asset Management in 2006, following an earlier acquisition of State Street Management and Research. Franklin Resources, another huge firm, is the result of the 1992 merger of giant Franklin Group and the giant Templeton Group. Invesco's acquisitions of AIM in 1996 and then of Morgan Stanley's Van Kampen subsidiary in 2009 also increased the firm's asset base manyfold.[9]

---

[9]Over the past 15 years, the concentration of fund assets at the five largest firms has soared—from 39 percent in 1997 to just short of 50 percent in 2012. The extent to which conglomeratization was one of the drivers of this trend is not clear.

Equally interesting is the number of fund management companies that have changed hands several times or more. Putnam, as I'll soon describe, moved from private to public, then to Marsh and McLennan, and most recently to Power Financial of Canada. Delaware moved from private to Lincoln Financial, to Macquarie. Dreyfus moved from private to public to Mellon to Bank of New York. Ownership of the venerable Scudder Stevens and Clark (now DWS Investments) went from private to Supervised Shares to Zurich Insurance to Deutsche Bank (which has been reported to be seeking a new buyer). Even this partial list of fund management companies being "shopped" from one firm to another is sufficient to validate the SEC's earlier-noted concern that public ownership would lend to "trafficking" in management contacts. So it has, but with no discernable benefit to fund shareholders.

The shift in ownership of a substantial minority interest in the manager of the American Century funds is yet one more example of this trafficking. Bought by JPMorgan Chase in 2003, it was sold for $848 million to Canadian Imperial Bank of Commerce (CIBC) in 2011. In subsequent litigation, arbitrators determined that JPMorgan Chase had repeatedly violated its contract with American Century, and ordered it to repay the firm $373 million. More subtle forms of acquisition of control of fund management companies have also developed.

In 1990, a firm called Affiliated Managers Group (AMG) began to acquire majority stakes from owners of previously private management companies. Today, the firm owns majority stakes in 27 different fund management companies. Its most recent acquisition was typical: AMG bought a controlling stake in Yacktman management, overseeing $17 billion of assets, adding to the total of $352 billion that AMG already oversees. (As the press headline read, "AMG Scoops Up Yacktman.") The managers get the money, although we never know how much. (Amazingly, the terms of these deals are not even disclosed.) But they continue to run their firms, and continue to receive compensation, though again, without disclosure. "Is this a great business, or what?"

Corporate Structure and Fund Performance

I can't "prove" with precise statistics that this conglomeratization of the fund industry has eroded the returns earned by fund shareholders. But

I can note that the fund groups that are privately held, including the one mutual firm, have been among the fund groups with distinctively superior returns, as measured by the ratio of above-average funds to below-average funds based on the Morningstar "star" ratings. For example, if a fund group placed 25 percent of its funds in the five- and four-star categories and 10 percent in the one- and two-star categories, the fund group would have a net rating of +15 percent. (As you might expect, the average rating of the 50 largest fund groups is essentially zero.) In Appendix I, I present the ratings for these fund managers during the 2001–2011 decade.

During the past decade, private firms predominated in the best performing groups—TIAA-CREF (+46); Vanguard (+44); Grantham, Mayo, Van Otterloo & Co. (GMO) (+19); and Dimensional Fund Advisors (DFA) (+22); all in solid positive territory. (It is more than coincidental that these fund groups are noted for their low operating costs.) American Funds (+7) and Fidelity (+6) are also above the average, if barely so.

Yes, some publicly held management companies have achieved excellent scores over the decade. Publicly held T. Rowe Price is a notable example, leading the list with a score of +51 during the past decade, slightly above Vanguard's +44. On the other hand, financial conglomerates hold a predominant position among the groups rated lowest by their Morningstar ratings: Goldman Sachs (−43),[10] Putnam (−40), Invesco (−21), Oppenheimer (−20), and Alliance Bernstein (−12)—all rate toward the very bottom among the large fund complexes. (These groups happen to be at the high-cost—or very high-cost—end of the scale.)

As you might imagine, each firm's score may vary significantly from one period to the next. But the statistical correlation of the ratings of each firm over time looks pretty solid (0.67, with 1.00 being perfect

---

[10]Goldman Sachs often claims to put the interests of their clients first, but with their funds having an average expense ratio of 1.37 percent—among the highest in the field—that doesn't appear to be the case. The average expense ratio for the 50 firms in this study is 1.16 percent. If Goldman simply reduced their expense ratios to that level, I suspect the firm would move up to average in terms of performance.

correlation). What's more, earning either a positive rank or a negative rank during one period is highly likely to recur during the subsequent period. Comparing rankings in Appendix I with a similar study completed five years ago, for example, 16 of the 17 fund groups with the highest positive scores remained in positive territory during the past decade and 10 of the 15 groups with the highest negative scores remained in negative territory.

Likelihood of Change

Unfortunately, a federal mandate requiring the internalization of large mutual fund groups is not a realistic goal. (The SEC considered such a change in 1960, in the report "Public Policy Implications of Investment Company Growth," but deferred action.) In the long run, considering the unmistakable fact that shareholder costs are far higher in conglomerate-controlled funds than in private fund complexes (and especially in the sole *mutual* complex), it seems likely that, sooner or later, investors will begin to vote with their feet, and move to funds that do their best to regard the interests of shareholders as their highest priority. Indeed, the industry's cash flows suggest that such "voting" is already taking place.[11]

In addition, it is at least conceivable that a time will come when the independent directors of the mutual funds in a large fund group will see the light, and act on their duty to serve the fund shareholders; perhaps they will do so overnight (or at least with 60 days' notice to the manager) or perhaps by gradually reducing management fees, with the ultimate goal of mutualization. Perhaps other circumstances or challenges will give directors no choice but to mutualize. In Box 4.2, I describe how that eventuality nearly became a reality, in recounting my attempt to have the Putnam Management Company, once a major factor in the industry, take that giant step into the brave new world of mutuality.

---

[11]In 2011 and the first quarter of 2012, Vanguard took in some $53.5 billion of cash flow in its stock and bond funds; the other 49 largest firms took in $126 billion. Vanguard represents fully 30 percent of the cash flow of the top 50 firms.

Box 4.2
Putnam's Brief Flirtation with Mutuality

In 2009, in the updated tenth anniversary edition of my book
Common Sense on Mutual Funds, I bemoaned the fact that my
hope for a radical restructuring (truly *mutual* mutual funds) that
places control of the funds in the hands of fund shareholders
had not been fulfilled. Five years earlier, however, my hope had
risen that the time had come. One of Vanguard's long time
peers, Putnam Management Company, became an almost
perfect candidate for mutualization.

From its beginning in 1936, Putnam had become a
respected industry leader. At first it operated a single balanced
fund (the George Putnam Fund of Boston) but gradually joined
the industry-wide trend in offering a broad line of funds with
varying objectives. Privately held by the Putnam family and
firm executives, the firm enjoyed solid growth through the
mid-1960s, when allowing founders and managers to cash in on
the firm's success became an industry-wide phenomenon.

In 1965, the management company turned to public
ownership via an IPO. In 1969, the firm agreed to be acquired
by the incredibly successful Government Employees Insurance
Company (GEICO), reaching, as the Putnam announcement
stated, "an agreement in principal" (sic) to combine the two
firms. (GEICO was later acquired by Warren Buffett's Berkshire
Hathaway.)

Enriching the Manager

That agreement never reached fruition. But just a year later in
1970, Putnam was acquired by the insurance broker Marsh &
McLennan. During the great bull market of the 1982–2000
era, under the aggressive leadership of new president Lawrence
Lasser, Putnam prospered. It became a goldmine for Marsh &
McLennan, earning the firm more than $3.3 billion in

2000–2007 alone. (Lasser too, prospered, often earning annual compensation of $20 million or more—$27 million in 1999 alone—plus another $78 million when he left the company and restricted stock in Marsh valued at another $29 million.)

But while Putnam earned these profits for its new owner, it was quite another story for the shareholders of its funds. While the manager's speculative bent produced good performance numbers for their aggressive equity funds to report, most shareholders didn't jump aboard the speeding train until the returns were history, and investor returns were small, even during the bull market.

Along the way, their once tiny Putnam High Income Government Trust grew to the mammoth size of $11 billion (the second largest in the field in 1987) driven largely by advertising a return of 12 percent when long-term U.S. Treasury bonds carried yields in the 6 percent range. (Don't ask.)

The strategy failed miserably. The Fund's annual distributions dropped from $1.54 per share in 1987 to $0.62 in 1994, ultimately falling to a low of $0.20 in 2004. Its net asset value fell from $12.47 per share to $8.09. Rather than firing the Fund's manager, the directors (wisely, I guess) changed the fund's name to Putnam American Government Income Fund. (In this business, it's easy to bury our mistakes.) Currently, the fund's assets total some $700 million, 93 percent below the peak.

In the early 2000s, when the stock market came back down to earth in the crash, these Putnam equity funds that had taken such high risks fared even worse. In the 1999 edition of *Common Sense on Mutual Funds*, I had written that the conditions for changing the traditional industry structure—focused on maximizing profits to fund managers—to a mutual structure—focused on maximizing returns for fund shareholders—might come from "investors who get badly burned by a long period of equity underperformance, or even by a significant plunge in stock prices."

(Continued)

Impoverishing the Shareholder

Now, having produced distinctly inferior performance in the great bear market of 2000–2003, Putnam faced both of those baneful circumstances. What's more, the firm was a major participant in the fund industry's "time-zone trading" scandals. Worse, nine of its portfolio managers were found to have been trading against the interests of the very funds that they were managing. Lasser was well aware of this obvious breach of fiduciary duty, but determined not to inform the funds' board of directors.

At that point, Marsh & McLennan accepted Lasser's resignation, and determined to get rid of its Putnam Management subsidiary. So I decided to approach the board of directors of the funds themselves and encourage them to take advantage of this valuable opportunity to mutualize—valuable to fund shareholders, but likely making the Marsh ownership stake worthless.

I telephoned the funds' independent board chairman John A. Hill, and he invited me to meet with him in New York City to discuss the issue. We enjoyed a pleasant luncheon together, and I made the case that the mutualizing option would better serve the fund shareholders. While he qualified as an "independent" director, I later learned that he had served as CEO of Marsh & McLennan Asset Management years before he became Chairman of Putnam, a fact not disclosed in the proxy statement. I later met with one of his fellow independent directors. In neither instance did I make any progress, and when Mr. Hill stopped returning my phone calls, I got the message: "No dice."

In 2008, Marsh sold its ownership of Putnam Management Company. The buyer was Power Financial of Canada, and the price, a cool $4 billion(!). But Putnam has yet to turn the corner. The shareholders of its funds have liquidated their shares unremittingly, and the firm has experienced net cash outflow in every year from 2000 through 2011. Fund assets have plummeted from $250 billion to just $53 billion as 2012 begins. It's hard to imagine that the Putnam fund shareholders would not have received huge benefits from mutualization. As it turned out, even the new owner of the management company seems unlikely to recoup its huge purchase price for many years, even decades. So bully (I guess!) to Marsh & McLennan for serving itself and its own shareholders so well, even at the expense of serving the Putnam fund shareholders to whom the firm owed a fiduciary duty.

Fund Organization Structure—It Makes a Difference

Most mutual fund investors don't consider how their mutual fund company is organized. Indeed, probably very few of us have given much thought to the structural organization of the funds that we own. Why should we care? Well, we should care simply because a fund's organizational structure can have an enormous impact on the returns earned by the mutual fund shareholders it serves.

With only a few significant exceptions, all mutual fund complexes operate under a common structure: a group of related mutual funds owned by their shareholders and governed by a common board of directors. This board, theoretically, is largely "independent" of the management of the funds' management company. Each fund in the group contracts with the external management company to manage its affairs in return for a fee. The management company provides the funds' officers and often the board's chairman, too. (I'm not kidding!) These officers typically are officials of the management company and are paid by the management company. The management company undertakes to provide substantially all of the activities necessary for the funds' existence: investment advisory services; distribution and marketing services; and operational, legal, and financial services.

In contrast to this traditional organization structure—in which the funds are essentially corporate shells—is the mutual structure, one in which the funds actually *own* the management company, which then operates on an at-cost basis. Here, the officers and directors of the funds are also the officers and directors of the management company, creating substantial advantages for the fund shareholders, discussed immediately following the structure chart in Exhibit 4.5.

Exhibit 4.5   Mutual Ownership Structure versus Traditional Corporate Structure

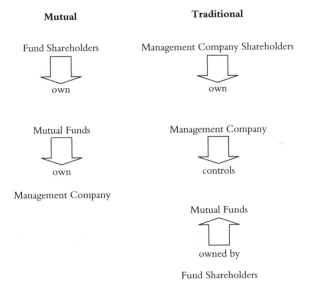

Strategy Follows Structure

Critical contrasts in strategy arise from the differences between, on the one hand, the conventional industry structure, designed to serve the often-conflicting interests of two sets of owners (fund shareholders and fund managers), and, on the other hand, the mutualized, internal-management structure, designed to serve solely the interests of the fund owners. With the exception of service strategy, these differences are profound.

Profit Strategy. Of course, the managements of both structures aim to earn the highest reasonable returns for their fund shareholders. But firms operating under the conventional structure also strive to maximize their own profits, which have proved to be very substantial. It is hardly counterintuitive to expect that the drive to make money for others—in this case, the fund shareholders—may not be as powerful as the drive to make money for oneself. Remember Adam Smith's earlier warning about managers "giving themselves a dispensation."

Pricing Strategy. The pricing strategy of the conventional (externally managed) fund complex, broadly stated, is to charge whatever the traffic will bear. Given the critical role that fund costs play in shaping fund returns (a principle described earlier in this chapter), perhaps the lack of concern by fund directors and fund shareholders arises from ignorance of the role of costs in shaping returns. In contrast, a firm with a mutual structure is in a position to offer funds on an at-cost basis—with costs that are far lower than what the traffic will bear.

Service Strategy. In both structures, the managers of funds strive not only to meet clients' expectations, but to exceed them. In the fund industry, service excellence is becoming a commodity—as it must be for any service industry. Both organizational structures honor the tenet, "Treat your customers as if they were your owners." But only the mutual organization can, with accuracy, tack on the phrase, "because your customers *are* your owners."

Risk Management Strategy. In conventionally operated mutual funds, investment strategy can, in the search for higher returns, be risk-tolerant, so long as a fund's risk—usually measured by its short-term price volatility—is consistent with the risks assumed by its peer funds. A mutual organization's investment strategy can afford to be risk-intolerant. With costs far below competitive norms, there is little need to reach for slightly higher returns on stock funds or higher yields on bond funds. Assuming portfolio quality is held constant, higher yields can be easily generated simply by lower costs.

"Product" Strategy. Conventional fund companies today eagerly develop new products designed for their perceived attractiveness to the investing public, irrespective of their intrinsic long-term merit. Raising additional assets produces additional fees and additional profits for the management company owners, at least in the short term. No similar premise faces a mutual organization. Its business is not to promote costly new business that does nothing significant to enhance shareholder returns. Its sole mandate is to earn optimal net returns for its fund owners.

Marketing Strategy. The financial benefits of asset growth in the fund industry accrue largely to management companies, not to fund shareholders. As a result, firms operating under the conventional industry structure are aggressive asset gatherers. So an aggressive marketing strategy is logical for a fund complex with the conventional structure. But a conservative marketing strategy would be the logical and productive strategy for a shareholder-owned complex, operating at cost and controlling its expenditures—in this case, its marketing costs—the best that it can.

Vanguard's Structure and Strategy

When Vanguard was created, it was these benefits to mutual fund shareholders that I had in mind. The mutual structure would minimize operating costs, put the shareholder in the driver's seat, and focus on offering funds that would perform in a highly predictable manner relative to their peers. Our creation of the stock index fund, just a few months after we began operations, was the firm's first major decision in implementing this strategy.

An abbreviated history follows, describing how Vanguard came to be. Here, you will learn how difficult it was to create this unique structure. But once completed, the firm has risen from its humble beginnings, overseeing just over $1 billion in assets, to become the largest fund complex in the world, now overseeing $1.8 trillion in fund assets. Perhaps you will wonder—as I do—why, 37 years later, Vanguard remains the only *mutual* mutual fund complex in our nation.

Box 4.3
How Did Vanguard Happen?

When in 1974 I had the idea of creating a new structure for fund management, the strong comparative advantage of the truly *mutual* structure was obvious to me. Vanguard's present position as the largest mutual firm in the world surely confirms that those very obvious strategies detailed above alone have paid off for our fund shareholders and for our firm. "Strategy follows structure" was my formulation, and it worked.

The story of Vanguard's creation is complicated and in a sense technical, so let me try to summarize it. In 1969, I was the CEO of Philadelphia's Wellington Group—11 associated mutual funds operated by Wellington Management Company, then managing assets of some $2.3 billion. The firm was largely owned by its executives, but had public shareholders as well, the result of an IPO in 1960. (It is now privately held by its partners.) Despite the travail that followed the demise of the boom in speculation during the preceding Go-Go era, the stock market was again rallying, on the way to its then-all-time high early in 1973, and the company was prospering.

Earlier, in 1967, with the so-called "currency" that its public stock had made available, Wellington Management had acquired the Boston investment counsel firm of Thorndike, Doran, Paine, and Lewis, Inc., and TDP&L's four partners came to hold some 40 percent of Wellington's voting power. TDP&L was the manager of Ivest Fund, a "Go-Go" fund (now long gone), one of the industry's premier performers during that era of speculation. It soon became a major generator of the Wellington group's capital inflows.

The Fiduciary Principle

Despite the remarkable success of the merger in its early years, I was pondering whether that public ownership structure was the optimal one for our funds' shareholders, and whether a new structure would improve both the lot of our fund shareholders as well as the firm's competitive position in the industry. I began to realize that, unless we changed, industry leadership would be unlikely. Speaking at the yearly meeting of the firm's partners in September 1971, I talked about the possibility of mutualization, beginning my remarks with a 1934 quotation from Justice Harlan Fiske Stone:

> Most of the mistakes and major faults of the financial era
> that has just drawn to a close will be ascribed to the

(Continued)

failure to observe the fiduciary principle, the precept as old as holy writ, that "a man cannot serve two masters." . . . Those who serve nominally as trustees but consider only last the interests of those whose funds they command suggest how far we have ignored the necessary implications of that principle.

I then set forth my concern: "An ancient prejudice of mine: *All things considered, it is undesirable for professional enterprises to have public shareholders.* Indeed it is possible to envision circumstances in which the pressure for earnings growth engendered by public ownership is antithetical to the responsible operation of a professional organization. Although the field of money management has elements of both a business and a profession, any conflicts between the two must, finally, be reconciled in favor of the client." I then suggested such a reconciliation might be achieved by "mutualization," whereby the funds would acquire the management company, airing an idea that would, against all odds, become a reality a short five years later. Then, in 1974, I would not only *talk the talk* about mutualization, but *walk the walk.*

Wellington's new business model began to fail in the early 1970s. As the 1973–1974 bear market took hold, the happy partnership formed by the 1967 merger fell apart. I was fired from my position as CEO of Wellington Management Company by the very money managers who, with me, had failed the stockholders of the management company and the shareholders of the funds as well. After my firing, however, I remained as chairman of the funds themselves, with their largely separate (and largely independent) board of directors—the conventional structure in the fund industry.

An Innovative Proposal

On January 12, 1974, even before my being fired, I had submitted to the board of directors of the Wellington funds a proposal to mutualize the funds and operate under an internally managed structure. I openly acknowledged that such a conversion to mutual status was "unprecedented in the mutual fund industry." The cautious fund board was interested enough to ask me to explore this option.

By March 11, my first report was completed, offering various structural options, beginning with full mutualization of the funds. The ultimate objective was "to give the funds an appropriate amount of corporate, business, and economic independence," through a structure that was specifically contemplated by the Investment Company Act of 1940 but no longer used. "The issue we face," I bluntly concluded, "is whether a structure so traditional, so long accepted, so satisfactory for our infant industry as it grew during a time of less stringent ethical and legal standards, is really the optimal structure for these times and for the future—or whether the funds should seek the greater control over their own destiny so clearly implied by the word *independence*."

On June 11, 1974, after months of study, the fund board made its decision. It rejected full mutualization and chose "limited internalization," under which the funds would employ their own officers and staff and assume responsibility for providing the funds' administration, accounting, legal and shareholder record keeping services, as well as responsibility for monitoring and evaluating the external investment advisory and distribution services, which would continue to be provided by Wellington Management Company.

Late in the summer, the board agreed that Wellington Management Company could retain its name, which thus could not be used as the identifier of our new firm. (I was not amused!) While Wellington Fund would also retain *its* name, a new name would have to be found for the administrative company soon to come into existence. In September, I proposed to call the new company "Vanguard" and the board—after heated debate—approved the name. The Vanguard

(Continued)

Group, Inc., was incorporated on September 24, 1974. By May 1, 1975, the SEC had cleared the funds' proxy statements that proposed the change; the fund shareholders had approved it; and Vanguard began operations, providing its services to the funds on an "at-cost" basis.

Completing the Mutualization

With the funds controlling only one leg of the operations/investment management/distribution tripod on which all fund complexes rest, I began to have second thoughts. Yes, I had won a victory of sorts, but, I feared, a Pyrrhic victory. The narrow mandate that precluded our engaging in portfolio management or distribution services would give Vanguard insufficient power to control its destiny. Why? Because success in the fund field is driven *not* by how well the funds are administered, but by what kinds of funds were created; how they were managed; whether superior investment returns were attained; and how—and how effectively—the funds were marketed and distributed. We had been given one-third of the fund loaf, as it were, but arguably the least important third in terms of realizing our vision. It was the other two-thirds that would make us or break us. I realized that the newly named Vanguard must control them as well.

We quickly seized the second one-third of the loaf. Only a few short months after the firm began operations, the board of the funds approved the creation of the world's first index fund, modeled on the Standard & Poor's 500 Stock Index. It was incorporated late in 1975, and its initial public offering was completed in August 1976. Less than five years after that halting entry into what was, arguably, equity investment management, the firm assumed full responsibility for the management of Vanguard's bond and money market funds in 1980, and later, management of funds relying upon actively managed quantitative techniques rather than fundamental analysis. External advisers—now 30 in number—continue to manage many of

Vanguard's actively managed equity funds, now constituting about 20 percent of the firm's $1.8 trillion of assets with 80 percent managed by Vanguard, including our classic index funds and most of our bond funds, all with distinct index-like characteristics (clear tracking standards, high quality, exceptionally broad diversification, and rock-bottom costs).

On February 9, 1977, only five months after the index fund IPO had brought investment management under Vanguard's aegis, we acquired the final one-third of the mutual fund loaf. The funds terminated their distribution agreements with Wellington Management and eliminated all sales charges. Overnight, Vanguard had eliminated its entire distribution system, and moved from its seller-driven, load-fund channel to a new buyer-driven, no-load distribution channel. The fledgling organization was now a complete mutual fund complex, in charge of administration and distribution of the funds and the investment management of the predominant portion of their assets. We were ready to set forth on a new and unprecedented course. "Mutualization" was now complete, and Vanguard began to make its mark.

Building a Fiduciary Society

While the challenges facing mutual funds and other institutional money managers today are inevitably different from those of the past, the principles are age-old, summed up by Adam Smith's nineteenth-century warning, which I repeat here: "Managers of other people's money rarely watch over it with the same anxious vigilance with which . . . they watch over their own." That failing continues to prevail among far too many of our nation's money manager/agents, often to the point of an almost complete disregard of their duty and responsibility to their shareowner/principals. Too few managers seem to display the "anxious vigilance" over other people's money that once defined the conduct of investment professionals.

So what we must do is build a new *fiduciary* society, one that guarantees that our last-line owners—not only mutual fund shareowners whose life savings are at stake, but pension fund beneficiaries as well—have their rights as investment principals protected. These rights must include:

- The right to have their institutional money manager/agents act solely on behalf of their principals. The client, in short, must be king.
- The right to rely on prudential standards, including due diligence and professional conduct, on the part of the money manager/agents who shape investment strategy and the securities analysts who appraise securities for the investment portfolios that are ultimately owned by the principals that they serve.
- The assurance that our agents will act as responsible corporate citizens, restoring to their principals the neglected rights and responsibilities of stock ownership, demanding that corporate directors and managers meet their fiduciary duty to their own shareholders.
- The right to demand some sort of discipline and integrity in the mutual funds and financial products that our manager/agents offer.
- The establishment of advisory fee structures that meet a "reasonableness" standard based not only on *rates* but on *dollar amounts*, and their relationship to the fees and structures available to other clients of the manager who are able to bargain at arm's length.
- The elimination of all conflicts of interest that could preclude the achievement of these goals.

This final provision would logically require financial conglomerates to divest their ownership and control of money management firms, the very form of organization that dominates the mutual fund industry today. (As I noted earlier, 33 of the 50 largest fund managers are now owned by these conglomerates.) Painful and disruptive as such a separation would be, conglomerate ownership of money managers is the single most blatant violation of the biblical principle that "no man can serve two masters."

"This Is a Fiduciary Business"

I've often felt a bit isolated in my long-standing quest to have mutual fund managers honor their duty as fiduciaries. So it was with considerable delight that I read *The Rise of Mutual Funds, An Insider's View*[12] by

---

[12]Oxford University Press (2008), 259–260.

Matthew P. Fink, long-time (now retired) President of the Investment Company Institute, the association and industry lobbyist that is hardly known for taking strong stands on principles. Here is his unequivocal statement on the issue:

> Mutual funds are not like other businesses. This is a fiduciary business. We and the management company are trustees. Therefore, the independent directors' role is to make sure that the fund management company acts as a fiduciary. The key to being a fiduciary is that the beneficiary's interests must come ahead of your own. That's the only test. Directors of a mutual fund have a unique role in a unique governance context.
>
> If many fund directors and management company officials believe that ensuring compliance with fiduciary standards is not their number one priority, the industry is in for some very rough times. There will be numerous ethical if not legal violations . . . draconian legislation [will result]. The industry will be homogenized, commoditized, and dumbed down, all to the detriment of fund shareholders. On the other hand, if industry participants strive to act as fiduciaries, the industry and fund shareholders will do well. The industry's future is in its own hands.

Matt Fink's comments are well taken. But I'm not so sure about his conclusion. The fact is that the industry's future remains in the hands of the investors it serves. If they "vote with their feet," moving their money (and their trust) away from funds whose managers can't reasonably pass the "stewardship quotient" test that I next describe in Chapter 5, and move their investments to those managers who pass the test with flying colors, the industry's future is bright.

But for action by masses of individual investors to reshape the industry, it will take years, probably decades. We need action now. The action that I advocate is the enactment of a statutory federal standard of fiduciary duty to foster the creation of a new mutual fund culture, one that adheres to its old values, one that is part of the fiduciary society that I've just described. We need an explicit statement in the law that makes unmistakable the principle that the federal government intends, and is capable of enforcing, standards of trusteeship and fiduciary duty that require money managers to operate with the *sole* purpose of serving the interests of their beneficiaries.

While such government action is essential, the new system should be developed in concert with the private investment sector. We need an Alexander Hamilton-like sharing of the responsibilities in which the Congress codifies the fiduciary standard, and private enterprise establishes the practices that are required to fulfill it. This task of returning capitalism to its ultimate owners will take time, true enough. But the new reality—increasingly visible with each passing day—is that the concept of fiduciary duty is no longer merely an ideal to be debated: It is a vital necessity to be practiced.

Until then, mutual fund investors in particular will need to evaluate the funds they own and determine whether or not they are meeting the fiduciary standard we have a right to expect of these stewards of our assets. How would an investor know? Chapter 5 presents some ideas for measuring "The Stewardship Quotients" earned by individual funds and their managers.

Chapter 5

Are Fund Managers True Fiduciaries?

The "Stewardship Quotient"

Give an account of thy stewardship, for thou mayest be no longer steward.

—Luke 16:2

The leaders of the mutual fund industry, and of its trade association, the Investment Company Institute, purport to represent mutual fund shareholders. But in fact they represent the management companies that operate the funds. The themes of the industry's annual General Membership Meetings ignore this conflict. Indeed, for three recent years, 1997, 2000, and 2008, the theme focused on "A Tradition of Integrity." In his remarks at the ICI's General Membership Meeting in May 2003, Matthew Fink, then president of the ICI, pointed with pride at the industry's then-rock-solid reputation.

Fink cited SEC commissioner Harvey Goldschmidt's glowing tribute just a few months earlier: "The mutual fund industry has been blessed—and blessed is the only word—by being relatively free of scandal." As he read those words, they were displayed as giant images on both sides of the dais. Fink then added: "The record is no accident . . . We have succeeded because the interests of those who manage funds are well-aligned with the interests of those who invest in mutual funds."

Fink's comments echoed those of ICI chairman and senior executive of the American Funds group Paul G. Haaga, Jr., the keynote speaker: "Our strong tradition of integrity continues to unite us . . . The word integrity has been the theme of every recent general membership meeting for one simple reason: integrity and the trust it engenders on the part of our shareholders is the basic foundation of our business. Our shareholders trust that their mutual funds are being managed with their interests in mind." Then he took on the industry's detractors, "former SEC chairmen, television talking heads, competitors, an oracle from Omaha—even a saint with his own statue (looking directly at me in the large audience when he said these words)—have all weighed in about our perceived failings. . . . It makes me wonder what life would be like if we'd actually done something wrong."[1]

Enter Attorney General Spitzer

Mr. Haaga didn't have long to wonder. Less than four months later, on September 3, 2003, a shocking scandal struck the mutual fund industry. New York's crusading attorney general Eliot L. Spitzer filed civil actions against four major mutual fund management companies, charging that they had conspired with, and even aided and abetted, certain preferred investors to undertake illegal acts. These preferred investors ultimately included some 400 hedge funds that identified their strategy as "mutual fund market timing." Based on late-breaking events that had taken place well after the U.S. market had closed, these investors would be allowed to buy and sell mutual fund shares of funds investing in non–U.S. securities, trading at closing prices that had been already set in foreign markets hours before the trades took place. Spitzer accurately compared

---

[1]The "Oracle from Omaha" was a thinly veiled reference to Warren Buffett. And Mr. Haaga was referring to me when he mentioned "a saint with a statue." I've often been called, certainly cynically, St. Jack, and, yes, a statue of me as Vanguard's founder reposes on our Valley Forge campus.

these practices to allowing favored investors to bet on a horse race after the horses have crossed the finish line.

Attorney General Spitzer's exposé of the fund industry's breach of trust constituted an eerie reprise to the scandals that came to light, first in the corporate sector with Enron in 2001 and again in 2012 in the investment sector with Wall Street scandals in which "sell-side" security analysts of firms in effect colluded with their investment banking colleagues to give high ratings to stocks that the firms were underwriting. (These analysts were hardly unaware of the quality of many of the underwritings they recommended. "Let's put some lipstick on this pig" was one of the characterizations that is fit to print.) Over the next year, the number of firms involved in the mutual fund scandals grew to 23, including many major industry participants. Their long-term fund assets totaled nearly $1.2 trillion, fully 25 percent of the industry's then $5 trillion total.[2] As the scandals unfolded, the reaction from fund investors turned from incredulity to revulsion, and then to action. Share liquidations at the firms that were involved in the scandal leaped upward.

The management companies involved finally settled the SEC claims against their violations of law—"without admitting or denying the charges," language that in early 2012 came under serious challenge by the judiciary—suffering well-deserved, if grossly inadequate, financial penalties, as well as some degree of opprobrium in the marketplace. Even the firms not charged with infractions seemed cautious about declaring their innocence, for it turned out that virtually all transactions in 401(k) thrift plans took place long after each day's 4 P.M. cut-off time for executing orders for regular purchases and sales of fund shares. The timely accounting for these high volumes of transaction activity is by its nature virtually impossible, so I can only assume that fraud was not involved, although as a result of this practice one of the two prime clearing houses for these transactions was forced out of business.

---

[2]The assets managed in smaller funds were generally insufficient to accommodate these trading volumes, so the percentage of these firms among funds large enough to engage in these practices could well have reached 75 percent. Not just a few bad apples, then, but a barrel of apples that was importantly contaminated. Among those who resisted at least this particular temptation to feather their own nests were American Funds, Fidelity, T. Rowe Price, and, I'm pleased to report, Vanguard.

The public judgment that these firms betrayed the trust of their clients coincides with my own. And I see no reason why the reaction of those clients should not be harsh. What's really the point of keeping your money with a firm that has betrayed your trust? Even Charles E. (Ed) Haldeman, brought in to serve as new CEO of Putnam after its participation in the scandals, agreed. "There were individuals here," he said, "who had a lapse of judgment and who put their interests first ahead of shareholders. . . . I believe that was the wrong judgment. *When an investment professional violates a fiduciary trust, you don't get a second chance.* And I don't think there's a statute of limitations." Amen!

Where Should Fund Investors Turn?

When fund investors and their advisers decide that their trust in a mutual fund's management has been violated, where should they turn? In my view, they should select funds from those organizations that have strived to strike a proper balance between the interests of fund shareholders and the interests of fund managers. They should select those funds that, if you will, have placed a far heavier weight on stewardship than on salesmanship. Those fund managers who have done their best to put service to shareholders above service to themselves. Those fund managers who have honored their fiduciary duty to investors.

Please understand that I'm not naïve about this subject. *Every profession has elements of a business.* No organization—whether it's a profit-making corporation or the noblest of nonprofit philanthropies—in which expenses consistently exceed revenues will long exist. Yet when I look at some of our nation's proudest professions—medicine, law, accounting, journalism, architecture, and, of course, trusteeship—I fear that the traditional balance has been gradually shifting away from that of trusted profession and toward that of commercial enterprise. Writing in *The New York Times Magazine* a few years ago, Roger Lowenstein bemoaned the loss of the "Calvinist rectitude" that had its roots in "the very Old World notions of integrity, ethics, and unyielding loyalty to the customer. . . . America's professions," he wrote, "have become crassly commercial . . . with accounting firms sponsoring golf tournaments." He might have added that mutual fund managers were not only doing the same thing, but also buying naming rights to stadiums for staggering costs. (Citigroup, before its fall, agreed to pay $400 million for the naming rights to the New York Mets' new baseball park.) "The battle for independence," he concluded, "is never won." And so it is in the field of investment management—the better to ensure that managers of other people's money (OPM) act solely in the interest of their investors.[3]

A Challenge to Judgment

I have no particular wisdom to offer other professions about returning to their roots. But I do have some ideas about the trusteeship of other people's money. There is much information available to investors to evaluate the firms that manage mutual funds, and the extent to which they appropriately balance the conflicts between business and profession. The fund scandals gave us the opportunity to address that balance in a new light. Those scandals have arisen because fund managers put their own interests in asset-gathering, business-building, and the maximization of fee revenues ahead of the interests of their fund shareholders and their right to financial integrity, fair treatment, reasonable costs, honest disclosure, and optimal investment returns.

The bane represented by the mutual fund scandals, truth be told, is a blessing in disguise. It has awakened investors to the shoddy, illegal, and unethical practices of mutual fund managers. These mutual fund managers conspired with hedge fund managers and used extreme forms of "market timing" to dilute the returns of—or even defraud—the long-term investors in the funds. The scandals also awakened investors to the damage done by the equally pernicious but far more subtle forms of mutual fund market timing in which all too many fund investors engage, and which the fund industry has aided and abetted. I'm speaking here of the creation of specialty funds focused on narrow and often speculative investment strategies, and, in recent years, on highly leveraged bets on

---

[3]OPM is an acronym that has come into general use. Less familiar is MOM—"My Own Money"—coined by Princeton professor Alan Blinder. Both acronyms are sending the same message: Put the investor first.

whether the stock market is going to rise or to fall. Such funds, almost inevitably, are bought today to be sold on some date near or far (or now, sold some minutes or even seconds later!), rather than truly diversified equity funds bought to be held, well, forever.

Happily, there are still funds and fund managers who have done their best to hold the fort against the industry's new paradigm in which marketing has superseded management. It is these firms that I believe investors should first consider, when and if they decide that they have had enough of the sharp practices and misbehavior that have characterized the scandal-ridden firms (and many others) and decide to move assets to another fund organization. Investors might consider using the standards I'll now present to reappraise how to think about *any* of the mutual funds that you favor with your trust, whether or not they were participants in the scandals.

The Stewardship Quotient

Since past performance has proved, over and over again, to be a highly unreliable guide to the returns funds earn in the future, I recommend that funds be considered (or, for that matter, ignored) depending upon the extent to which they have placed the interests of their shareholders ahead of the interests of their managers. This very principle is at the heart of the Investment Company Act of 1940. When the Act says that mutual funds must be "organized, operated, and managed" in the interests of shareowners *rather than* in the interests of "investment advisers and underwriters" (meaning fund distributors), it places the stewardship of investor assets above the salesmanship of the "products" offered by fund managers. Through what I call the *Stewardship Quotient* (SQ), we can measure fifteen important elements that reflect the degree to which the fund managers balance these two distinct and often-competing interests.

Before I describe these elements, a disclaimer: *What I offer you is a highly subjective viewpoint that was the driving force in my creation, some 38 years ago, of a firm that would hold stewardship as its highest principle.* Even though my career has reflected these values of stewardship imperfectly, I have done my best. Please feel free to regard my listing of these elements as self-serving, especially since the model that I created in 1974 of a fund group with a shareholder-owned, truly *mutual* mutual fund structure has yet to be emulated or even copied by any other fund organization. But please know that I gain no pecuniary benefit by fostering these standards, only the profound conviction that they are the right ones for nearly all fund investors and, in the long run, the right ones for the fund industry.

Exhibit 5.1 will help you follow my reasoning. It lists 15 of what I consider to be the major differentiators that determine the degree to which a fund organization's priorities lie in serving the interest of its fund owners, versus the interest of its own officers, employees, and stockholders. Please be my guest in thinking about how you'd rate your fund's manager on each of these criteria. Fill in the grid in the box—three points being the highest; zero being the lowest. Then calculate the manager's SQ by adding up its scores and dividing the sum by 15, resulting in an average score, then multiply the result by 100. For example, a firm with two points in each category—a total of 30 points—would have an SQ of 200. A firm with the maximum of three points per category (45 points), would score 300. Now let's cut to the chase, and examine the 15 standards shown in the scoresheet in Exhibit 5.1.

Standard 1: Management Fees and Operating Expense Ratios

Nowhere is the inherent conflict between fund managers and fund shareholders more sharply and obviously manifested than in the level of management fees and operating expense ratios—from 1.95 percent for the high-cost quartile of equity funds, to 0.65 percent for the low-cost quartile. This represents a 1.30 percentage point differential that accounts for even more than the 1.20 percent enhancement in annual returns earned by the low-cost quartile over the past 20 years—8.82 percent versus 7.62 percent.

As shown in Exhibit 5.2, the cumulative growth of a $10,000 initial investment in these two sets of differences in costs is dramatic. In the expense ratio grouping, the low-cost group produces an extra $10,800 over the two decades; the low-turnover group, $10,000 extra; and in the low-total cost group, an extra $13,400. That added value comes without any increase in risk—"found money," if you will. The relationship between expense ratios and returns is consistent not only over time, but

Exhibit 5.1   Scoresheet for the Stewardship Quotient

Manager Name _____

The Stewardship Quotient*
SQ Scores

	3	2	1	0	Score
1. Management fees and operating expense ratios	Very low	Below average	Roughly average	Above average	___
2. Equity portfolio turnover	Under 30%	30%–50%	50%–100%	Over 100%	___
3. Equity diversification	Owns total market	Large cap-blend	Other broad style	Sector fund	___
4. Marketing orientation	Sells what it makes	Gives in, but rarely	Gives in sometimes	Makes what will sell	___
5. Advertising	None	Limited	Extensive	Performance	___
6. Pays for distribution	No	Broker-dealer low pay	Broker-dealer high pay	Supermarket "shelf-space"	___
7. Sales commissions	Strictly no-load	No-load with small 12b-1 fee	Low-load	Substantial sales loads +12b–1 fees	___
8. Shareholder stability (redemptions as a percent of fund assets)	Under 20%	20–40%	40–50%	Over 50%	___
9. Limitations on fund size	Willing to limit size	Closings when appropriate	Rare fund closings	No limits on size	___
10. Experience, stability of portfolio managers	More than 10 years	5–10 years	Less than 5 years	New manager	___
11. Insider ownership of fund shares	Large, and in many funds	Moderate, and in many funds	Moderate, but in few funds	Small or none	___

146

12. Organization of fund manager	Mutual	Privately owned	Publicly owned	Conglomerate subsidiary	
13. Composition of fund board	Independent of manager	Largely independent	Many insiders	Many links to manager	
14. Chairman of fund board	Unaffiliated with adviser	Separate from chief executive	Official of conglomerate	Head of conglomerate board	
15. Regulatory infractions	None or insignificant	No recent major infraction	Minor infraction	Major infraction	

Stewardship Quotient for manager[*]
(Total score ÷ 15) × 100

SQ[*] ___

Exhibit 5.2   Equity Fund Costs and Returns

20-Year Returns: Low-Cost Funds versus High-Cost Funds

Quartile	Group by Expense Ratio		Group by Turnover		Group by Total Cost	
	Expense Ratio	Total Return	Turnover	Total Return	Total Cost	Total Return
Low-cost	0.65%	8.82%	14.3%	8.94%	0.96%	9.02%
High-cost	1.95	7.62	130.9	7.86	2.86	7.55
Difference	−1.30%	1.20%	116.6%	1.08%	−1.90%	1.47%
Appreciation in Value of $10,000 Initial Investment						
Low-cost	$44,200		$45,400		$46,300	
High-cost	$33,400		$35,400		$32,900	
Difference	$10,800		$10,000		$13,400	

SOURCE: Morningstar.

over styles as well. Such a gap, of course, is intuitively obvious: If all of these expert professional fund managers, competing with one another, are—indeed as they *must* be—average *before* the deduction of costs, then it is costs that will differentiate them.

The principle that fund costs are the prime determinant of fund returns used to have few adherents. Today, the issue no longer is in doubt. Jack Otter, executive editor of CBS *MoneyWatch*, is just one more believer. Writing in *The New York Times* in April 2012, he notes that "the single best predictor of a mutual fund's performance is fees," meaning that lower fees can point to better performance. One major aspect of stewardship, then, is setting management fees at reasonable levels, reconciling the clear conflict between managers who seek to maximize their fees and shareholders who benefit by minimizing them. Lower fee rates reflect a higher commitment to stewardship. Since lower expense ratios clearly lead to higher returns, it is only common sense for fund advisers to do their fund shopping in the low-cost quartile.[4] So let's

---

[4]It's also a good idea to look at the *dollar* amount of fees as well as the fee *rate*. A 1 percent fee for a $100 million dollar fund may seem reasonable, but even one-quarter of 1 percent for a $30 *billion* fund—$75 million per year—may be excessive.

give three stewardship points to the tiny handful of firms with *very* low costs, and none to those above the presently high industry norms.

Standard 2: Portfolio Turnover

A similar inverse relationship exists between a fund's portfolio turnover and its returns: *Higher turnover correlates with lower returns* (see Exhibit 5.2). Turnover measures how much trading the portfolio manager does. For example, the lowest-turnover quartile of equity funds, with an average turnover of 14 percent per year, earned more than 1 percentage point of extra annual return—8.94 percent versus 7.86 percent. The highest-turnover quartile churned portfolios to an amazing *average* turnover of 131 percent per year. (For taxable investors, however, turnover also increases the tax burden.) Let's award three stewardship points for lower turnover, say, below 30 percent, and none at above 100 percent.[5]

Interestingly, if we look at funds on a *total* cost basis, we find a combined cost/benefit ratio that is even *stronger* than its two individual parts. Here, I define total costs as the total of expense ratios and turnover costs, which I've estimated at a conservative 1 percent of the turnover rate, that is, a cost of 0.25 percent for portfolio sales and 0.25 percent for purchases—a total of 0.5 percent—for a fund with a portfolio turnover of 50 percent. The combined expense/turnover cost ratio for the lowest-cost quartile is 0.96 percent, and for the highest-cost quartile 2.86 percent, a cost advantage of fully 1.90 percentage points per year.

This cost gap helped drive an even larger 1.5 percentage-point advantage in annual performance—9.0 percent versus 7.5 percent (see Exhibit 5.2). Since the high-cost funds (annual standard deviation of 19.8 percent) have assumed about 30 percent *more* risk than the low-cost funds (standard deviation of 17.5 percent), the gap in risk-adjusted returns is even larger.

Please do not underestimate the impact of what might seem moderate differences between returns and costs. Based on an actual investment of $10,000 20 years ago, a fund earning 9.0 percent over the past 20 years

[5]Like management fees, there may be special considerations regarding turnover. Quantitative funds, for example, often report portfolio turnover in excess of 100 percent, but they typically have been effective at minimizing transaction costs.

would have produced a profit of $46,000; at a 7.5 percent rate, the profit would be just $32,500—a 40 percent increase in capital appreciation.

Whether we like it or not, the jury is in. It has rendered its verdict: *Cost matters.* Funds that are managed with a view toward low operating costs and turnover costs for their investors reflect a significantly higher concern for the stewardship of investor assets than their peers, a concern that results in far higher returns for their investors.

Standard 3: Equity Diversification

Fund companies can earn high stewardship grades for organizing, operating, and managing mutual funds that have low costs and low turnover. Fund companies can also get high stewardship marks if they offer mutual funds that are very broadly diversified and designed to be held for the long term. At one extreme lies the all-stock-market index fund, which owns essentially all of the publicly traded equities in the United States and essentially holds them forever. At the other extreme, we have the specialty funds, which invest in narrow market sectors such as telecommunications or technology, ultimately created for investors to trade. In the middle lie the funds following various style specialties— mid-cap value, small-cap growth, and so forth. These styles are a bet that, at least from time to time, one particular style will outpace the market as a whole, and that a style can be owned as part of a portfolio and/or traded on an opportunistic basis.

In its early era of stewardship, the fund industry was dominated by broad-market-oriented funds (see Exhibit 5.3). But in the recent era of salesmanship, such funds have found themselves in the minority, surrounded by an army of more specialized funds with narrow investment policies.

I admit to a strong bias toward highly diversified funds, but especially low-cost index funds. Why? Because index funds deliver no more nor less than what they promise—as close to 100 percent of the stock market's annual rate of return as is achievable. Because of costs, beating the market is by definition a loser's game for investors as a group. So earning the market return itself is a virtual guarantee that an investor will, over the long term, accumulate more assets than his neighbors. I'd award three stewardship points for highly diversified funds, including all-market-index funds, and none for sector funds.

Exhibit 5.3 From Broad Market Diversification to Narrow Market Slices

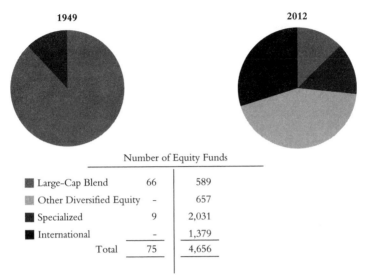

	Number of Equity Funds	
■ Large–Cap Blend	66	589
▨ Other Diversified Equity	–	657
▩ Specialized	9	2,031
■ International	–	1,379
Total	75	4,656

SOURCE: 1949 Wiesenberger, 2012 Morningstar.

Standard 4: Marketing Orientation

What is more, the record is clear that the gap between the returns earned under the highly diversified, low-cost, broad market concept, relative to the more concentrated funds-as-individual-stocks concept, is far larger than the cost differential. Why? Because the cost differential reflects only the *economic* component of the investment management service. But there is also a large *emotional* component to the returns earned by investors. Since buying and holding the entire market is apt to entail far less trading and far less emotion, investors who own the entire stock market (at low cost) actually capture their fair share of the market's return.

But when fund managers act as salesmen of specialized funds, investors seem, far too often, to buy and sell their shares at the *wrong* time. Fund marketers favor the fads that are in the momentary limelight, with the expectation that investors will take the bait. Partly because of their own greed, investors do exactly that, jumping opportunistically into the fund *after* a particular style peaks, and just *before* it goes out of style. As a wise man said, "the issue is not people with *investment* problems, it is investments with *people* problems."

Exhibit 5.4   Boom and Bust in Tech Funds

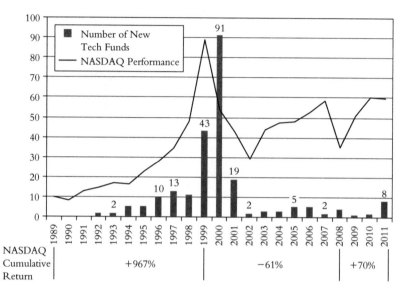

SOURCE: Morningstar.

Fund managers cannot possibly be unaware that the best time to *sell* an exciting new fund concept is usually the worst time to *buy* it. This trend is best illustrated by the industry's forming more and more technology funds as their prices soared. Early in the 1990s, for example, it was rare to see more than a single new tech fund created in a single year. But in 2000 alone, 91 new tech funds were created. After the subsequent fall of tech stocks, of course, the number plummeted, and an average of only three tech funds have been created each year since 2002 (see Exhibit 5.4). Fully 75 percent of these new funds were exchange-traded funds, designed for speculators.

The manager's range of choice in the funds it offers, usually called "products,"[6] is a powerful reflection of its emphasis on stewardship versus salesmanship. Is the manager choosing solid, diversified funds that

---

[6]To me, a product is something that is made to be sold. Period. During my quarter-century as CEO, I banned the use of the word "product" from the Vanguard lexicon. A mutual fund, on the other hand, is a financial service, or, even better, a trust.

largely reflect the stock market as a whole, or narrow, specialized funds whose popularity blows back and forth with the market winds? The highest stewardship is reflected by managers with the strongest discipline against pandering to the public taste for the hottest new investment ideas. Those managers who limit their offerings to what they do well—maybe a single fund or even a half-dozen—reflect the most stewardship of all. Managers *who make what will sell*—for example, jumping on the "New Economy" bandwagon of the 1990s—lure hundreds of billions of investor dollars into them, before the bubble inevitably bursts and those funds go up in smoke. No stewardship points for them; three points for managers who *sell what they make*.

Standard 5: Advertising

When it comes to advertising, the stewardship-salesmanship orientation is patently obvious. Who *pays* for it? Answer: the existing shareholders of the fund. Who *benefits* from it? Answer: the managers who gain revenues by enticing new shareholders to invest in the fund. It is often argued that the manager is spending "its own money" to promote the fund, but of course it is the fees paid by shareholders that are the source of this money, which could otherwise be waived and returned to the fund. There is no evidence whatsoever that advertising benefits fund investors by bringing in an amount of new assets adequate to create economies of scale that offset the amount spent. (On the other hand, there is considerable evidence that building fund assets above a certain size impinges on the manager's ability to create superior performance.)

Because they generate costs to fund investors, advertising expenditures raise a serious question about stewardship. Spending massive sums to promote fund growth suggests that salesmanship is in the driver's seat. For whatever reason, most large fund firms find it necessary to spend shareholder dollars to promote new and existing funds, whether through media advertising, or incentives to brokers, or other means of achieving success in the fund marketplace and building market share. So I'd award the three-point maximum to firms that don't advertise, two points to those that do so only on a limited basis, and one point to those whose advertisements are rife. Keep your eyes open!

But zero points go to funds that advertise their performance. Why? Because, almost universally, we advertise only our most successful funds, and we do so only *after* they have generated high returns. When they fail or when the stock market has tumbled, we lapse into complete silence. Ads that follow this pattern strike me as inherently misleading. For example, at the stock market's peak in March 2000, 44 funds advertised in *Money* magazine, preening about returns that averaged an astonishing 85.6 percent during the preceding year alone. In view of what happened next, the fund advertisers look more like greedy opportunists. Could those fund advertisers really have been focused on stewardship? Within five years, their actions seemed to be mere salesmanship. Of those 44 funds, nine had gone out of existence. The average return of the funds that survived came to *minus* 39.5 percent, a mere 125 percentage points short of the gains their managers had so recently touted.

Standard 6: Shelf Space

When funds pay for "shelf space" to build distribution, fund advertising finds a baneful counterpart—spending shareholders' money to gain even more assets. When the first of today's mutual fund supermarkets came into existence in the 1990s, it was a transforming moment for the industry. No longer would investors pay their own commissions or transaction costs when they shopped there. Rather, the managers whose funds were effectively listed for sale would pay for what came to be known as "shelf space," a common marketing concept in the retailing business. Few observers expressed concern that the apparent ability to make what appeared to be "free" transactions would lead to a rise in market timing or to a high-turnover mentality by investors; or that the fund's other shareholders were effectively paying for the shelf space even though they were not using the service.

It wasn't long, of course, before the national wire houses that did *not* view themselves as supermarkets demanded similar treatment. Then, the going rate for bringing in assets rose—from 0.20 percent to 0.25 percent, to 0.30 percent, to what now seems to be 0.40 percent. Firms that never considered their funds to be "products" for "supermarkets" soon found that sharing their management fees with brokers was a requisite for broker support. Somewhere along the way, an important line was crossed. Salesmanship crossed the line, and stewardship was on the wrong side of it. So three points for funds that will have no part of paying for shelf space, one or two points for funds that are paying for broker-dealer space, and zero for funds that are spending their shareholders resources (directly or indirectly) on supermarkets.

Standard 7: Sales Loads

It is no secret that the fund industry, like the financial services industry in general, has become a marketing business. Indeed, the industry would be but a fraction of its giant size today had there *not* been, in the industry's early years, securities brokers and salesmen to carry our message to investors who otherwise might have learned about mutual funds not only far later, but with far less information. Although its costs obviously detract from the returns investors earn, that information service is essential. It has value. But I'm not at all sure that we are getting the *right* information to investors. We focus on past performance, knowing that, if it is not *negatively* correlated with future returns, the linkage is anything but causal. To earn their keep, advisers should focus their clients not on "picking winners" but on factors such as sound asset allocation, broad diversification, low cost, tax-efficiency, simplicity, and even estate planning.

But when investors have already paid sales commissions to own the funds involved in the scandals—especially if they have done so recently—they should consider reinvesting in funds that don't carry commissions. They've already bought the ticket for their investment voyage, and they shouldn't have to buy it again. So they should seek out funds that meet the standards of stewardship that have been, to some degree at least, ignored in the funds they held. Even if they are subject to penalty sales charges when they redeem, it's probably better to move out rather than continuing to pay 12b-1 fees for years more.

As a broad generalization, salesmanship is used to sell load funds for more than no-load funds. After all, the purpose of the load is to compensate a salesman. So I'd award three stewardship points to *pure* no-load firms, and drop it to two points if a small 12b-1 fee is charged. While there are a number of good fund managers with reasonable sales charges and 12b-1 fees, the fact is that these costs are a significant drag on returns. So consider awarding no stewardship points for these funds.

Standard 8: Shareholder Stability

During my first two decades in this business, market timing was anathema. Shareholder redemptions averaged about 8 percent of equity fund assets, suggesting a holding period of 12-plus years for the average investor. But the redemption rate then began to steadily rise, reaching a high of 41 percent (!) in 2002, a holding period of just 2.4 years for the average fund investor. The average redemption rate for international funds was more than 100 percent per year!

With the reaction created by illegal late-trading and by international time-zone trading described at the outset, the equity fund redemption rate has now retreated to the 30 percent range, still a remarkably short average holding period of only three-plus years. We've created an industry populated importantly by a horde of funds with relatively narrow styles and funds focusing on concentrated market sectors; funds, if you will, bought to be sold by investors, not to be held for an investment lifetime. That the investors who engage in such foolishness are playing a loser's game is only the tip of the iceberg. (Unless, of course, they're given free rides through late trading and time-zone trading!) The problem is that substantial trading volumes generate costly portfolio turnover for the fund itself, a disservice to investors who trusted the fund managers to be their faithful stewards.

Once again, the proof of the pudding is in the eating. If funds are heavily focused on stewardship, they're likely to have low redemption rates—in today's foolish high-fund-turnover environment, of no more than about 20 percent. About 1,800 equity funds, or one fifth of the total, meet this test. (For the record, the redemption rate of Vanguard's actively managed equity funds in 2011 averaged about 10 percent and its index funds averaged about 7 percent.)

While even 20 percent seems like a high number to me, let's award these funds three full stewardship points, two points for those with rates somewhat below the current 30 percent norm—say 20 percent to 40 percent—and a stingy one point if the redemption rate stays below 50 percent. But let's give zero points when rates exceed that level, along with a warning that when redemptions exceed 100 percent of fund assets (there are, unbelievably, 1,133 equity funds in that category!), there might well be heavy market timing going on.[7] If you want to *subtract* a stewardship point for firms that countenance—or even encourage—high levels of trading activity, or *add* a point for those that have voluntarily imposed a redemption fee on short-term trades, please be my guest.

Standard 9: Limitations on Fund Size

Many, perhaps most, managers are in the business of gathering the maximum possible amount of assets, so they can increase their fee revenues. Yet it is no secret that, in the field of investment management, "nothing fails like success." Promoted aggressively, funds with apparently superior performance records draw large amounts of capital, and eventually get muscle-bound; their investible universe shrinks; the impact of their portfolio transactions on the prices at which they buy and sell rises; soon their ability to recover the glory of their early days has vanished. A perfect example is Magellan Fund, for nearly a decade giant Fidelity's crown jewel. In its glory era of 1978–1983, its average annual return of 26 percentage points above the S&P 500's return of 12 percent carried its assets from $30 million to $2 *billion* (see Exhibit 5.5). It did fine in the *next* 10 years, too (+4 percentage points a year ahead of the Index), growing to $31 billion in 1992, on the way to $102 billion in 1999. But the performance momentum had long since come to an end. Magellan has fallen short of the Index return in 7 of the past 10 years, and its return has lagged the Index by an average of 2 percent per year in 1993–2012; the fund's assets plummeted to $15 billion as 2012 began.[8]

In letting funds grow beyond the ability to manage them with distinction, salesmanship is clearly in the driver's seat, and any notion of

---

[7]Some idea of a fund's interest in serving long-term owners lies in the number of round-trip transactions allowed to a shareholder during a 12-month period. Two round trips is on the low side (though it seems a lot to me!). If eight or more are allowed, no stewardship points.

[8]Peter Lynch, Magellan's highly talented original portfolio manager, resigned in 1990. So we'll never know how effectively he might have managed the fund's massive asset growth during the late 1990s and early 2000s. More information on Magellan's (inevitable) reversion to the mean (RTM) is presented in Chapter 9.

Exhibit 5.5   Magellan: Too Big to Succeed

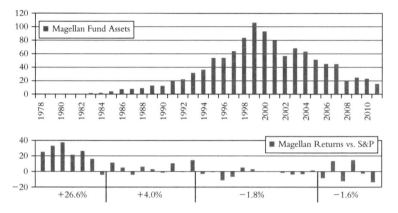

SOURCE: Strategic Insight Simfund/MF Desktop.

stewardship seems powerless to influence the speed and direction of the automobile. While some funds are relatively immune to the burdens of "too big to manage" (for example, index funds and other funds with very low turnover), most funds are not. So I'd award three stewardship points to firms that do not announce in advance any limitations on assets (and when they announce them, live by them!); two points to those that appropriately close funds to new investors so as to preserve their investment characteristics for existing shareholders; just one point to firms that have closed funds, even if infrequently and too late, or, even worse, have announced the closing *in advance*, a sure-fire way to *increase* cash flow; and a zero to funds that are allowed to grow without concern for the obvious and near-certain long-term consequences.

Standard 10: Experience and Stability of Portfolio Managers

A critically important part of measuring stewardship is what happens behind the scenes of fund management. Do the managers act like, well, *stewards*? It is not easy to measure trust and confidence and integrity, but information about the age, education, professional experience, and tenure of fund executives and portfolio managers is widely available. In general, I would cast my lot with the veterans who have worked through at least a few market cycles, who can clearly articulate their philosophy and strategy, and who run portfolios that give living expression to those factors. Typically, it seems to me, such managers, whether they emphasize what are called (rather crudely) value stocks or growth stocks, also tend to focus on the long term.

Morningstar reports that the typical portfolio manager runs a fund for only *five years*, which seems a long way from stewardship to me. Consider a typical shareholder who owns five funds—and holds them, however unlikely that may be, over an investment lifetime. Employing 50 different portfolio managers over 50 years seems much more like a choice of "products" than the selection of a trustee. So I'd reserve three stewardship points for managers with something like 10 to 15 years of experience and tenure, with no points, except under special circumstances, for new managers.

While we've come to think about the "portfolio manager" as our prime consideration, please don't ignore funds run by *teams* or *investment committees*. We now know that many seemingly well-qualified portfolio manager *stars* have turned out to be more like *comets*, burning out after a few years in the limelight, their ashes floating gently back to earth. The wisdom of the collective seems more suggestive of stewardship, especially since the individual "stars" are often promoted with dazzling salesmanship. I'd not hesitate to award three points to funds run by experienced investment committees.

Standard 11: Insider Ownership

I prefer fund directors, executives, and portfolio managers who "eat their own cooking" by investing importantly in the shares of the funds they direct or manage, but not necessarily to the exclusion of other funds in the same fund complex. A few firms even take this philosophy to an extreme, requiring their insiders to invest *all* of their liquid assets in their funds, but that will not always be possible. In any event, three stewardship points for managers who meet those standards, and for others who approach that goal in spirit, if not quite in letter. After all, we can expect a steward to take a special interest in the oversight of his own investments. If there's little or no ownership by the fund insiders, award zero points.

Unfortunately, there's little solid information on this vital issue, and no requirement that management company officials and portfolio managers disclose their transactions in the shares of their funds. As the timing scandals showed, some fund managers were even engaging in market timing in the shares of the very funds they were managing. The SEC now requires the disclosure of portfolio manager holdings, but disclosure of their transactions is also essential. If the answer is that it is "none of your business," consider investing in funds in which the stewards are not only willing, but eager, to disclose their policies, their holdings, and their transactions alike.

As to fund holdings by directors, a serious, indeed inexplicable, information gap continues to exist. Somehow, the Investment Company Institute persuaded the SEC to exempt fund directors from disclosure of the precise number of shares they own, the standard for *all* other public corporations. Rather, fund directors need only disclose the *range* of their holdings: none; $10,000 or less; $10,000 to $50,000; $50,000 to $100,000; over $100,000, both for the fund and for all funds in the group. That *may* be better than no disclosure at all.

But why shouldn't an investor know if a director of the fund has increased his investment from say, $101,000 to $1,000,000? Or, perhaps even more important, reduced it from $1,000,000 to $101,000. Yet that information remains secret, and present regulations suggest that it's indeed "none of your business." (That information gap persists in the SEC's position that the compensation paid to mutual fund senior executives from the fund itself and from the management company need not be disclosed. Again, a standard applied to all other public corporations.) The sooner we revise the regulations to provide exact disclosure rather than inscrutable ranges, the better.

Standard 12: Organization of Manager

When I came into this industry all those years ago, virtually *all* fund management companies were small partnerships or corporations, closely held by their principals. They were but a step removed from the funds they managed, and looked at themselves as trustees, stewards of the assets entrusted to their care. They considered themselves members of the profession of investment management. By 1958, this sound structure was on the way out. As I discussed in Chapter 3, public offerings of management company shares became possible, and numerous management company IPOs quickly followed. At that point, managers were sorely tempted to focus on the price of their company stock and the interest of their own *public* owners, often at the expense of the welfare of their own *fund shareholders*. A primary goal became to build on the fund group's asset base and its market share, and to increase management fee revenues, market aggressively, and to make as much profit as they could.

But as described in the previous chapter, that was only the beginning. Gradually, both public and private management companies were purchased by giant financial conglomerates, who were not necessarily seeking to maximize the return on the capital of the *fund investors* they served, but on the return on *their own* capital. If a bank bought a fund manager for $1 billion, by golly, it had to earn its, say, 15 percent cost of capital—$150 million per year—come hell or high water. As a result, *professional* interests—the stewardship of shareholder assets—were superseded by *business* interests—more salesmanship, more marketing, and more revenues.

You are free to agree or disagree with my awarding three stewardship points to firms that choose the mutual structure (so far, we're all alone!), two points to the firms that remain private, and one point for those that are publicly held. But if you agree that the spirit of stewardship is vastly diminished when a fund manager is owned by a conglomerate far-removed from the fund's operations, a score of zero seems the right judgment for funds operating under that structure.

Standard 13: Composition of Boards

The true independence of the independent directors of mutual funds (those not affiliated with the fund's investment adviser) cannot be measured. But we can look to the credentials, backgrounds, and experience of directors. We can also measure the duration of their service. I confess that, at least up to a point, I favor directors with longer tenure. How can a director come close to understanding his or her responsibilities in fewer than, say, three to five years of service? Even then, how can a director of 100 or 200 funds possibly understand every one of them (or even know their names!). Excessive director's fees are also a concern, for disproportionally large fees may bias a director in favor of the very management that determines his or her compensation. Awarding these scores is inevitably crude and involves guesswork as well as judgment, but let's use both, awarding three points to those funds that seem *generally* to excel in those areas, zero points to those who need substantial improvement; and one or two points to those in between.

Standard 14: Board Leadership

Chairman of the board of a fund is a position that has substantial potential power, albeit almost never used. The chairman leads the board, sets the agenda, and is, or is supposed to be, the principal person in charge of fund governance. The fund's chief executive, on the other hand, usually runs the fund management company. The passage of time—and the increased focus on board independence in our society— has persuaded me that the positions of fund chairman and fund chief executive should be separated, giving the board clear authority over the management. (Full disclosure: I served in both positions at Wellington Management Company and also at Vanguard. But as Lord Keynes said: "When conditions change, I change my mind. What do you do?") So three points for funds that have implemented that separation, and zero points for funds with the ultimate conflict: the *management company* chairman (or president) also serves as chairman of the *mutual fund* board. We'll award one or two points to situations that fall between these two extreme models of governance.

Standard 15: Regulatory Issues

We must ask: how often have the fund and/or its manager gotten in trouble with our principal federal regulatory authorities, the SEC, FINRA (formerly the NASD), or state securities commissioners? When problems came to light, what were the terms of settlement? These settlements are too often resolved with the defendants "neither admitting nor denying the charges." (I don't care for that convention. Management company officials should either admit their wrongdoing, or deny the charges and go before a judge—or a jury—and let the chips fall where they may.) Were they alleged to be violations of civil law, or of criminal law? As it happens, five of the industry's largest fund groups were not involved in the timing scandals, but one highly respected giant faced significant regulator challenges, and was rebuked and fined.[9] Three points for those fund managers with a clean regulatory slate, but zero points for firms that have faced significant regulatory problems. (Four specific examples are shown in Box 5.1.)

Looking at other industry participants, you'll find, I think, that very few fund firms have SQs much above 200, and many have SQs below 75. It is a *very* safe bet, in my hardly objective view, that during the decade that lies ahead, the former group will deliver significantly higher returns to their shareholders than their peers. Ultimately, firms that manifest a bias toward stewardship will come to dominate the fund industry. Shareholders, looking after their own best interests, will vote with their feet, and they will move mountains.

I strongly urge investors to consider these fifteen elements of the Stewardship Quotient and to select and hold the shares of funds that measure up to them. None of these standards are precise. So feel free to add other elements of your own, and then make your own judgments. But entrust your investments largely to managers whose mutual funds strike a proper balance between stewardship and salesmanship, a balance that places professional standards over business pressures. The Steward-ship Quotient—however halting, however subjective—is designed to measure the extent to which fund managers meet fiduciary principles and are worthy of your trust.

Is the Fox in the Henhouse?

My ratings show that Vanguard's SQ of 267 (out of a maximum of 300) is a virtual tie with much smaller Longleaf's SQ of 247. American Funds fell short, largely because of size and regulatory issues; and Putnam's near-rock-bottom 67 results largely from the actual data (high expense ratios, high turnover, sales loads, and conglomerate ownership), not merely my own opinion. The Morningstar statistical service also rates fund families

---

[9]In 2008 American Funds' manager, The Capital Group, was fined $1 million by FINRA for directing fund brokerage commissions to investment brokers based on their sales volume in the funds' shares, a violation of FINRA rules. On appeal, the verdict stood, but the fine was reduced to $100,000, essentially because "everybody was doing it." Now that's an interesting point!

Box 5.1
"Where Angels Fear to Tread":[*]
A Few Specific Examples

	Stewardship Quotients			
	Vanguard	American	Longleaf	Putnam
1. Management fees and operating expense ratios	3	2	2	0
2. Equity portfolio turnover	3	3	3	0
3. Equity diversification	3	2	2	1
4. Marketing orientation	2	2	3	0
5. Advertising	3	3	3	0
6. Pays for shelf space	3	1	3	1
7. Sales commissions	3	0	3	0
8. Shareholder stability (redemption rate)	3	3	3	1
9. Limitations on fund size	2	0	2	1
10. Experience, stability of portfolio managers	2	3	3	0
11. Insider ownership of fund shares	2	3	3	1
12. Organization of manager	3	2	2	0
13. Composition of board	3	3	1	2
14. Chairman of board	2	2	1	2
15. Regulatory issues	3	0	3	1
TOTAL	**40**	**29**	**37**	**10**
Stewardship Quotient	**267**	**193**	**247**	**67**

[*]This title suggests my hesitancy in playing the dangerous game of comparing Vanguard with our rivals.

with their own "Stewardship Grades." Vanguard's average grade is A (although we received a very low grade on "manager incentives." I'm not sure what the heck to make of that!); American Funds A−, Longleaf B+, and Putnam B−. Their independent ratings range from A to C, and reflect roughly the same general pattern of my own ratings in Box 5.1.

In assigning these ratings, I've relied on my review of a few of the largest—but I think highly representative—funds managed or supervised by each of the four managers. (Nearly all large fund complexes offer funds spanning a wide range of objectives, policies, and strategies, and even costs.) My system is rather complex, and may even seem a bit superficial. If my judgments are deemed overly simple, I can hardly overemphasize the need for some judgment on the part of readers to take into account not only the 15 categories that I use to generate the Stewardship Quotient, but other factors you deem relevant.

Readers should be properly suspicious when the fox is minding the hen house. So I'm vaguely embarrassed about the high ratings that I've awarded Vanguard in most—but not all—of the 15 categories. But the fact is that I founded Vanguard with a truly mutual structure, designed to meet the sternest standards of fiduciary duty. That choice is reflected in the client-oriented culture that I did my utmost to instill in the firm. Even 38 years later, that culture has remained largely intact. Of course, it is unarguable that Vanguard: (1) is by far the lowest-cost provider in the industry, (2) is the most committed to low-turnover broad-market index funds, (3) is offering its fund shares on a no-load basis, (4) is enjoying the highest shareholder stability rates, and (5) does no advertising of fund performance. All of the other factors may be debatable, so feel free to debate them, and to challenge the ratings I've awarded.

Perhaps obviously, Vanguard champions—and heavily relies upon—index funds (and funds with index-like characteristics) with high predictability of returns relative to comparable stock and bond market segments operated at rock bottom costs. That strategy has been a major factor in testing our stewardship ethic. The contrast between actively managed traditional mutual funds and passively managed index funds is a story unto itself. So is the story about how index funds that operate in a culture of long-term investment are being crowded out in the marketplace by index funds with a culture of short-term speculation. In Chapter 6, "The Index Fund," I tell that story.

Chapter 6

The Index Fund

*The Rise of the Fortress of Long-Term Investing
and Its Challenge from Short-Term Speculation*

The stone that the builders rejected became the chief cornerstone.

—*Psalm 118*

Part I

*A Brief History of the First Index Mutual Fund:
The Paradigm of Long-Term Investment*

On August 31, 1976, the world's first index mutual fund came into formal existence. Named First Index Investment Trust, it was sponsored by The Vanguard Group of Investment Companies, the new mutual fund complex that itself had begun operations only 16 months earlier. While the index fund began with a tiny asset base, its creation recently was hailed, in Morningstar's words, "as a seminal event in investing . . . a steady revolution that continues today." Almost 36 years have rolled by since its formation, and what I considered the paradigm of long-term investment has now become the largest pool of

167

equity in the world. Now named the Vanguard 500 Index Fund, today's six series of that original index mutual fund have assets exceeding $205 billion.

On Wall Street, the index fund was not a popular idea. The implicit claim that passive management would outpace active management was criticized and ridiculed. Until then, the mutual fund industry's universal strategy was active management and the first index mutual fund was referred to as "Bogle's Folly." Index funds were described as "un-American." Yet today, indexing has earned incredibly broad, if still begrudging, acceptance. Assets of index mutual funds now total $2.4 trillion, accounting for more than one fourth of all equity fund assets. And the trend is accelerating. Over the past five years, while actively managed equity funds have suffered cash *outflows* of $372 billion, equity index funds have enjoyed cash *inflows* of $571 billion. Indexing has clearly proven to be an idea whose time has come. The lesson of Psalm 118 described it well: *The stone that the builders rejected became the chief cornerstone.*

At the time of the index fund's creation, my associates at Vanguard shared my confidence that indexing would ultimately reshape the mutual fund industry. After all, equity mutual funds as a group were destined to roughly track the returns of the entire stock market, but only before the high costs they incurred. These costs included management fees and operating expenses, averaging about 1.5 percent of assets per year; hefty sales loads paid to brokers on most sales of fund shares; embedded (and undisclosed) transaction costs of portfolio turnover; and excess tax costs incurred by shareholders of actively managed funds. All-in, these costs of active management could easily reach 3 percent per year on an after-tax basis, virtually guaranteeing that investors in actively managed funds would, as a group, experience a substantial shortfall compared to the market.

Creating the First Index Fund   In contrast, that first index fund, based on the Standard & Poor's 500 Index: (1) paid no advisory fees since it required no active management; (2) was expected to maintain an expense ratio of 3/10 of 1 percent per year (by 2011, the expense ratio on Vanguard 500 Index shares had plummeted to 6/100 of 1 percent, or just six "basis points"); (3) would, following its initial public offering, eliminate all sales loads; (4) would incur minimal portfolio turnover costs; and (5) would enjoy a high level of tax efficiency. As a result, the index fund would virtually guarantee that its investors would earn their fair share of stock market returns, even after the deduction of those tiny costs.

My partners in the development of the investment concepts and the marketing plan for the index fund included James S. Riepe, then a truly remarkable young businessman. He would later become a highly regarded industry leader and serve as chairman of the Investment Company Institute and managing director of T. Rowe Price. Another partner was a young Princeton graduate and Wharton School MBA, Jan M. Twardowski, who would later become President of Frank Russell Securities Company. He did the awesome statistical work required for us to make our case for the index fund with completeness, accuracy, and professionalism. As the summer of 1975 began, the three of us enthusiastically set to work to make that case. At their board meeting on September 18, 1975, I presented the formal proposal to the Vanguard directors.

At the meeting, most of the discussion focused on whether this unique venture would be within our new company's mandate. Formed less than a year earlier, Vanguard was precluded from engaging in investment advisory or marketing services. Our limited mandate was to provide all fund administrative services, and even that limited mandate had been won only after a considerable internal struggle. But we were able to persuade the Board that no investment advice would be involved and that a public underwriting could be handled by an outside syndicate of brokerage firms.

We presented the board with a table showing the historical record: the average annual return of all equity mutual funds for the period 1945–1975 was +9.7 percent, compared to +11.3 percent for the S&P 500 Index, an excess return for the Index of 1.6 percentage points per year. That seemingly small percentage-point edge represented a reasonable, if possibly conservative, approximation of the long-term advantage an index fund could provide.

That percentage margin might have seemed persuasive on its own, but to drive the point home we assumed an initial investment of $1 million in the Index and in the average fund; then we compounded the investment over the entire 30-year period. Result: index fund, $24,024,000; average mutual fund, $15,387,000—an enormous edge of almost $9 million. That seemingly unbelievable outcome was a tribute to *the magic of compounding of returns*, overwhelming (as I would later describe it) *the tyranny of compounding of costs*. (The year-by-year returns and cumulative returns are presented in Appendix II.)

In those days, the only way to raise capital for a new mutual fund was to persuade a group of Wall Street's investment banking firms to underwrite an initial public offering (IPO). For our index fund, I spent months trying to assemble a syndicate, but finally persuaded four of the largest retail brokers on Wall Street—Dean Witter; Bache Halsey Stuart; Paine, Webber, Jackson & Curtis; and Reynolds Securities—to lead the effort. (Ironically, not one of these firms remains today.) A successful offering—their target was $150 million—would be a slam dunk. Or so we thought.

It was not to be. The official underwriting of First Index Investment Trust came in at just $11.3 million, a 93 percent shortfall from our goal, tiny proceeds that were insufficient for the Trust to own all 500 stocks in the S&P 500 Index. When the underwriters brought me the news of the failure, they suggested that we just call the whole thing off and cancel the deal. I remember saying: "Oh, no we won't. Don't you realize that we now have the world's first index fund?"

The Professor, the Student, and the Index Fund

Nobel Laureate economist Paul Samuelson played a major role in the creation of the first index fund. More than 25 years earlier, I'd hinted at the idea of an index fund in my 1951 Princeton University senior thesis, titled "The Economic Role of the Investment Company." I had always loved contrarian ideas that challenged the status quo, and was often inspired to take the road less traveled by. And, yes, just as Robert Frost promised, "that has made all the difference." Dr. Samuelson was much more direct and forceful. He *demanded* an index fund. His words strengthened my backbone for the hard task ahead: taking on the industry establishment.

In the autumn of 1974, Dr. Samuelson's "Challenge to Judgment" was the lead article in the inaugural edition of the *Journal of Portfolio*

Management. It caught me at the perfect moment.[1] The professor pleaded "that, at the least, some large foundation set up an in-house portfolio that tracks the S&P 500 Index—if only for the purpose of setting up a naïve model against which their in-house gunslingers can measure their prowess. . . . The American Economic Association might contemplate setting up for its members a no-load, no-management-fee, virtually no-transaction-turnover fund." He noted, however, the perhaps insurmountable difficulty was that "there may be less supernumerary wealth to be found among 20,000 economists than among 20,000 chiropractors." He laid down an express challenge for *somebody, somewhere* to start an index fund.

Presented with that challenge, I couldn't stand back any longer. While all of our peers had the *opportunity* to create the first index fund, Vanguard alone had the *motive.* For reasons that I described in the previous chapter, the newly formed Vanguard Group, ought to be "in the vanguard" of this new concept, which was simple, elegant, and logical. Why? Because our goal was to offer well-diversified funds operating at minimal costs, focused on the long term. We were the only *mutual* mutual fund complex; and the index fund was a perfect fit. It was a marriage made in heaven, strongly supported by the unequivocal data that I had assembled on fund performance relative to the S&P 500 over the previous three decades.

Simple Arithmetic: An Unarguable Conclusion   Few commentators have recognized that two distinct intellectual ideas formed the foundation for passive investment strategies. Academics and sophisticated students of the markets—"quants," as they are known today—rely upon the EMH—the *Efficient Market Hypothesis*, first articulated by University of Chicago Professor Eugene Fama in the mid-1960s. This theory suggests that by reflecting the informed opinion of the mass of investors,

---

[1]A year later, another article, "The Loser's Game," by investment professional Charles D. Ellis, published in the *Financial Analysts Journal*, also gave me encouragement. Even earlier, in the first edition of his remarkable book *A Random Walk Down Wall Street* (1973), Princeton professor Burton G. Malkiel also issued a challenge for someone to start "a mutual fund that simply buys the hundreds of stocks making up the market averages." Alas, I didn't read his book until the early 1980s.

stocks are continuously valued at prices that accurately reflect the totality of investor knowledge, and are thus fairly valued.

But, as I've often noted, we didn't rely on the EMH as the basis for our conviction. After all, sometimes the markets are highly efficient, sometimes wildly inefficient, and it's not easy to know the difference. Rather, we relied on a theory that it is not only more compelling, but unarguably universal. The CMH—the *Cost Matters Hypothesis*—is all that is needed to explain why indexing must and will work. In fact, the CMH enables us to quantify with some precision *how well* it works. *Whether or not the markets are efficient, the explanatory power of the CMH holds.* As I've noted in several earlier chapters, *gross* return in the stock market, minus the (high) cost of obtaining that return, equals the *net* return actually received by investors. Yes, it *is* as simple as that.[2]

It was the opportunity of a lifetime: to *at once* prove that indexing would work in practice as well as in theory, and work effectively. And it would mark this upstart of a firm as a pioneer in a new wave of industry development. After all, "Vanguard" means, among other definitions, "leadership of a new trend." With Dr. Samuelson's inspiration, and with luck and hard work, the idea that had begun to germinate in my mind in my Princeton thesis would finally become a reality (see Box 6.1).

Dr. Samuelson's *Newsweek* Column   The initial press reception to the underwriting had been reasonably good, but bereft of a single hint that the index fund represented the beginning of a new era for the mutual fund industry. The most enthusiastic comments came from Professor Samuelson himself. Writing in his *Newsweek* column in August 1976, he expressed delight that there had finally been a response to his earlier challenge: to create an index fund "that apes the whole market, requires no load, and keeps commissions, turnover and management fees to the feasible minimum."

Now such a fund lay in prospect. "Sooner than I dared expect," he wrote, "my explicit prayer has been answered. There is coming to market, I see from a crisp new prospectus, something called the First Index

---

[2]My thinking has long been informed by a fifteenth-century maxim known as Occam's Razor (after English philosopher Sir William of Occam): When there are multiple solutions to a problem, pick the simplest one.

Box 6.1
Ideas versus Implementation

Ideas are a dime a dozen; implementation is everything. I've expressed that mantra all through my career, and it surely applied to the creation of the world's first index mutual fund.

It was way back in 1951 that I first developed at least a vague idea of the index fund. After examining the statistics on equity fund returns relative to various market indexes, I concluded in my Princeton University thesis that mutual funds "should make no claim to superiority over the market averages." Others have interpreted that thought as a precursor of my later interest in matching the market with an index fund. Honestly, I don't know whether it was or not. Nonetheless, if I had to name the moment when the index fund seed was planted, that would be it. That seed finally germinated into my proposal to the Vanguard Board in 1975 that we form the first index mutual fund based on the S&P 500 Index.

By the late 1960s, many analysts and academics had begun to seriously pursue the indexing idea. In 1969–1971, Wells Fargo Bank, working from complex mathematical models, developed the principles and techniques leading to its version of index investing. John A. McQuown, William L. Fouse, and James Vertin pioneered the bank's effort. As McQuown said, "Before we had computers, data, and good models, we didn't know which procedures were right and which were wrong. We missed a lot, but we did come out with some clear ideas." Their work led to the construction of a $6 million index account for the pension fund of Samsonite Corporation in 1971.

The idea was solid, but the implementation was, by one description, "a nightmare." For the strategy was based on an *equal-weighted* index of New York Stock Exchange equities, creating "cumbersome record-keeping and bean-counting, and

(Continued)

requiring day-to-day management." That strategy failed, and was finally abandoned in 1976. The new index it chose, of course, was a *market-cap-weighted* index—the S&P 500 Index, the very same index that we had selected as the standard for Vanguard's new offering a year earlier. Wells Fargo used the new strategy for its own pension clients, and later for Illinois Bell.

In 1971, Batterymarch Financial Management of Boston independently decided to offer the idea of index investing to its advisory clients. The developers were Jeremy Grantham and Dean LeBaron, two of the founders of the firm. Grantham described the idea at a Harvard Business School seminar in 1971, but found no takers. For its efforts, Batterymarch won the "Dubious Achievement Award" from *Pensions & Investments* magazine in 1972. It was two years later, in December 1974, before the firm finally attracted its first pension client.

By that time, the American National Bank in Chicago had created a common trust fund—also modeled on the S&P 500 Index—requiring a minimum investment of $100,000. The idea had begun to spread from academia—and from these three firms that were the first professional advocates—to a public forum.

Two other failed attempts to develop the index fund concept should also be noted. In 2002, former American Express executive George Miller sent me a note enclosing a copy of a preliminary "red-herring" prospectus for "The Index Fund of America" filed with the SEC on February 22, 1974, by American Express. The fund was "loosely modeled" on the S&P 500 and required a minimum investment of $1 million. But before the year was out, American Express senior management lost heart for the challenge. The offering was withdrawn and the project was abandoned.

In September 2011, *The Wall Street Journal* published a letter to the editor written by Mr. Miller briefly describing this history. By that point, yet another claim to be the creator of an index fund chimed in. An executive of TIAA-CREF reported that, way back in 1971, the firm received a letter from Nobel

Laureate economist Milton Friedman, who served on the board of CREF (College Retirement Equities Fund). Dr. Friedman proposed that the CREF variable annuity should eliminate all investment analysis and "adopt a mechanical formula whereby CREF simply brought into a Standard & Poor's 500 Index." This idea also fell by the wayside, never to reach fruition.

This multilayered history of the development of the indexing concept confirms my thesis that it is not the idea itself, but its actual implementation, that ultimately wins the day. In all of these other forays into indexing: idea A+; implementation F. Only Vanguard earned the double grade that is required if any innovation is to reach its fruition: Idea A+, implementation A+.

Investment Trust." He conceded that the fund met only five of his six requirements: (1) availability for investors of modest means; (2) proposing to match the broad-based S&P 500 Index; (3) carrying an extremely small annual expense charge; (4) offering extremely low portfolio turnover; and (5) "best of all, giving the broadest diversification needed to maximize mean return with minimum portfolio variance and volatility."

His sixth requirement—that it be a no-load fund—had not been met but, he graciously conceded, "a professor's prayers are rarely answered in full." As it happened, his final prayer would be answered only six months later, when in February 1977, all of the Vanguard funds eliminated their sales charges and made an unprecedented conversion to a "no-load" distribution system.

A Long Relationship   In a curious way, the relationship of this reasonably intelligent but hardly brilliant college student with "the foremost economist of the twentieth century" (as *The New York Times* called Dr. Samuelson) had begun much earlier. At the beginning of my sophomore year at Princeton University, I took my first course in economics; our textbook was the first edition of Dr. Samuelson's *Economics: An Introductory Analysis*. (My marked-up copy still graces the shelves of my library at home.) Truth told, I found the book tough going, and fared poorly in my first stab at this subject, which was then new to me. My midterm grade, in the autumn of 1948, was 4+ (D+ in today's lexicon). I was required to maintain an average of at least 3− (C−) to maintain the full scholarship that Princeton had provided me. If I did not improve by the end of the semester, my college career would be over.

I struggled, but I made the grade that I needed by semester's end, gaining the 3 that I coveted, even though it was on the margin. My grades continued to improve. Thanks largely to the high grade that I was awarded on my senior thesis on the mutual fund industry (a long way from the macroeconomics of Dr. Samuelson's book!), I graduated *magna cum laude* in Economics. On July 5, 1951, I entered the mutual fund industry, joining Walter Morgan's pioneering Wellington Management organization.

A Priceless Endorsement From that lowly beginning in 1948, and then through his support for that first index mutual fund in 1975, my association with Paul Samuelson grew ever closer and warmer. In 1993, I asked him to endorse my first book—*Bogle on Mutual Funds*. He demurred. But to my utter astonishment he told me that he would prefer to write the foreword. Some excerpts:

> The same surgeon general who required cigarette packages to say: "Warning, this product may be dangerous to your health" ought to require that 99 out of 100 books written on personal finance carry that same label. The exceptions are rare. Benjamin Graham's *The Intelligent Investor* is one. Now it is high praise when I endorse *Bogle on Mutual Funds* as another. . . . I have no association with The Vanguard Group of funds other than as a charter member investor, along with numerous children and innumerable grandchildren. So, as a disinterested witness in the court of opinion, perhaps my seconding his suggestions will carry some weight. John Bogle has changed a basic industry in the optimal direction. Of very few can this be said.

Mutual Admiration Paul Samuelson and I met face-to-face perhaps only a half-dozen times during what was arguably our 61-year relationship. But he often sent me notes, and must have made at least a score of telephone calls to me in my office. When he called, I'd quickly grab a yellow legal pad and pen, for I knew he'd be giving me a rapid-fire series of ideas to improve that first index mutual fund, in ways large and small. At first I was intimidated (of course!), but as time went on, I appreciated not only his brilliance, but his warmth, his friendliness, his wry sense of humor, and his patience with a mind far less powerful than his own.

One brief handwritten note dated "mid-summer day" comes to mind. Late in June 2005 he wrote: "Any small influence on you has been more than offset by what Vanguard has done for my 6 children and 15 grandchildren. May Darwin bless you!" The culmination of our mutual admiration society came when, with his permission, I dedicated my 2007 book—*The Little Book of Common Sense Investing: The Only Way to Guarantee Your Fair Share of Stock Market Returns*—to Paul A. Samuelson. The final words of the dedication, "Now in his 92nd year, he remains my mentor, my inspiration, my shining light." Even after his life's long journey ended in 2009, he continues to inspire me.

A Simple Idea Becomes a Huge Reality   Today, the assets of the Vanguard funds modeled on the S&P 500 Index exceed $200 billion, together constituting the largest equity fund in the world. The second largest, at $180 billion, is the series of Vanguard Total Stock Market Index funds. This fund's portfolio is dominated by the large-cap stocks that constitute the S&P 500, but it also holds the stocks of mid-cap and small-cap companies. Obviously, investors have given their stamp of approval both to our index fund concept and its implementation. Investors have voted with their wallets, and they continue to do so.

Surely Paul Samuelson's highest accolade for the index fund came in his speech at the Boston Security Analysts Society on November 15, 2005: "I rank this Bogle invention along with the invention of the wheel, the alphabet, Gutenberg printing, and wine and cheese: a mutual fund that never made Bogle rich but elevated the long-term returns of the mutual-fund owners. Something new under the sun." Those words from an intellectual giant about a mere mortal who has scraped by without a great intellect—but with great intellectual curiosity and relentless determination—are among the greatest rewards of my long career.

Economics, one might say, makes strange bedfellows. But together, the professor and the student who joined forces gave the world its first index mutual fund.

The Triumph of Indexing

The creation of Vanguard's index fund in 1975 resulted in a plethora of negative reactions and disdainful comments. There was zero competitive response. The industry, as the saying goes, "couldn't have cared less." Indeed, it was not until nine years later that the fund industry's second index fund was formed. In 1984, Wells Fargo created its Stagecoach Corporate Stock Fund. But it was burdened with an initial sales load of 4.5 percent and an annual expense ratio of 1 percent. At that cost level, it didn't deserve to succeed; it would inevitably fall far short of the performance of the very index it was designed to emulate.[3] Now known as Wells Fargo Advantage Index Fund, its assets total but $130 million, a drop in the bucket of index fund assets.

In 1986, the major equity index offering was Colonial Index Trust, which carried a sales load of 4.75 percent. In effect, the public was being offered an index fund that began "behind the eight ball"—the amount of the initial sales commission—and, due to an annual expense ratio of about 1.50 percent, would fall further behind the eight ball with each passing year. The marketplace proved discriminating. The flawed fund drew limited investor assets and was put out of its misery in 1993.

For 10 long years, indexing remained a tiny portion of equity mutual fund assets—less than one-half of 1 percent share at year-end 1986. Still, there were strong signs of life in the private pension fund arena, where indexing had by then attracted nearly 15 percent of pension assets. An uptrend in indexing was beginning to take shape.

The acceptance of index mutual funds, so frustratingly slow at the outset, would all too soon become an avalanche. Equity index fund assets grew from that paltry $11 million in 1976 (0.3 percent share of the assets of equity funds), leaped six-fold to $600 million a decade later (0.4 percent share), and then to $91 billion in 1996 (5.5 percent share).

---

[3]That high cost was justified by a Wells Fargo spokesperson because "we (the manager) can make a lot of money. The fund is our cash cow."

Exhibit 6.1 The Rise of Indexing—Growth in Assets of Index Mutual Funds (1977–2012)

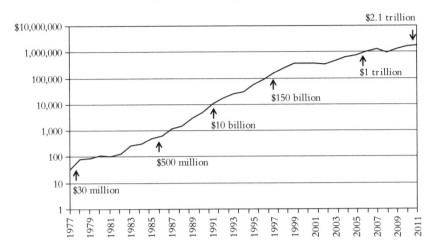

SOURCES: Morningstar (1977–1984), Strategic Insight (from 1984).

By 2001, index funds had leaped to $340 billion (11 percent share), and finally to $1.1 *trillion* in early 2012, fully 28 percent of equity fund assets (see Exhibit 6.1). The triumph of indexing could hardly be clearer.

The Power of Simplicity What commends the index fund to institutional investors and individual investors alike is its simplicity. In its original incarnation, it essentially owned the U.S. stock market, as measured by the S&P 500 Index. Buy the market and hold it forever (or at least until you retire). Don't worry about portfolio managers who will come and go, and don't speculate on which manager may be lucky enough or smart enough to outperform the market for a time. Own an index fund, get a life outside of finance, and relax.[4]

For better or worse, with the growth of the index fund came diversity. While in the early years, all index funds followed the S&P 500

---

[4] The typical investor owns about four equity mutual funds; the typical fund manager lasts for five years. So in the course of, say, a 60-year investment lifetime, the investor's portfolio will have been managed by almost 50 different managers. It seems to me that it would be, well, inconceivable for such an investor to even approach the returns earned by an index fund.

model, indexing soon expanded to subsume the total U.S. stock market (which was fine). Indexing then expanded to cover various market sectors, such as growth and value; large-cap, mid-cap, and small-cap; then to developed international markets and later to emerging markets. This broadening, too, didn't bother me. Then, in the early 1990s, a new strain of index fund entered the arena. The traditional index fund (TIF), which could be purchased or redeemed at the close of business on any day, was challenged by a new exchange-traded fund (ETF), an index fund that could be bought and sold instantly, all day long. But ETFs came to offer a huge range of funds with even-narrower market segments. My concern with this trend has become almost palpable.[5]

In any event, there are now two distinctive kinds of index funds (with some, but surprisingly few, overlaps between them in the index portfolios each offers). So let's turn first to consider the TIF, whose portfolio composition looked like Exhibit 6.2 as 2012 began.

This exhibit is noteworthy on many levels. First, U.S. broad market index funds—designed to be held for a lifetime—total $485 billion, constituting almost 65 percent of all TIF assets. If we include three more kinds of funds—(1) "completion" funds, designed to be paired with S&P 500 funds to gain full market exposure; (2) large-cap style funds that reflect the total market's large-cap bias; and (3) index funds investing in the world's developed markets—the total grows to 134 funds and $655 billion. Broad-market index funds, then, represent nearly 90 percent of total TIF assets of $770 billion. This dominance by mainstream traditional index funds suggests that the focus on long-term investment that the first index fund model established as the paradigm of long-term investing remains the paradigm today.

The Proof of the Pudding   Yet again, the proof of the pudding is in the eating, so let's see how well that first index fund served its original investors. Curiously enough, thanks to a 2006 dinner marking the 30th anniversary of

---

[5]Over the past decade, the ETF has become the new paradigm of indexing, reflected in this burgeoning, now dominant, strain of the index fund. As you will see, the asset profile of ETFs in Exhibit 6.5 looks vastly different from the profile of TIFs in Exhibit 6.2.

Exhibit 6.2 Traditional Equity Index Funds Today: Dominated by Long-Term Portfolios

Type	Portfolio Count	Total Assets (in millions)
S&P 500 Index	51	$304,855
Total Stock Market	9	180,200
Total Broad Market	**60**	**$485,055**
Completion Index	5	$23,459
Core/Growth/Value Styles		
Large–Cap	36	$47,077
Mid–Cap	19	33,780
Small–Cap	25	40,510
Total Large/Mid/Small	**80**	**$121,367**
Developed International	33	$99,589
Emerging Markets	5	14,140
Total International	**38**	**$113,729**
Other	34	$27,309
Total Traditional Equity Index Funds	**217**	**$770,919**

the fund, I can easily answer that question. At this celebration, attorney Steven West of Sullivan & Cromwell, counsel for the fund's underwriters, reported to the group that he had actually purchased 1,000 shares at the original offering, at a price of $15.00 per share, including an initial sales charge of 6 percent for its distributors. He had held on to that $15,000 investment ever since, making no redemptions and reinvesting all dividends. He pulled from his pocket his most recent Vanguard statement and proudly announced that the value of his holding in that statement had grown to $461,771. As 2012 began, despite the steep bear market of 2007 through early 2009, the value of that initial investment has actually continued to grow—to $550,134. That achievement would seem to require no comment.[6]

[6]Well, maybe one comment. Of the 360 equity mutual funds in existence in 1976, only about 135 remain. Some 225 funds have vanished from the scene.

So the simple answer to the simple question—"How did the charter investor fare?"—is "very well, indeed." But a second question—more sophisticated and totally fair—remains. "How have the returns earned by that passively managed Index 500 Fund compared with the returns earned by actively managed funds under professional supervision?" The only answer is, "Extraordinarily well!" Vanguard 500 Index Fund's relative performance over the years has been truly remarkable. Over the past quarter-century, relative to its large-cap blend peers (also holding both growth and value stocks), Index 500 has been in the top two quartiles 16 times, and not once was it in the bottom quartile. I'm not sure any single peer has ranked so high so often, with nary a single bad stumble.[7]

These are simple facts. But a more precise answer is surprisingly elusive. Equity funds come and go at a surprising rate, so taking into account the generally inferior returns of funds that have gone out of business is imprecise at best.[8] There's no way to accurately account for the value of the index fund's substantial tax-efficiency, the result of its miniscule portfolio turnover, nor is there any precise method for calculating the amount of sales commissions paid by the investors in managed funds, about two-thirds of which impose sales loads, now averaging about 5 percent per year.

But we try to present all of the facts. Here's what the data tell us:

- The total rate of return of Vanguard Index 500 from its inception in 1976 to the beginning of 2012 has been 10.4 percent. Based on an initial investment of $10,000, the final compounded value is $328,838.
- The total rate of return of the average large-cap blend fund (the most relevant comparative standard), was 9.2 percent; total compound return on a $10,000 investment, $226,253.

---

[7]Thinking of this extraordinary performance, I once had a dream that when I started the fund, I decided not to disclose that it was an index fund. I told investors that I would be the portfolio manager. In the dream, I was named the most successful equity-fund manager of the past quarter-century. When I awoke, I began to think. . . .

[8]Vanguard recently conducted a study for the 20-year period 1990–2010. It found that after accounting for survivor bias, 72 percent of actively managed U.S. equity funds failed to beat the S&P 500.

- Annual index advantage of 1.2 percentage points; cumulative advantage $102,585, an enhancement in total capital accumulation of almost 50 percent. Remarkably, that margin happens to be almost identical to the adjusted margin of 1.6 percentage points that I presented in my crude study to the Vanguard directors in 1975, described earlier in this chapter.[9] That remarkable consistency over nearly six decades provides a powerful message about the sustained superiority of the index fund.

However, even this comparison is biased in favor of the active managers. Why? Four reasons may explain the difference: (1) The adjustments noted in the table are, I'm confident, significantly understated. (2) The index fund tax advantage is ignored, but would come to an added advantage of at least another 1 percent per year. (3) As the 500 Index Fund's costs have plummeted, the gap between the 500 Index

Exhibit 6.3   Passive Fund Returns Have Outpaced Active Equity Fund Returns by 1.2 Percent Annually—Average Annual Returns (1976—2011)

Period	S&P 500 Index	Vanguard 500 Index Fund**	Average Large Cap Blend Fund***	Vanguard 500 Index vs. Avgerage Large Blend Fund
1976*—1981	8.8%	8.1%	12.1%	−4.0%
1981—1986	19.9	19.3	16.8	2.5
1986—1991	15.4	15.0	12.2	2.8
1991—1996	15.2	15.1	12.6	2.5
1996—2001	10.7	10.7	8.7	2.0
2001—2006	6.2	6.1	5.0	1.1
2006—2011	−0.2	−0.2	−1.9	1.7
1976*—2011	10.6	10.4	9.2	1.2
Growth of $10,000	$356,276	$328,838	$226,253	$102,585

*From the 500 Index Fund's inception on August 31, 1976, to year end.

**Investor shares through 2000, Admiral shares thereafter.

***Author's calculation based on Morningstar data minus 0.50% for estimated survivor bias and 0.30% for the estimated impact of sales loads.

SOURCE: Morningstar.

---

[9]See footnote 3 in Chapter 4 on page 112 for more detail.

Fund return and the S&P Index return itself dwindled from 0.7 percent to virtually zero in 2011. (4) We clearly picked a poor time to launch the fund, for the launch of the fund in 1976 followed a period (1972–1975), during which returns of the S&P 500 were abnormally high relative to those of actively managed funds. So it was hardly surprising that some reversion to the mean would take place during our first five years. That period, as it happens, was the only one of the seven five-year periods in which the S&P failed to meet the test of superiority over active managers. To be fair, the excellent results for the 500 Index fund during the next three periods may reflect, well, some reversion of that reversion.

The Responsibilities of the Innovator   Even before the first index mutual fund began to make its mark, we expanded our index offerings. Of course, that first fund would finally prove to be both an amazing artistic (investment performance) and commercial (asset-gathering) success. As the pioneer of the original S&P 500 index fund, Vanguard was determined to lead the way in developing new kinds of index funds offering the same kinds of advantages, but designed to serve investors with more specialized needs. The industry was virtually certain to evolve in that direction. (Just as it has.) Given the skills and experience of Vanguard's investment and administrative staff and the firm's ability to operate at rock-bottom cost, we felt that we had the responsibility to continue to dominate the index fund field. So we quickly pursued a strategy of expanding the original indexing concept to broader uses.

The process moved forward quickly and easily. In the years that followed the creation of our stock index fund, we moved first into the bond index area. Thereafter, we would build an index fund "family" that would greatly expand our mandate. Here are the highlights.[10]

Vanguard Index Fund Family Milestones (1976 to 1996)

- **1986: The Bond Index Fund.** We took this obvious step to build on our reputation as an index manager. Its story is told in greater depth in Box 6.2.

---

[10]More detailed information on this history is presented in my booklet *Vanguard— Index Pioneer*, privately published in 1995. Electronic copies are available on my eBlog: www.johncbogle.com.

Box 6.2
The Bond Index Fund

In 1986, the first decade of Vanguard's stock index fund came to a close. Its assets would soon top the $1 billion milestone. Its performance success and its growing, if modest, acceptance— led to an obvious idea: If indexing worked so well in the stock market, why wouldn't it also work in the bond market? What's more, compared to the huge divergence in the annual returns of equity funds, the annual returns earned by bond funds would fall in a far narrower range. That's because bond fund returns are driven largely by changes in the general level of interest rates, rather than the varied degrees of skill among bond managers. Conclusion: A low-cost bond index fund would not only nicely outpace actively managed bond funds as a group, but would do so consistently, and would make the index fund advantage not only more assured, but more obvious to investors.

So as 1986 came to a close, we took our second plunge into index waters. Vanguard formed the first bond index fund for individual investors. (A bond index fund for institutional investors had been started earlier in the year.) Because most bond funds were grossly overpriced, often carrying both high expenses and excessive sales charges, there was no question in my mind that bond index funds would come to meet a major need in the marketplace. A low-cost, no-load index fund seemed certain to fill much of that need.

With the formation of Vanguard Bond Market Fund, Vanguard was again the pioneer. Since the SEC would not accept the notion that an index fund could own a relatively small number of individual bonds and hope to closely replicate the performance of an index that included 4,000 bonds, the Commission staff would not permit our use of the name

(Continued)

Vanguard Bond *Index* Fund. We had been laying the ground-work for a bond index fund during much of 1986, but the final inspiration—this is true!—came when *Forbes* magazine, writing about the second-rate returns and high costs of most fixed-income mutual funds, expressed the crying need for a low-cost bond index fund.

A Second Cri de Coeur

The magazine plaintively asked, "Vanguard, where are you when we need you?" Thus, yet another cri de coeur—an echo of the plea of Paul Samuelson a decade earlier for a stock index fund—provided the final impetus. Once again, we responded. In the ensuing years, our bond index fund would again prove a great artistic and commercial success. The Bond Index Fund admirably tracked the returns in the Lehman Brothers Bond Index of U.S. investment grade bonds (now called Barclays Capital Aggregate Bond Index.) By the end of its first decade, the fund had become one of the industry's 10 largest bond mutual funds.[11]

While it has taken time, the now (finally) aptly named Vanguard Total Bond Market Index Fund has emerged as the second-largest bond fund in the industry. As 2012 began, the assets of its two linked portfolios totaled $160 billion, second only to PIMCO's Total Return Bond Fund, up in the strato-sphere with $250 billion of assets, thanks to the superior returns it has earned under the direction of fixed-income industry legend Bill Gross. But no other bond fund even approaches those levels. Together, the next 10 largest funds hold assets averaging but $34 billion.

---

[11]This is not to say that closely matching a bond index is easy. In 2002, the return of Vanguard Total Bond Market Index Fund lagged the Barclay's Aggregate Index by 2 full percentage points. Paradoxically, despite this remarkable shortfall, the Total Bond Market Index Fund still outpaced the average managed bond fund by 0.75 percentage points.

That dominant size reflects the fact that the Vanguard Total Bond Market Index Fund has fully measured up to its performance potential. Its now 24-year lifetime rate of annual return averaged 6.9 percent, a nice margin of 1.2 percentage points (again!) over the average 5.7 percent rate of return of its taxable peers. That superiority comes despite the Fund's assuming far less credit risk, for the fund (and the bond market index itself) typically hold more than 70 percent of assets in securities backed by the U.S. Treasury and its agencies, including mortgage pass-through certificates. Compounded, the appreciation of a $10,000 investment made at the close of 1986 was remarkable: average actively managed bond fund $29,900; Vanguard Total Bond Market Index Fund, $42,600, or a difference in profit of more than 40 percent. This stunning advantage once again reaffirms the timeless truism: Never forget either the *magic* of long-term compounding of returns, nor the *tyranny* of long-term compounding of costs.

Learning from Experience

Certainly the marketplace of bond investors has learned from that truism. In 1989, the assets of Vanguard's bond index fund didn't reach even $100 million, and represented 0.1 percent of the total assets of all taxable bond funds. But by 1996, assets of our bond index funds had soared to $4 billion, some 1 percent of the assets of all taxable bond funds, and by 2006, $45 billion or 4 percent. As 2012 began, assets of Vanguard's bond index funds totaled $190 billion, a record-high share of nearly 9 percent of all taxable bond fund assets.

Perhaps even more significantly, bond index funds as a group now claim a record high 17 percent market share among taxable bond funds—$370 billion of the $2.4 trillion total. What's more, during 2011, bond index funds accounted for fully 40 percent of the investor cash flow into taxable fixed-income funds as a group.

(Continued)

This penetration is a harbinger that the trend toward bond indexing will continue to strengthen, just as has the trend toward stock indexing. This accelerating trend confirms what Peter Fisher, talented head of the fixed-income group for giant global money manager BlackRock, has observed: "We're moving to the second phase of the index revolution. The world is a frightening, uncertain place, and investors want to make their (bond) portfolios much simpler so they can sleep at night."

With an annual expense ratio now averaging 0.10 percent (10 basis points), Vanguard Total Bond Market Index Fund remains a ferocious competitor. Peer bond *index* funds are charging an average of 0.40 percent (40 basis points). Peer *actively managed* taxable bond funds are charging an average of 1.05 percent (105 basis points). In the majority of cases, peer actively managed funds also charge hefty sales loads. It is hard to imagine that the superiority of the bond indexing strategy will not continue to prove itself over the long term.

CAVEAT: If there is a weakness to the case for the all-bond-market-index funds, it is that Barclay's Aggregate Bond Index itself is so heavily weighted by U.S. Treasury and agency securities and federally backed mortgage bonds (GNMAs). In 1986, in the first annual report of the Vanguard's bond index, I noted that U.S.-government-related bonds accounted for 77 percent of assets. In the Fund's most recent annual report, it was only slightly lower, at 72 percent. With Treasury yields recently near their lowest levels since the 1940s—just 1.6 percent for the 10-year Treasury note—the risk of rising rates cannot be ignored.

So it's time to create yet another bond index fund, a Total Corporate Bond Index Fund. Its estimated yield in May 2012 is 3.3 percent, versus 1.9 percent for the Total Bond Market Index Fund. A corporate bond index fund would be useful to investors who require higher income without assuming undue risk. An investor who transferred, say, half of his bond holdings in the total bond index portfolio into an investment-grade corporate bond portfolio would have a 35 percent position in U.S. government securities. As low interest rates continue for the foreseeable future, and spreads between corporates and Treasurys remain at current levels, it can only be a matter of time until a total corporate bond index fund is made available to investors.

- **1987: Extended Market Portfolio.** As good as it was, an index fund modeled on the S&P 500 Index was in some sense not quite good enough. It provided a means to match approximately 80 percent of the U.S. stock market, but it did not include stocks with medium and small-size market capitalizations. The "Extended Market" portfolio covered the "non-500" position required to replicate the Wilshire 5000 Equity Index.
- **1989: Vanguard Small Capitalization Stock Fund.** An actively managed fund run by an external investment adviser, this fund provided distinctly inferior results during 1985–1988. We converted it into a small-capitalization index fund, modeled on the Russell 2000 Index.
- **1990: Two International Funds.** We first considered an international fund modeled on the Morgan Stanley Capital International Europe, Australia, Far East (EAFE) stock index. But we were concerned about the substantial risk of a bubble in the Japanese stock market at that time. We came to grips with the dilemma by starting *two* international funds—one indexed to the European portion of the EAFE Index and the other to the Pacific portion. Fortuitous or smart, our fears about the Japanese market proved correct, and the decline that began in 1989 has continued to the present day.
- **1990: An Index Fund for Large Institutions.** Vanguard Institutional Index Fund was also modeled on the S&P 500 Index, but designed for institutions with substantial assets. The minimum initial investment was $10 million per account, with an annual expense ratio of just 0.09 percent, compared with a then-cost of 0.22 percent for our basic 500 Portfolio.
- **1992: Balanced Index Fund.** We had proven that stock indexing worked, and then that bond indexing worked. The logical conclusion: Start a balanced index fund, 60 percent in the total U.S. stock market

index, 40 percent in the U.S. bond market index. This concept was the precursor of our later formation of LifeStrategy Funds, and, in 2005, our Target Retirement Funds, both of which are based on our underlying index funds in the various asset classes. (See below.)

- **1992: Growth and Value Index Funds.** Persuaded by the proven success of "all-market" indexing, we determined to offer separate growth and value index funds. When Standard & Poor's at last created these indexes in 1992, we quickly followed suit. The idea was to offer a growth index fund for an investor's accumulation phase and a value index fund in his distribution phase. Alas, too many investors used these portfolios to speculate on which market sector would do best in the future (a loser's game, of course), and their potential has yet to be realized.

- **1993: Defined-Maturity Bond Index Funds.** In March 1993, we created the industry's first specific-maturity bond index funds—the Long-Term Bond, Intermediate-Term Bond, and Short-Term Bond Portfolios were modeled on the comparable segments of the Lehman Brothers Aggregate Bond Index.[12] We had originated this maturity segmentation concept in 1976 with the formation of our three-tiered municipal bond fund. These tax-exempt portfolios were not technically index funds, but were managed under indexing principles.

- **1993: Emerging Markets Index Fund.** Later that year, we decided to form an emerging markets stock fund, based on the MSCI emerging markets index. Although emerging markets had soared to what seemed to be speculative heights, we believed in the long-term utility of such a portfolio. Happily, procedural and regulatory issues delayed our offering until May 1994, by which time the bubble in the emerging markets had burst.

- **1993: Tax-Managed Index Funds.** Also in 1993 (busy year!), we began the development of a new index fund concept that would

---

[12]These funds carried extremely low costs and were available only to investors who could meet the requirement of a $25,000 minimum investment. We gave them the designation *Admiral*. Ultimately, we parlayed this idea into share classes with lower expense rates for larger investors (given their economies of scale) in nearly all of the remaining funds in the Vanguard Group. These new low-cost classes also carried the Admiral name. Admiral shares now represent more than 30 percent of Vanguard's fund assets.

optimize its potential tax advantages. We formed not one, but three, index-oriented tax-managed funds—Growth and Income, Capital Appreciation, and Balanced, with assets divided 50/50 between lower-yielding stock portfolio and intermediate-term tax-exempt municipal bonds. We wanted to avoid the "hot money" of speculators, so we levied penalties on shareholders who redeemed their shares in these portfolios within five years of purchase.

- **1994: LifeStrategy Index Funds.** Each of our four LifeStrategy Portfolios maintains varying allocations to stocks, using existing Vanguard index funds. Income, 20 percent; Conservative Growth, 40 percent; Moderate Growth, 60 percent; Growth, 80 percent. The balance was composed of our bond index funds. (For a time, the LifeStrategy Portfolios also held modest commitments in Vanguard Asset Allocation Fund.)
- **1996: Total International Index Fund; REIT Index Fund.** The Total International Portfolio was a "fund of funds," a composite of our underlying European, Pacific, and Emerging Markets Portfolios. The REIT (real estate investment trust) index fund, which provided a low-cost way for investors to diversify into the real estate "asset class," was launched in May 1996.

When I stepped down as Vanguard's chief executive in 1996, the most fertile ground for index funds had already been plowed. During the next few years, we rounded out our index offerings, forming index funds to complete our participation in all nine Morningstar "style box" categories, namely: growth, value, and blended index funds for small-, mid-, and large-cap stocks. We formed more tax-managed index funds, along with a "social index" fund based on an external index of corporations said to honor the principles of "corporate social responsibility." In 2004, we created index funds for the 10 industry segments of the S&P 500, including financial, health care, energy, and information technology.

In 2006, recognizing the vital role of dividend income in shaping long-term stock market returns, we created two more index funds, one focused on dividend appreciation and one on high dividend yield. And in 2010, as the number of indexes proliferated, we created a series of six index funds reflecting the basic categories of the Russell indexes, mimicking those we had earlier created based on the S&P indexes.

As 2012 begins, Vanguard administers 62 broad market index funds and 12 broad sector index funds, plus another four LifeStrategy Funds and eight Target Retirement Funds, both of which use our existing Vanguard index funds as their underlying investments. These two series of index-oriented asset allocation funds have grown rapidly, with aggregate assets totaling $130 billion as 2012 begins.

Part II

The Invasion of the ETF

Today, Vanguard remains at the pinnacle of the index mutual fund field, as we have for 35 years, accounting for more than 50 percent of the industry's index fund assets. While our growth in index fund assets from 1986 through the 1990s had come entirely from our traditional index funds (TIFs), most of our growth since then has been driven by "nontraditional" index funds known as "exchange-traded index funds." ETFs have existed only since 1992, but by 2000 they had become a major force in index investing. By 2008, ETF assets actually exceeded TIF assets and lead by an even wider margin today—$1,129 billion for TIFs; and $1,210 billion for ETFs (see Exhibit 6.4). Along the way, in 2001, Vanguard jumped on the ETF bandwagon. In early 2012, Vanguard's ETF assets totaled $205 billion and represented 16 percent of ETF assets, and accounted for 28 percent of 2011 ETF cash flow.

While the TIF and the ETF are often said to compete with one another, that can't be true. How can they be "competitors" when both are index funds; both are (generally) mutual funds in form; and the major index participants operate funds in both categories. Uniquely in Vanguard's case, both the TIF portfolios and the ETF portfolios actually share ownership in exactly the same underlying stock holdings. But those duplicate identities end right there. Beyond form, two sharp differences in substance exist:

1. **Trading Volumes—Investment versus Speculation:** Conventional index funds are overpoweringly used by long-term investors, with redemption rates by TIF shareholders running around 10 percent per year. ETFs, on the other hand, seem largely used by short-term investors with staggeringly high trading activity.

Exhibit 6.4   Growth in Assets of Index Mutual Funds (1992–2012)

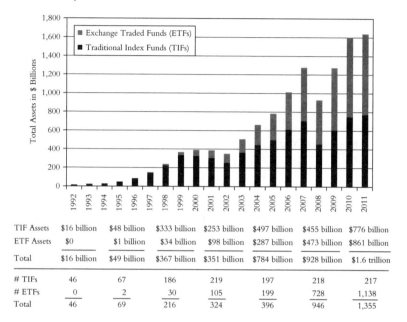

TIF Assets	$16 billion	$48 billion	$333 billion	$253 billion	$497 billion	$455 billion	$776 billion
ETF Assets	$0	$1 billion	$34 billion	$98 billion	$287 billion	$473 billion	$861 billion
Total	$16 billion	$49 billion	$367 billion	$351 billion	$784 billion	$928 billion	$1.6 trillion
# TIFs	46	67	186	219	197	218	217
# ETFs	0	2	30	105	199	728	1,138
Total	46	69	216	324	396	946	1,355

Annual turnover rates average 1,400 percent, with turnover as high as 10,000 percent or more in some ETFs. These rates are obviously leagues above the turnover rates of TIFs, and also many times the turnover rates of even the most actively traded individual common stocks. The stock of General Electric, a widely-traded stock issue, usually runs at about 150 percent per year.

2. **Narrower Portfolio Focus and Higher Selection Risk:** Fully 96 percent of individual ETFs and 87 percent of ETF assets are highly specialized and far less focused on broad market indexes such as the S&P 500. Rather, they are more heavily focused than TIFs on extremely narrow market segments such as individual market sectors; specific countries; commodities (especially gold); and on funds that leverage daily market returns for those wishing to make heavy bets on the direction—up or down—of momentary stock prices.

When we combine the remarkably high turnover among most ETFs with their focus on ever-narrower market segments, the difference in degree of ETFs from TIFs becomes a difference in kind. The difference, if you will, is between long-term investment and short-term speculation. Exhibit 6.5 presents a radically different profile for ETF index funds than for TIFs. This chart depicts a revolution in process. The TIF clearly dominated indexing into the early 2000s, but burgeoning acceptance of the ETF in the marketplace quickly developed. It continues to this day. It is not that TIFs are declining; it is that ETFs are at present the engines of index fund growth.

But if the amounts of assets in each category are similar, the number of funds in each category is anything but similar. In 2005, there were almost 200 TIFs, and also 200 ETFs. Currently, the number of equity TIFs remains flat at 217, while the number of equity ETFs has surged to 1,138. (It's said that some 1,000 more are planned in 2012.)

Consider the strikingly different profile of ETFs in Exhibit 6.5 compared to the profile of TIFs presented earlier in Exhibit 6.2. There are but 11 U.S. broad market ETFs among the total of 1,138, holding 15 percent of the field's $870 billion total. But in TIFs there are 60 broad market funds holding 65 percent of the $717 billion total. Looking more closely at ETFs, there are 223 industry sector ETFs, 95 individual country ETFs, 142 commodity ETFs, and 191 leveraged and inverse levered ETFs. Almost all of these categories are conspicuous by their absence from the TIF matrix in Exhibit 6.2. One obvious purpose for these narrowly focused ETFs is to enable investors to speculate on future returns in industry and country segments, and on the momentary movements of stock prices. Appendix VII presents the growth in the number of funds and assets of these two distinctly different approaches to the principles of indexing.

In sum, long-term investment has been the major driver of the TIF business. Short-term speculation has become the major driver of the ETF business. While broad-market ETFs can easily and beneficially be used by long-term investors—they may even compare favorably with their comparable TIF cousins in some cases—no one can be certain of the extent of this usage. But it seems likely that the major component of the ETF asset base is large investment institutions that use ETFs (largely the SPDRs and QQQs) for hedging purposes, implementing complex strategies, and for equitizing cash balances for short periods. A significant portion of the remaining ETF base is likely comprised of

Exhibit 6.5   Exchange-Traded Equity Funds Today: Long-Term Portfolios Are a Small Portion

Type	Portfolio Count	Total Assets (in millions)
S&P 500 Index	3	$113,926
Total Stock Market	9	24,864
Fundamental Index ETFs	44	11,434
Total Broad Market	**56**	**$150,224**
Specialized ETFs Core/Growth/Value Styles		
Large-Cap	102	$135,236
Mid-Cap	36	42,148
Small-Cap	52	39,877
Total Large/Mid/Small	**190**	**$217,261**
Developed International	70	$79,823
Emerging Markets	33	82,066
Country Specific	95	52,150
International Sector	53	9,287
Total International	**251**	**$223,325**
Sector Funds	**223**	**$106,114**
Gold	28	$110,175
Other Commodities	114	22,752
Total Commodities	**142**	**$132,927**
Leveraged ETFs	75	$11,310
Inverse ETFs	96	12,518
Long/Short/Market Neutral	20	755
Total Alternative Strategies	**191**	**$24,583**
Currency ETFs	20	$5,151
Other	65	8,342
Total Specialized ETFs	**1,082**	**$717,703**
Total Equity ETFs	**1,138**	**$867,927**

individuals who like the opportunity to engage in short-term trading. We simply don't know the amount of assets held by long-term investors. I'd guess (probably generously) that their share is about 15 percent. Have ETF investors been able to enhance their returns with their hyperactive trading in ETFs? The evidence suggests that they do quite the reverse—reducing their returns.[13]

One can only wonder what Nathan Most, the visionary who had the original idea for the ETF structure and, lest we forget, who had the relentless drive to implement his idea, would be thinking if he were alive today. (He died in 2004.) His contribution has gone largely unnoticed, so I'll introduce him to you in a moment.

A Brief History of the ETF

When I first studied the mutual fund industry six decades ago, I was struck by the promise of "daily liquidity." Investors could liquidate their share of the funds they owned each day, essentially at an asset value determined at the subsequent close of business. I thought such a promise was remarkable, and it was honored almost without exception during the ensuing 60 years. Daily liquidity, along with professional management, diversification, convenience, and shareholder service were the keys to the fund industry's enormous growth, which took place largely during the great bull market of 1982–1999. Fund industry assets soared from $2.5 billion in mutual fund assets when I joined the industry in 1951, to more than $6 trillion in 2000. While asset growth then slowed, it continued at a more reasonable 5 percent rate; with assets reaching $11 *trillion* as 2012 begins.

Early in 1992, a visitor came into my office in Valley Forge, Pennsylvania, and tried to persuade me that the daily liquidity we offered for our index funds was not nearly good enough. He presented a design for a new "product" in which shares of the Vanguard 500 Index Fund could be traded instantaneously throughout the market day, and proposed that we partner with him. He was convinced that if Vanguard Index 500 shares could be traded on the nation's stock exchanges just like individual stocks, it would vastly increase our client base by

---

[13]A recent paper—"Do ETFs Badly Serve Investors? Testing the Bogle Hypothesis"—by Professor Edward Tower and Ming Xie of Duke University confirms my intuition. Professor Tower concludes that ETF investors "make bad decisions in the short term as well as in the long term, and their style drift subtracts even more value than their decisions over short-term horizons."

attracting a new breed of investors. (Of course, it would also attract speculators, though he did not use the word.)

Think of it, he said: in addition to the diversification, the portfolio transparency, and the low expense ratios that Vanguard already offered, investors would gain the ability to sell shares short or buy them on margin; to trade easily on foreign exchanges; possibly to enhance tax-efficiency; and to attract hedge funds and other institutional investors by enabling them to fine-tune their risk exposures on a moment-by-moment basis. My visitor, soft-spoken though he was, was clearly a missionary for his concept.

Meet Nathan Most. His name was Nathan Most, and he was head of product development at the American Stock Exchange. He laid before me a plan for a breakthrough innovation that would become known as the exchange-traded mutual fund. I listened to his presentation with interest and gave him my reactions: (1) there were three or four flaws in the design that would have to be corrected in order for the idea to actually function; and (2) even if the new design solved the problems, our Index 500 Fund was designed for long-horizon investors. I feared that adding all that extra liquidity would attract largely short-horizon speculators whose interests would ill-serve the interests of the long-term investors in our index fund. So, we found no community of interest. But we parted amicably, and would enjoy a nice friendship over the years that followed.

As Nate Most told the story, on his train ride back to New York City he figured out how to fix the operational problems that I had found in his design. He then resumed his search for a partner, soon finding one at giant State Street Global Advisers. In January 1993, State Street introduced the Standard & Poor's Depository Receipts. The "SPDRs," based on the S&P 500 Index (SPY on the New York Stock Exchange) have dominated the ETF marketplace ever since. Despite the amazing influx of new ETFs, year after year, the SPDRs remain the world's largest exchange-traded fund—and now the world's most actively traded stock—with assets of $90 billion as 2012 begins.

The Idea Catches On. ETF assets have grown, I'm certain, far beyond Nate's highest expectations. With some $1.2 trillion now invested in ETFs, it is without hesitation that I describe Nathan Most's visionary creation of the first ETF as the most successful *marketing* idea of the modern age of the securities business. Whether it proves to be the most successful *investment* idea of the age, however, remains to be seen. I have my doubts. So far, ETFs, in general, have not served their investors well. Indeed, how could ETFs possibly serve investors well? With 1,446 ETFs in early 2012—tracking an incredible 1,056 indexes(!)—picking an ETF is just like picking a stock, with all of the attendant risks. (I freely concede that speculating in index funds generally carries significantly less risk than speculating in individual stocks.)

So, it's hard for me to imagine that today's ETFs will become the Holy Grail of investing—that ever-sought after way to beat the returns of the stock market. Yes, some ETFs offer the temptation to bet on narrow segments of the stock market, some now employ exotic leveraged strategies, and some make betting on commodities relatively easy. But six decades of investment experience have reinforced my basic tenet that short-term trading—yes, let's call it speculation—is by definition a loser's game, and long-term investing is by definition a winner's game (see Chapter 1.)

". . . All Day Long, in Real Time."   The early advertisements for the SPDR expressed its marketing proposition bluntly: "Now, you can trade the S&P 500 Index all day long, in real time." I can't help but wonder, if you'll forgive the coarse language, "What kind of a nut would do that?" Yet day after day, the SPDR lives up to its promise—invariably the most actively traded stock in the entire world, with average daily trading volume of 220 million shares, or an astonishing $6.8 *trillion* in 2011 alone. With SPDR assets averaging about $90 billion for the year, that's a turnover rate of 7,311 percent. I concede the success of the ad's message: Investors are indeed trading the S&P 500 Index all day long in real time—in huge amounts, and in unimaginable volumes. Nate Most, I think, would be proud that his dream has been realized.[14]

---

[14]But I'm not at all sure that he would be pleased that the original SPDR has now morphed into 113 separate SPDRs! A recent advertisement listing each SPDR was entitled "Next time you go to the market, take this shopping list." To foreshadow what I will point out on the next few pages, if you're not sure which to pick, "just throw a dart!"

But the SPDR has spawned a whole host of followers, and the diversity of investment options seems to have reached far beyond the furthest reaches of what even an innovator like Most would have found appropriate. "Name an exotic product—any product you can imagine—and we'll create it," is the war cry of the new breed of ETF entrepreneur. These marketers are in the game, not necessarily because their so-called "product" may be good for investors, but because they may hit the jackpot, attract a lot of assets, and make a personal fortune. Some ETFs, used properly, are good for investors, while others are not. But the temptation for fund marketers to jump on the bandwagon of a hot new product is almost irresistible. During my career, I've seen scores of innovations, but I know of only a handful that has served the enduring needs of long-term investors. And ETFs hardly meet that standard.

"I'm Shocked, Shocked. . ." The simple fact is that there is far more short-term speculation than long-term investment going on in the ETF field, not only among traders in specialty and leveraged funds, but in middle-of-the-road funds covering broad market segments such as the total U.S. stock and bond markets, or the total international (non-U.S.) market. The dimension of that speculation is staggering: in 2011 the dollar value of trading in U.S. ETFs alone came to $18 *trillion* dollars. Denying that this huge turnover exists reminds me of the classic line from Captain Louis Renault, the police chief in *Casablanca*: "I'm shocked, shocked to find that gambling is going on in here."

Yes, much of that gambling in ETFs is done by financial institutions that speculate, or hedge, or equitize cash holdings, or have margin lending on tap. No one seems to know how these numbers play out, but I'd estimate that 75 percent of ETF assets are held by institutional investors and the remaining 25 percent by individuals. Further, I'd also guess that about two-thirds of the individual holders follow trading strategies of one type or another, and only one-third follow a strict buy-and-hold strategy akin to that of the original TIF paradigm. (This would mean that less than 10 percent of ETF assets are held by long-term investors.)

Exhibit 6.6 below shows the 2011 turnover rates for the major players in the ETF game, ranging from a high of 15,813 percent to a low of 342 percent. The exhibit also presents the turnover rates of a selection of individual ETFs, ranging from 12,004 percent to 207 percent. More

Box 6.3

Just Throw a Dart!

ETFs listed in the Wall Street Journal on January 3, 2012

Given the astonishing array of more than 1,400 ETF options available, perhaps interested investors and speculators that are tempted by the ETF promise should just throw a dart to make their selection. (To fit this space, this table of listings includes "only" 750 ETFs. It is said that another 1,000 ETFs are in the pipeline for 2012!)

EXCHANGE-TRADED PORTFOLIOS 2011 TRADING SUMMARY

wsj.com/ETFresearch

Exhibit 6.6   2011 ETF Turnover

Selected ETF Managers	2011 Average Total Assets (in millions)	2011 Total Dollar Trading Volume (in millions)	2011 Turnover
BlackRock	$448,469	$5,055,158	1127%
State Street (SPDRs)	246,164	10,038,971	4078
Vanguard	159,551	545,730	342
ProShares	23,338	1,387,600	5946
WisdomTree	11,037	48,281	437
Direxion	6,634	1,049,071	15813

Selected ETFs	2011 Average Total Assets (in millions)	2011 Total Dollar Trading Volume (in millions)	2011 Turnover
ProShares Ultra S&P500	$1,622	$194,674	12004%
iShares Russell 2000 Index	15,880	1,298,192	8175
SPDR S&P 500	92,636	6,876,297	7423
iShares MSCI Emerging Markets Index	39,976	722,399	1807
SPDR Gold Shares	60,768	670,638	1104
Vangaurd MSCI Emerging Markets ETF	43,592	260,881	598
Vanguard Total Stock Market ETF	18,726	38,765	207

SOURCE: Morningstar, Strategic Insight, Indexuniverse.com

NOTES: ETF dollar trading volume is the sum of daily share volume multiplied by the daily closing market price.

often than not, the more speculative (or non-mainstream) the strategy, the higher the turnover.[15] It seems obvious that the lure of speculation is the main driver of the ETF boom. (Note in the exhibit, not only the

---

[15]I want to be clear that these turnover rates apply to trading in ETFs by market participants, not to the turnover rates of the ETFs themselves. For example, the SPDR portfolio had a portfolio turnover rate of just 1 percent, and the turnover rate of the Vanguard Total Stock Market ETF was just 5 percent. (Source: Morningstar.)

rates themselves, but the astonishing dollar volumes, often in the trillions of dollars.)

Vanguard and Vipers. Impressed with the growth and potential of ETFs, Vanguard joined the parade in 2001. Gus Sauter, head of Vanguard's investment group, led the charge and (as I understand it) was relentless in demanding the decision. He became the enthusiastic leader of its implementation. Sauter created a novel, patented structure in which each ETF would simply be a new share class of the portfolio of one of the firm's existing TIFs. The firm's original ETFs were named "Vipers"—an odd choice when you realize that a viper is a poisonous snake with large fangs (or a treacherous person)—and the name was soon dropped.

After its first Total Stock Market ETF was launched in 2001, Vanguard expanded its entry into the existing conventional broad market styles such as growth, value, small-cap, and so forth. The firm also gradually expanded into fairly broad market sectors such as energy, health care, and information technology; into broad international indexes; then into a wide array of bond index funds; and in 2010 added S&P- and Russell-based broad index funds. To its credit, the firm is clearly taking the high ground in ETF-land, ignoring the most risky sectors and narrow speculative sectors that encourage betting on the unknown.

Vanguard's relatively disciplined strategy has attracted both long-term investors and short-term speculators. Its ETF turnover rates are amazingly high relative to its TIFs, but they are only a fraction of those of other ETF sponsors. Such marketing discipline is rarely rewarded in the mutual fund field, but the growth of Vanguard's ETFs belies that presumption. The firm's share of ETF assets has grown unremittingly from just 3 percent in 2004 to 8 percent in 2008; and to 16 percent as 2012 begins. In 2011, Vanguard's share of ETF inflow had grown to 28 percent, the largest in the field, and some 10 percentage points more than the second-ranked firm. Exhibit 6.7 shows the number of ETFs and the assets supervised by the leading providers, along with brief descriptions of their "product lines."

While it took Vanguard almost a decade to enter the ETF fray, its peers have been far slower to react. Late in 2011, Fidelity announced that it would sharply expand its ETF business beyond the single ETF (NASDAQ

Exhibit 6.7   The ETF Field Today: Leading ETF Managers: Total Assets and Number of Funds

Manager Name	Fund Count	Total Assets (in Millions)	Comments
BlackRock (iShares)	270	$500,494	25 subsector (tech-software, mortgage finance); 41 individual country (Thailand, Turkey, India Nifty 50).
State Street (SPDRs)	109	289,752	33% of assets in S&P 500 SPDR; 45 sectors.
Vanguard	64	205,001	80% of assets in broad market funds; No country or sub-sector funds.
Invesco PowerShares	125	58,537	5 funds over $1 billion; half of assets in Nasdaq QQQs; 20 "dynamic" funds.
ProFunds	132	23,535	Leveraged, inverse, and leveraged inverse funds; Largest funds: Ultra Short U.S. Treasury 20+ years; Short and Ultra Short S&P 500.
WisdomTree	48	15,691	WisdomTree Total Dividend (original strategy, now 1% of assets); 9 currency funds.
Guggenheim Investments	36	7,946	10 currency funds (ruble, pound, peso, etc.).
Direxion Funds	56	6,862	Bulls (3 × leverage); Bears (3 × inverse leverage).

Index) it had run since 2003. Early in 2012, PIMCO launched an actively managed ETF modeled on its flagship Total Return Fund. Alliance Bernstein, Dreyfus, Janus, and T. Rowe Price have all filed the necessary applications with the SEC to begin offering actively managed ETFs. But foolish as it is to speculate on momentary movements in the stock market, isn't it even more foolish to speculate on whether a particular manager is significantly outperforming or underperforming the market itself on a minute-by-minute basis?

Others such as American Funds and Franklin Resources may feel the press of competition and join the ETF parade, likely to follow the actively managed model. (Most fund firms dislike index funds, especially their rock-bottom costs.) But given the overwhelming dominance of indexing, born of the general failure of active managers to earn consistently superior long-term returns, I believe that the actively-managed ETF model is unlikely to drive the industry and that BlackRock's iShares, State Street's SPDRs, and Vanguard's index-based ETFs will continue to dominate the field.

The Un-Proof of the Pudding

But overall, if "the proof of the pudding is in the eating," the ETF meal is not very tasty. The evidence continues to roll in on how ETF investors, who so often are really speculators with extremely high trading volume, actually fare. But we know that even many of the relatively solid ETF offerings are falling short of their promise. Exhibit 6.8 tracks the returns *reported* by a sampling of ETFs compared to the returns *actually earned by investors* in those ETFs. We include the returns earned by investors in ETFs that are narrowly focused on sectors, and in ETFs making leveraged bets on the direction of short-term movements in stock prices up or down, called leveraged ETFs and inverse ETFs. We call these returns, respectively, *time-weighted fund* returns and *dollar-weighted investor* returns.

With but one exception, the ETFs in this selected list that focused on leverage, inverse bets, and other extreme strategies have delivered returns to their investors that severely lagged the indexes they tracked. While this group's cumulative ETF returns for the five years averaged +21.3 percent, the returns of investors in these ETFs averaged +0.8 percent, a negative gap of more than 20 percentage points. (Imagine the size of that accumulated shortfall if we'd had a full decade to evaluate it!) It is a curious paradox that investors betting on a bear market (S&P 500 Short ETF) suffered a 52 percent relative loss of capital, while investors betting on a bull market (S&P Ultra 500 ETF) gained a 41 percentage point edge even though their cumulative return was only 0.3 percent. (Please don't ask me to explain that difference!) Note also that even the best sectors of the era left their investors well behind the eight ball. (Brazil, minus almost 50 percent; gold, minus 28 percent.)

By contrast, investors in the broad-based ETFs fared much better, averaging an annual negative gap of −1.3 percentage points, or −6 percentage points for the five years. That heavy trading in the SPDR,

Exhibit 6.8 ETF Investor Returns Seriously Lag the Returns of Their Funds

Fund Category	Five-Year Annual Return			Five-Year Cumulative Return		
	ETF	Investors	Investor Lead/Lag	ETF	Investors	Investor Lead/Lag
Broad Based ETFs						
SPDR S&P 500	-0.2%	-3.7%	-3.5%	-1.1%	-17.4%	-16.3%
Vanguard Total Stock Market Index	0.4	2.3	2.0	1.9	12.3	10.4
iShares Russell 3000 Index	0.0	-1.0	-1.0	-0.2	-5.1	-4.9
iShares MSCI EAFE Index	-4.0	-6.6	-2.6	-18.5	-29.0	-10.5
Average	-1.0%	-2.3%	-1.3%	-4.8%	-10.8%	-6.0%
Narrow/Inverse ETFs						
SPDR Gold Shares	21.8%	19.2%	-2.7%	168.5%	140.4%	-28.1%
iShares MSCI Emerging Markets Index	2.9	2.0	-0.9	15.4	10.5	-4.9
Vanguard MSCI Emerging Markets Index	3.8	1.2	-2.5	20.4	6.3	-14.1
iShares MSCI Brazil Index	9.5	1.5	-8.0	57.4	7.9	-49.4
Ultra S&P 500 ProShares	-10.0	0.1	10.0	-40.8	0.3	41.1
Short S&P 500 ProShares	-4.4	-23.1	-18.7	-20.2	-73.1	-52.8
Average	3.9%	0.2%	-3.8%	21.3%	0.8%	-20.5%

SOURCE: Author's calculations, using data from Strategic Insight, through November 2011.

however, apparently cost those traders more than 16 percentage points in potential capital. Investors in Vanguard's Total Stock Market ETF, where annual turnover at 207 percent is modest (for this field), actually earned *higher* returns than the index itself. Perhaps that is because its assets were tiny at the outset, but gradually grew to more than $1 billion by the end of the five-year period. But clearly most of the more focused and the more speculative ETFs have ill-served investors, with huge gaps averaging a 20 percent relative loss of capital in this five-year example.

To be fair, it's a bit too early in the ETF game to come to definitive conclusions about the impact of providing the moment-by-moment liquidity of ETFs compared to the daily liquidity of the traditional mutual funds. A few years from now, we'll be able to evaluate a full decade of returns. For those few funds that have already been around for a decade or more, the results are not encouraging. I found just 62 ETFs with enough history to calculate a 10-year investor return. The average annual return on those ETFs over the past 10 years was 6.9 percent. ETF investors (or, perhaps more appropriately, speculators) earned only 4.2 percent per year, a staggering cumulative shortfall of almost 50 percent over the last decade.

In Chapter 4, we have already seen that the returns earned by investors in traditional actively managed equity funds, across the board, have also fairly consistently lagged the returns reported by the *funds* that they own, typically by 1 to 3 percentage points over the past 15-year period. While these longer-run data cannot be fairly compared with the five-year data for ETFs, we saw earlier (Exhibit 4.4) persuasive evidence that there is a positive correlation between higher volatility and lower returns by investors; the more volatile the fund, the larger the negative gap. In less volatile funds such as TIFs, the negative gap is smaller. If that principle holds in the ETF field—as it has done thus far in its relatively brief history—the substantially higher volatility of the ever-narrower sectors bodes ill for the returns that ETF investors actually earn.

ETFs have continued to move away from simplicity and toward complexity. As this trend accelerates (I assume to no one's surprise), obvious problems have arisen. While leveraged ETFs were designed to multiply the stock market's gain for the bulls (or multiply its gains for the short-selling bears), it turns out that while the multiplier (now usually *triple* leverage) works well on a daily basis, it fails to deliver on that goal as days turn to months and then years. For example, the ProShares Ultra S&P 500 ETF seeks to double the return of the S&P 500 on a daily basis. But over the last five years, the ETF has produced a total return of −25 percent, while the index itself provided a return of 10.5 percent.

Early in 2012, yet another glitch came to light. Credit Suisse suspended the offering of its "Velocity Shares Daily 2XVIX Short-Term" ETN (Exchange Traded Note), promising double the return of a set of CBOE Market Volatility Index futures. (I'm not making this up!). To this aging Luddite, betting on market volatility seems the essence of absolute absurdity; leveraging such a bet seems even crazier. In any event, in mid-March, surging demand for USD2XVIX exceeded issuer Credit Suisse's internal limits, at which point the bank stopped creating new units; the price soared, and then, in a two-day sideways market, dropped 50 percent. *Barron's* warned investors to "stay away." I concur.

There are some 200 ETNs in the ETF universe. But a note is simply an uncollateralized loan to an investment bank, and not subject to the protection offered by the Investment Company Act of 1940. Manager fees are deducted from a "shadow NAV" based on the before-fee performance since the ETN's inception. Apparently, ETNs are one of the few ways to buy commodity funds, which have quite enough problems even if they could be created in ETF form. I believe you should eschew all this complexity and risk, and—if you decide on a buy-and-hold strategy—stick to the simplicity of the standard garden-variety ETF. Even better, if you are an investor who can resist anything but temptation, focus on the original paradigm of long-term investment—the all-market TIF.[16]

---

[16]There is a serious question as to whether these high levels of turnover on ETFs increase stock market risk. In their article entitled "How Index Trading Increases Market Vulnerability" in the March/April 2012 issue of *Financial Analysts Journal*, editor Rodney Sullivan and James X. Xiong argue that the sharply increased trading in ETFs has *decreased* the benefits of diversification for all styles of stock portfolios . . . with *increased* market volatility. The authors conclude that heavy trading in ETFs—now accounting for an astronomical 35 percent of trading volume on U.S. exchanges (versus a mere 5 percent a decade ago)—has severely increased the fragility and systemic risk of the U.S. stock market.

ETFs: An Independent (and Intelligent) Appraisal

Rarely are my views on ETFs aptly characterized. So let me be clear: I remain positive on the concept, but only when the right kinds of ETFs are (a) used properly and (b) used for investment and not speculation. I'm decidedly negative about the remarkable range of foolish extremes that have characterized their implementation. So I'm happy when *The Economist* of London, a newspaper noted for its balance and perspective, says essentially what I'm saying about ETFs in this chapter. Here are some excerpts from its issue dated June 23, 2011.

Box 6.4

Exchange-Traded Funds: A Good Idea in Danger of Going Bad

The Risks Created by Complicating a Simple Idea

"In finance, the simple ideas are often the best. . . . The original idea was to create portfolios of shares replicating a stock market index, such as the S&P 500. Index-tracking funds had been available to institutional investors since the 1970s. Companies such as Vanguard offered them to individuals in the form of mutual funds. However, as the name suggests, the key feature of an ETF was that it was itself listed on a stock market, so that investors could buy and sell it easily. . . . When the public took to plain-vanilla ETFs, the financial services industry decided it should also offer egg-custard and blue-banana flavours. Investors (around the world) can choose between 2,747 funds covering everything from Asian property to water companies.

"The new types of ETF . . . have become a means for hedge funds to speculate on the market throughout the trading day, allowing them to make complex bets on illiquid asset

(Continued)

classes. And the portfolios of some ETFs consist not of a broad range of stocks but of a derivative position with an investment bank as a counterparty. In theory, this gives investors all the tools they need to design the portfolio which closely matches their risk preferences and economic outlook."

Not What It Says on the Tin

"One risk relates to liquidity. In some sectors, like emerging markets, it is easier for investors to buy and sell an ETF than to trade in the underlying illiquid assets. But the liquidity risk has not gone away. During the market turmoil known as the "flash crash" in May 2010, the Dow Jones Industrial Average briefly dropped 1,000 points as liquidity evaporated: 60–70 percent of the trades that subsequently had to be canceled were in ETFs.

"Another risk concerns a change in the nature of ETFs— the development of "synthetic ETFs" and related products such as exchange-traded notes (ETNs). These funds do not own assets like shares or bonds; instead they arrange a derivative deal with an investment bank, which guarantees to deliver the return of the targeted benchmark, exposing the ETF investor to the risk that the bank fails to pay up. . . .

"It would be a shame if reckless expansion spoiled a good innovation. Even some in the industry are nervous about the profusion of new vehicles. A failure might diminish the appeal of ETFs as a whole. . . . That would be a shame. Fund managers' fees have always eaten into investors returns; ETFs were a splendid way of letting investors keep more of their money. But like a hyperactive child, the finance sector can never leave a good thing be."

The Future of Index Funds

There can be no question that both the TIF and the ETF are here to stay. For the time being at least, both TIFs and ETFs continue to grow, not only in the absolute, but relative to the assets of actively managed equity funds. It seems increasingly apparent, however, that the paradigm of long-term investing represented by the TIF and the paradigm of short-term speculation so often represented by the ETF are, in general, competing only at the margin for the capital of the same investors.

The clash of the cultures in the index fund arena, then, is a clash between two very different philosophies. The first philosophy is *buy and hold* a widely diversified portfolio of stocks and bonds. The second is *buy such a portfolio and sell at will,* and do the same with narrow portfolios of, well, anything, including heavily levered portfolios through which bets are magnified. Seldom has the choice between investment and speculation been so starkly drawn.

To be fair, we must make a distinction between the use of ETFs by individual investors and financial institutions. It is increasingly clear that institutions—hedging equity portfolios, equitizing cash positions when not fully invested in stocks, and sheer short-term speculation on momentary fluctuations in the stock market—account for a dominant share of ETF trading activity. While there is little solid data available on this point, there is surely a significant group of individual investors who use ETFs in a productive fashion—buying broadly-diversified funds and holding them, and enjoying the relatively lower expense ratios that largely passive ETFs generally provide when compared to actively-managed funds.

A survey by Morningstar shows that most individual investors use ETFs for trading purposes, albeit at only a fraction of the huge aggregate turnover rates of institutional trading. Some 54 percent of the individual investors polled say they tend to trade their ETF portfolio only once every few months to a year. Only 11 percent plan to trade once a month, and only 3 percent say they would trade intraday. Of course, surveys are only surveys, and conclusions drawn from investor surveys are not necessarily a sound guide to their actual actions in the past or in the future. Over time, of course, the data will give us the facts.

As I have earlier demonstrated, the higher the trading activity, the greater the lag behind the market target is likely to be. If such foolishness cannot be regulated away—and I don't see how that would be possible, no matter how desirable—investors will have to learn from their own hard-won and costly experience the eternal message: In the long run, investors win and speculators lose. To be sure, such speculation is hardly limited to ETFs. In very different degrees and in very different ways, speculation plays a major role in the operation of our nation's retirement plan system, creating challenges and risks that we must work to resolve in the interests of our citizen/investors. I'll discuss that subject in depth in Chapter 7.

Chapter 7

America's Retirement System

Too Much Speculation, Too Little Investment

It is within our reach to move capitalism in a direction that is more wealth creating, more sustainable, less crisis-prone, and more legitimate than the "headwinds" capitalism we have today . . . to "pension fund capitalism." . . . It requires the redesign of pension fund organizations so that they themselves become more effective and hence more productive stewards of the retirement savings of young workers and pensioners alike.

—Keith Ambachtsheer

An Introductory Note

We don't usually think of the retirement systems of our nation as, well, speculative. But, in fact, our defined benefit (DB) pension plans entail two distinct kinds of speculation. First, our pension managers are hardly free of the same counterproductive biases and emotions as their

213

individual investor counterparts. Second, the defined benefit payments promised by pension plans to our retired citizens are, in effect, based on speculation as to whether today's highly optimistic projected investment returns will actually be earned. If not, the providers of these plans will prove to have made too little investment, and corporations will face huge shortfalls in funding.

Corporate sponsors of private pensions would have to raise their annual contributions to fund the plans—no mean task for corporations now aggressively seeking to slash costs in order to increase the earnings they report to their shareholders. For our state and local governments—now struggling to hold down costs—future budgets calling for higher annual plan contributions would not be popular with taxpayers. Even the necessary changes to Social Security are a matter of speculation. Can we rely on a Congress that is at an impasse—conflicted by partisan wrangling and gridlock—to ensure that future payments will continue to be made at present levels to retirees from this backstop of our national retirement system?

In our defined contribution (DC) plans, too many individual plan participants have behaved much like speculators. To name the major faults of these retirement plan investors: excessive turnover of their fund investments; betting on the selection of funds that are expected to outperform their peers in the future; gambling that fund managers can, despite their excessive costs, outpace the market; and failing to adequately diversify by making ill-considered asset allocation choices. It turns out that individual investors make the same mistakes in their retirement savings plans as they do in their personal investment portfolios. (How could one expect an individual investor to have two different mindsets?) Together, those particular chinks in the armor of sound long-term investment combine to result in the biggest speculation of all: the odds that participants will earn returns on their savings plans that will be adequate to ensure their comfortable retirement.

This chapter discusses the "Seven Deadly Sins" of the retirement system, and five of its obvious flaws. Where there are sins and flaws, I note, there are opportunities to fix them, including my proposal to create a Federal Retirement Board to oversee the diffuse and complex elements of our multiple variety of defined contributions plans—IRAs, 401(k) thrift savings plans, and 403(b) plans offered by nonprofit organizations—and focus on serving the needs of our nation's citizen/ investors.

I conclude the chapter with some provocative ideas on "The New Pension Plan," suggesting a redesign of today's system in the interests of the investors who are saving for their retirements. I present recommendations and simplifications, including reducing Wall Street's over-sized role in today's system, and focusing not only on investment risk, but longevity risk as well. These reforms should serve to increase in the long-term wealth accumulations by DB plans, by DC plans, and by IRA investors. In all, these reforms would move us away from today's culture in which speculation is rife, and far closer to a culture of long-term investing.

Today our nation's system of retirement security is imperiled, headed for a serious train wreck. That wreck is not merely waiting to happen; we are running on a dangerous track that is leading directly to a serious crash that will disable major parts of our retirement system. Federal support—which, in today's world, is already being tapped at unprecedented levels—seems to be the only short-term remedy. But long-term reforms in our retirement funding system, if only we have the wisdom and courage to implement them, can move us to a better path toward retirement security for our nation's families.

The Inadequacy of Our National Savings

Underlying the specific issues affecting our retirement plan system is that our national savings are inadequate. We are directing far too little of those savings into our retirement plans in order to reach the necessary goal of self-sufficiency. "Thrift" has been *out* in America; "instant gratification" in our consumer-driven economy has been *in*. As a nation, we are not saving nearly enough to meet our future retirement needs. Too few citizens have chosen to establish personal retirement accounts such as IRAs and 403(b)s, and even those who have established them are funding them inadequately and only sporadically. These investors and potential investors are, I suppose, speculating that their retirement will be fully funded by some combination of Social Security, their pensions, their unrealistically high expectations for future investment returns, or (as a last resort) from their families.

Broadly stated, we Americans suffer from a glut of spending and a (relative) paucity of saving, especially remarkable because the combination is so counterintuitive. Here we are, at the peak of the wealth of the world's nations, with savings representing only about 3 percent of our national income. Among the emerging nations of the world—with per capita incomes less than $5,000 compared to our $48,000—the saving rate runs around 10 percent, and in the developed nations such as those in Europe, the savings rate averages 9 percent, with several major nations between 11 and 13 percent. Our beleaguered pension system is but one reflection of that shortfall.

Box 7.1

Rebalancing the Financial Priorities of Our Citizens

The failure of American citizens to adequately fund their retirement plans is but one manifestation of our national preference for spending over saving. "I'll enjoy the consumer goods I can buy today (and even borrow from the future so I can enjoy them now) and worry about far off needs later on." As Scarlett O'Hara famously said, "I'll worry about it tomorrow." As if tomorrow will never come.

Paradoxically, our economy depends on consumer spending. Some 70 percent of our gross domestic product (GDP) is accounted for by spending. Not only on the daily necessities—food, shelter, medical care—but on luxury goods that represent "conspicuous consumption." I don't argue with that as such, but by shortchanging our needs for retirement, our lives will not be as we might expect when the time comes. We must save more (and borrow less), for in the long run, a healthy U.S. economy depends on the financial stability of our households. Yet our household savings rates, while they have risen during the recent recession, are far below historic norms.

As the following exhibit shows, from the 1960s through the 1980s, household savings ranged around 9 percent of income.

Then the rate began a gradual decline all the way down to the 2 percent range—a 75 percent decline—during 2000–2007, recovering to about 6 percent thereafter. But the most recent report shows a U.S. savings rate at just 3 percent.

U.S. Household Savings Rates (1960-2012)

Paradoxically, although we are one of the world's wealthiest nations (average household income of $48,000), we save relatively less than the citizens of most others. Household wealth in Germany is similar to ours ($44,000), but their savings rate is 11 percent. (Other major European nations average about 9 percent.) And even in the world's emerging economies, where annual household incomes run from $1,500 (India) to $5,200 (China), savings rates can easily run far higher than ours.

What's to be done? Better investor education; more efficient regulation; substantial protection against financial fraud for our citizens (the new Consumer Financial Protection Bureau, for example); greater tax incentives for our less wealthy brethren to save; and more rigorous credit standards for borrowers. More profoundly, we must move over time toward an economy less dependent on short-term spending and more dependent on long-term saving.

"The Seven Deadly Sins"

Let's now move from the general to the particular, and examine some of the major forces in today's retirement systems that have been responsible for the dangerous situation we now face.

Deadly Sin 1: Inadequate Retirement Accumulation

The modest median balances so far accumulated in 401(k) plans make their promise a mere shadow of reality. At the end of 2009, the median 401(k) balance is estimated at just $18,000 per participant. Indeed, even projecting this balance for a middle-aged employee with future growth engendered over the passage of time by assumed higher salaries and real investment returns, that figure might rise to some $300,000 at retirement age (if these assumptions prove correct). While that hypothetical accumulation may look substantial, however, it would be adequate to replace less than 30 percent of preretirement income, a help but hardly a panacea. (The target suggested by most analysts is around 70 percent, including Social Security.)

Part of the reason for today's modest accumulations are the inadequate participant and corporate contributions made to the plans. Typically, the combined contribution comes to less than 10 percent of compensation, while most experts consider 15 percent of compensation as the appropriate target. Over a working lifetime of, say, 40 years, an average employee, contributing 15 percent of salary, receiving periodic raises, and earning a real market return of 5 percent per year, would accumulate $630,000. An employee contributing 10 percent would accumulate just $420,000. If those assumptions are realized, this would represent a handsome accumulation, but substantial obstacles—especially the flexibility given to participants to withdraw capital, as described below—are likely to preclude their achievement. (In both cases, with the assumption that every single contribution is made on schedule—likely a rare eventuality.)

Deadly Sin 2: The Stock Market Collapse

One of the causes of the train wreck we face—but hardly the only cause—was the collapse of our stock market, on balance taking its value from $17 trillion capitalization at the October 2007 high in U.S. stocks, to a low of $9 trillion in February 2009. Much of this stunning loss of wealth has been recovered in the rally that followed, and as 2012 begins, the market value totals $15 trillion. Nonetheless, our nation's DB pension plans—private and government alike—are presently facing staggering deficits. And the participants in our DC plans—thrift plans and IRAs alike—have accumulations that fall short of what they will need when they retire.

Deadly Sin 3: Underfunded Pensions

Our corporations have been funding their defined benefit (DB) pension plans on the mistaken assumption that stocks would produce future returns at the generous levels of the past, raising their prospective return assumptions even as the stock market reached valuations that were far above historical norms. And the DB pension plans of our state and local governments seem to be in the worst financial condition of all. (Because of poor transparency, inadequate disclosure, and nonstandardized financial reporting, we really don't know the dimensions of the short-fall.) The vast majority of these plans are speculating that future returns will bail them out.

Currently, most of these DB plans are assuming future annual returns in the 7.5—8 percent range. But with stock yields at 2 percent and, with the U.S. Treasury 30-year bond yielding 3 percent, such returns are a pipedream. It is ironic that in 1981, when the yield on the long-term Treasury bond was 13.5 percent, corporations assumed that future returns on their pension plans would average just 6 percent, a similarly unrealistic—if directly opposite—projection as 2012 begins.

Corporations generate earnings for the owners of their stocks, pay dividends, and reinvest what's left in the business. In the aggregate, the sole sources of the long-term returns generated by the equities of our businesses should provide investment returns at an annual rate of about 7—8 percent per year over the next decade, including about 2 percent from today's dividend yield and 5—6 percent from earnings growth. Similarly, bonds pay interest, which is the sole source of their long-term returns. Based on today's yield, the aggregate return on a portfolio of corporate and government bonds should average about 3.5 percent.

A portfolio roughly balanced between these two asset classes might earn a return in the range of 5—6 percent during the coming decade.

Deadly Sin 4: Speculative Investment Options

A plethora of unsound, unwise, and often speculative investment choices are available in our burgeoning defined-contribution (DC) plans. Here, individuals are largely responsible for managing their own tax-sheltered retirement investment programs—individual retirement accounts (IRAs) and defined-contribution pension plans such as 401(k) thrift plans that are provided by corporations, and 403(b) savings plans provided by nonprofit institutions. Qualified independent officials of their employers seem to provide little guidance. What's more, they often focus on spurious methodology that is too heavily based on *historical* data, rather than the timeless *sources of returns* that actually shape the long-term investment productivity of stocks and bonds, misleading themselves, their firms, and their fellow employees about the hard realities of investing.

Deadly Sin 5: Wealth-Destroying Costs

The returns in our stock market—whatever they may turn out to be—represent the *gross* returns generated by the publicly owned corporations that dominate our system of competitive capitalism (and by investment in debt obligations). Investors who hold these financial instruments—either directly or through the collective investment programs provided by mutual funds and defined benefit pension plans—receive their returns only *after* the cost of acquiring them and then trading them back and forth among one another. Don't forget that our financial system is a greedy one, consuming from 1 to 2 percentage points of return, far too large a share of the returns created by our business and economic system. So we must recognize that individual investors and pension funds alike will receive only the net returns, perhaps in the 4—5 percent range, after the deduction of those costs. To significantly enhance that return, as shown in Box 7.2, less conventional portfolios using "alternative" investments will have to deliver returns that far exceed their own historical norms. To say the least, that is one more speculative bet.

Box 7.2
The Elusive 8 Percent

With reasonable expectations for a nominal return of roughly
7 percent on stocks over the coming decade, and, with somewhat more assurance, a return of roughly 3 percent on bonds, a
traditional 65/35 stock/bond policy portfolio of a defined
benefit (DB) pension plan might reasonably expect to earn a
5.5 percent annual return. Given the cost efficiencies in managing and administering portfolios with substantial assets,
I assume a cost of 1 percent, bringing the return to 4.5 percent.
Let's be generous and call it 5 percent.[1]

So is that the return that our corporate DB plans are pro-
jecting? No, it is not. The typical return projection is 8 percent,
with a few plans—corporate and local government alike— as
high as 9 percent and a few as low as 7 percent, or even slightly
less. (Berkshire Hathaway is using a 6.9 percent assumption.)
Where do these estimates come from? Well, here is what one
large corporation tells us: "We consider current and expected
asset allocations, as well as *historical* and expected returns on
various categories of plan assets . . . evaluating general market
trends as well as key elements of asset class returns such as
expected earnings growth, yields and spreads. Based on our
analysis of future expectations of asset performance, *past return
results*, and our current and expected asset allocations, we have
assumed an 8.0 percent long-term expected return on those
assets" (italics added, General Electric Annual Report, 2010).
Such disclosure has become sort of annual-report boilerplate.

All well and good, but, as they say, let's add some "granu-
larity" (a word I don't much care for), making some assumptions

(Continued)

---

[1]While the returns that I describe are measured in *nominal* terms (current dollars),
even an inflation rate of only 2 percent would result in a *real* return of just
3 percent.

that are arbitrary but not unrealistic. The table below shows one version of how various markets and asset-class managers must perform in order for a pension plan to reach that elusive goal.

A Template for DB Returns During the Coming Decade

				(2 + 3)		(4 − 5)
	1.	2.	3.	4.	5.	6.
			Value			
		Projected	Added	Adjusted	Less	
		Annual	by	Annual	Investment	Net
Class	Allocation	Return	Managers	Return	Costs	Return
Traditional Policy Portfolio						
Equities	40%	7.0%	+2.5%	9.5%	−1.0%	8.5%
Bonds	30	3.0	+0.5	4.0	−0.5	3.5
Alternative Investments						
Venture Capital	10	12.0	+3.0	15.0	−3.0	12.0
Hedge Funds	20	12.0	+3.0	15.0	−3.0	12.0
Total	**100%**	**7.3%**	**2.2%**	**9.5%**	**−1.5%**	**8.0%**

In effect, I present in the chart the very analysis that at least some corporations use—yet without their disclosure of the specific numbers they use. Here's the Exxon Mobil explanation for the process that underlies the corporation's expected return assumption of 7.5 percent for its pension plan: "a forward-looking, long-term return assumption for each asset class, taking into account factors such as the expected return for each." (Note that the firm totally ignores the costs of investing.)

Now let's consider how realistic the data in the table might be. First, the stock and bond returns are fully consistent with the reasonable expectations cited earlier. The returns for venture capital are generous but perhaps not unreasonable. But the required returns for hedge funds are far above historical norms. As to the value added by managers, my long experience tells me that it is extremely unlikely that any manager can possibly deliver the 3 percentage points of excess return that are required. Good luck in picking one in advance. What's more, for DB plan managers as a group—competing with one another—zero Alpha is the expected outcome. (In fact, with the typical costs that I've assumed, pension managers will, in the aggregate, produce *negative* Alpha.) Even if our asset class returns for equities and bonds are realized, venture capital and hedge funds would have to earn returns that are far above historical norms. If those asset classes fail to do so, the actual realized return for this example would fall by 2 percentage points, to 6 percent per year.

Mark your calendars for 2022, 10 years hence, and see who's made the best estimate. For me, subjectively, even 6 percent is an ambitious goal. (The 10-year U.S. Treasury bond is presently yielding less than 2 percent, the 30-year Treasury about 3 percent.) And even if that 6 percent return is in fact achieved, the financial implications of the cumulative deficit from the 8 percent assumption will be staggering, particularly when today's cumulative deficit in corporate pensions is almost $500 billion. By then, I hope, our corporations will be required to report the *actual* 10-year returns of their DB plans, a disclosure that, absurdly, has never been mandated.

Deadly Sin 6: Speculation in the Financial System

Speculation is rife throughout our financial system (and our world). As Chapter 1 discusses, high stock market volatility; risky, often leveraged, derivatives; and extraordinary turnover volumes have exposed the markets to mind-boggling volatility. As I note earlier, some of this hyperactivity is necessary to provide the liquidity that has been the hallmark of the U.S. financial markets. But trading activity has grown into an orgy of speculation that pits one manager against another—one investor (or speculator) against another—a "paper economy" that has, predictably, come to threaten the real economy where our citizens save and invest. It must be obvious that our present economic crisis was, by and large, foisted on Main Street by Wall Street—the mostly innocent public taken to the cleaners, as it were, by the mostly greedy financiers.

Deadly Sin 7: Conflicts of Interest

Conflicts of interest are rife throughout our financial system: Both the managers of mutual funds that are held in corporate 401(k) plans and the money managers of corporate pension plans face potential conflicts when they hold the shares of the corporations that are their clients. It is hardly beyond imagination that when a money manager votes proxy shares against a company management's recommendation, it might not sit well with company executives who select the plan's provider of investment advice. (There is a debate about the extent to which those conflicts have actually materialized.)

But there's little debate in the mind of Lynn Turner, former chief accountant of the SEC: "Asset managers who are charging corporations a fee to manage their money have a conflict in that they are also trying to attract more money which will increase their revenues, and that money often comes from companies who set up retirement accounts for their employees. There is not disclosure, from the asset manager to the actual investors whose capital is at risk, of the amount of fees they collect from the companies whose management they are voting on. It appears the institutional investors (including managers of mutual funds) may vote their shares at times in their best interests rather than the best interests of those whose money they are managing."

In trade union plans, the conflicts of interest are different, but hardly absent. Insider dealing among union leaders, investment advisers, and money managers has been documented in the press and in the courts. In corporate defined benefit pension plans, corporate senior officers face an obvious short-term conflict between minimizing pension contributions in order to maximize the earnings growth that market participants demand, versus incurring larger pension costs by making timely and adequate contributions to their companies' pension plans in order to assure long-term security for the pension benefits they have promised to their workers. These same forces are at work in pension plans of state and local governments, where the reluctance (or inability) to balance budgets leads to financial engineering—rarely disclosed—in order to justify future benefits.

Extracting Value from Society

Together, these Seven Deadly Sins echo what I've written at length about our absurd and counterproductive financial sector. Here are some excerpts regarding the costs of our financial system that were published in the Winter 2008 issue of *Journal of Portfolio Management*: ". . . mutual fund expenses, plus all those fees paid to hedge fund and pension fund managers, to trust companies and to insurance companies, plus their trading costs and investment banking fees . . . have soared to all-time highs in 2011. These costs are estimated to total more than $600 billion. Such enormous costs seriously undermine the odds in favor of success for citizens who are accumulating savings for retirement. Alas, *the investor feeds at the bottom of the costly food chain of investing*, paid only *after* all the agency costs of investing are deducted from the markets' returns. . . . Once a profession in which business was subservient, the field of money management has largely become a business in which the profession is subservient. Harvard Business School Professor Rakesh Khurana is right when he defines the standard of conduct for a true professional with these words: '"*I will create value for society, rather than extract it.*' And yet money management, by definition, extracts value from the returns earned by our business enterprises."

These views are not only mine, and they have applied for a long time. Hear Nobel laureate economist James Tobin, presciently writing in 1984: ". . . we are throwing more and more of our resources into financial activities remote from the production of goods and services, into activities that generate high private rewards disproportionate to their social productivity, a 'paper economy' facilitating speculation which is short-sighted and inefficient." (In validating his criticism, Tobin cited the eminent British economist John Maynard Keynes. But he failed to cite Keynes's profound warning, cited earlier, that business enterprise has taken a back seat to financial speculation.) The multiple failings of our flawed financial sector are jeopardizing not only the retirement security of our nation's savers but also the economy in which our entire society participates.

Our Retirement System Today

The present crisis in worker retirement security is well within our capacity to measure. The picture it paints is not a pretty one:

Social Security. While it is the massive backstay of our nation's retirement system, its future is speculative. Today, we can only guess whether Congress will continue to support its deficits. Or will the grit and resolve to make the simple changes required to assure its long-term solvency prevail?[2] All it would take is some combination of a gradual increase in the maximum income level for wage earners paying into the plan; a change from the wage-increase-based formula for increasing benefits to an inflation-based formula; a gradual increase in the retirement age to, say, 69; and a modest means test, limiting retirement payouts to those citizens with considerable wealth. (If Congress wishes to appoint me as the czar to implement these reforms, I'd be glad to accept the challenge.)

Defined Benefit Plans. Until the early 1990s, investment risk and the longevity risk of pensioners (the risk of outliving one's resources) were borne by the defined benefit (DB) plans of our corporations and our state and local governments, the pervasive approach to retirement savings outside of that huge national DB plan we call Social Security. But in the face of a major shift away from DB plans in favor of DC plans, DB growth has essentially halted. Largely because of the stock market's sharp decline, assets of corporate pension plans have declined from $2.1 trillion as far back as 1999 to an estimated $1.9 trillion as 2012 began. As noted at the outset, these plans are now severely underfunded. For the companies in the Standard & Poor's 1500 Index, pension plan

---

[2]If Congress does nothing, however, Social Security will continue. But according to a recent report, payments to retirees would fall to about 75 percent of today's levels by 2033.

assets to cover future payments to retirees face a deficit of almost $500 billion as 2012 begins. The deficits in state and local pension plans have been estimated at over $4 *trillion*, even as promises for higher future benefits continue to rise.

This deficit is reflected in the sharp drop in funding ratios of the pension plans (plan assets as a percentage of plan liabilities). The funding ratios for the giant corporations in the S&P 500 have fallen from 105 percent in 2007 to 80 percent in 2011; the ratio for public plans from 95 percent to 75 percent. What's more, the corporate plans show little sign of improvement; their average investment return of 4.4 percent in 2011 was barely one-half of their typical 8 percent return assumption. With bond yields in early 2012 remaining near their historic lows, only highly aggressive returns earned by the plans' equities and alternative investments will bail out these pension plans, a most speculative assumption, as shown in Box 7.2. If that desideratum does not happen, our companies will incur far larger pension expenses.

The Pension Benefit Guaranty Corporation. This federal agency, responsible for guaranteeing the pension benefits of failing corporate sponsors is itself faltering, with a $14 billion deficit in mid-2011. Early in 2008—just before the stock market's collapse—the agency made the odd decision to raise its allocation to diversified equity investments to 45 percent of its assets, and add another 10 percent to "alternative investments," including real estate and private equity. The decision to double the PBGC's equity participation came at what turned out to be the worst possible moment. (We don't yet know how that change worked out.) The fact is that the PBGC will ultimately require more funding if it is to meet its obligations. We don't know whether or how the issue will be resolved; we can only speculate.

Defined Contribution Plans. DC plans are gradually replacing DB plans, a massive transfer of *investment risk and return* as well as the *longevity risk* of retirement funding from business enterprises to their employees. While DC plans have been available to provide the benefits of tax-deferral for retirement savings for well over a half-century,[3] it has only been with the rise of employer thrift plans such as 401(k)s and 403(b)s, beginning in 1978, that they have been widely used to accumulate retirement savings. The growth in DC plans has been remarkable. Assets totaled $500 billion in 1985; $1 trillion in 1990; $3 trillion in 2000; $4.5 trillion in 2010. The 401(k) and 403(b) plans dominate this total, with respective shares of 67 percent and 21 percent, or 88 percent of the DC total.

Individual Retirement Accounts. IRA assets presently total about $4.7 trillion, about the same as the $4.8 trillion total in 2007, before the stock market crash. Mutual funds (now some $2 trillion) continue to represent the largest single portion of these investments. Yet with some 49 million households participating in IRAs, the average balance is but $55,000, which at, say, a 5 percent average return, would provide but $2,750 per year in retirement income for a household, a nice but far-from-adequate increment in a case where the wage-earner retired today. Younger workers with such a balance would of course see it grow remarkably over time. For example, such a balance assuming a 6 percent future return on the account, would grow to $565,000 over the next 40 years.

Focusing on 401(k) Retirement Plans

Defined contribution pension plans, as noted earlier, have gradually come to dominate the private retirement savings market, and that domination seems certain to increase. Further, there is some evidence that DC plans are poised to become a growing factor in the public plan market. The federal employees' Thrift Savings Plan is the largest single factor. With assets of about $250 billion, it has operated as a defined

---

[3]I have been investing 15 percent of my annual compensation in the DC plan of the company (and its predecessor) that has employed me ever since July 1951, when I first entered the work force. I can therefore give my personal experience that tax-deferred defined-contribution pension plans, added to regularly; reasonably allocated among stocks and bonds; highly diversified, managed at low cost; and compounded over a long period, are capable of providing wealth accumulations that, after my 61 years of participation, seem little short of miraculous.

contribution plan since its inception in 1986. As 401(k) plans have come to dominate the DC market, mutual fund shares have come to dominate the 401(k) market. Assets of mutual funds in DC plans have grown from a mere $35 billion in 1990 (9 percent of the total) to an estimated $2.3 trillion in 2012 (53 percent).

Given the plight in which our defined benefit plans have found themselves, and the large (and, to some degree, unpredictable) bite that future funding costs will take out of corporate earnings, it is small wonder that what began as a gradual shift became a massive movement to defined contribution plans. Think of General Motors, for example, as a huge pension plan, now with perhaps $94 billion of assets—and likely even larger liabilities—surrounded by a far smaller automobile business, operated by a company with a current stock market capitalization of just $38 billion.

I would argue that the shift from DB plans to DC plans is not only an inevitable move, but a move in the right direction in providing worker retirement security. In this era of global competition, U.S. corporations must compete with non–U.S. corporations with far lower labor costs. So this massive transfer of the two great risks of retirement plan savings—investment risk and longevity risk—from corporate balance sheets to individual households will relieve pressure on corporate earnings, even as it will require our families to take responsibility for their own retirement savings. A further benefit is that investments in properly designed DC plans can be tailored to the specific *individual* requirements of each family—reflecting its prospective wealth, its risk tolerance, the age of its bread-winner(s), and its other assets (including Social Security). DB plans, on the other hand, are inevitably focused on the *average* demographics and average salaries of the firm's work force in the aggregate.

The 401(k) plan, then, is an idea whose time has come. *That's the good news.* We're moving our retirement savings system to a new paradigm, one that ultimately will efficiently serve both our nation's employers—corporations and governments alike—and our nation's families. *Now for the bad news:* Our existing DC system is failing investors. Despite its worthy objectives, the deeply flawed implementation of DC plans has subtracted—and subtracted substantially—from the inherent value of this new system. Given the responsibility to look after their own investments, participants have acted contrary to their own best interests. Let's think about what has gone wrong.

A Deeply Flawed System

Since it has become the dominant force in pension funding, I now turn to the defined contribution plan. The major flaws that continue to exist in our 401(k) system (and, to some extent, in our IRA system) require radical reform. For our task is to give employees the fair shake that must be the goal if we are to serve the national public interest and the interest of investors. In addition to the shortfall in national savings illustrated in Box 7.1, the major problems in our retirement plan system that cry out for reform lie in the following five areas.

Too Much Flexibility.   401(k) plans, designed to fund retirement income, are too often used for purposes that subtract directly from that goal. One such subtraction arises from the ability of employees to borrow from their plans, and fully 20 percent of participants do exactly that. Even when—and if—these loans are repaid, investment returns (assuming that they are positive over time) would be reduced during the time that the loans are outstanding, a dead-weight loss in the substantial savings that might otherwise have been accumulated at retirement.

Even worse is the dead-weight loss—in this case, largely permanent—engendered when participants "cash out" their 401(k) plans when they change jobs or when their family circumstances change. The evidence suggests that fully 60 percent of all participants in DC plans who move from one job to another cash out at least a portion of their plan assets, using that money for purposes other than retirement savings. To understand the baneful effect of borrowings and cash-outs, just imagine in how much worse shape our beleaguered Social Security System would find itself if the contributions of workers and their companies were reduced by borrowings and cash-outs, flowing into current consumption rather than into future postretirement pay. It is not a pretty picture to contemplate.

Another kind of excess flexibility, clearly demonstrated during the recent recession, is the freedom given to corporations to modify, suspend, or even abandon their employee retirement plans. Counter-productively, this means that the benefits of "dollar cost averaging" are often suspended during tough times, just when stock prices tend to be most attractive for long-term investors. The IRA situation, sadly, is even more flexible, for sticking to a regular payment schedule is totally at the option of the IRA owner, and withdrawals can be made easily, albeit subject to significant penalties.

Inappropriate Asset Allocation and Faulty Investment Selection. One reason that 401(k) investors have accumulated such disappointing balances is due to unfortunate decisions in the allocation of assets between stocks and bonds.[4] While virtually all investment experts rec-ommend a large allocation to stocks for young investors and an increasing bond allocation as participants draw closer to retirement, a large segment of 401(k) participants fails to heed that advice.

Nearly 20 percent of 401(k) investors in their 20s own zero equities in their retirement plan, holding, instead, outsized allocations of money market and stable value funds, options that are unlikely to keep pace with inflation as the years go by. On the other end of the spectrum, more than 30 percent of 401(k) investors in their 60s have more than 80 percent of their assets in equity funds. Such an aggressive allocation likely resulted in a decline of 30 percent or more in their 401(k) balances during the present bear market, imperiling their retirement funds precisely when the members of this age group are preparing to draw upon it.

Company stock is another source of unwise asset allocation deci-sions, as many investors fail to observe the time-honored principle of diversification. In plans in which company stock is an investment option, the average participant invests more than 20 percent of his or her account balance in company stock, an unacceptable concentration of

---

[4]These data are derived from a Research Perspective dated December 2008, published by the Investment Company Institute, the association that represents mutual fund management companies, collecting data, providing research, and engaging in lobbying activities.

risk. Those who are far too conservative, those who are far too "aggressive," and those who bet the ranch (or a large part of it) on tying their careers to their retirement plan are all speculating about what the future holds, rather than true investing, diversifying those risks (but not market risk itself) away.

ERISA restricts a pension plan's allocation in company stock to 10 percent of assets (still far too high a concentration for any individual equity). No similar restriction exists for 401(k) plans, although a recent Department of Labor regulation requires corporations to allow employees to diversify out of company stock after a certain period of time. Concerns about the concentration of assets in company stock, which can be exacerbated by employer matches issued in the form of company stock, led FINRA to issue an alert warning investors against this behavior. According to a 2009 study conducted by the Employee Benefit Research Institute, over one-half of employees having the option to invest in company stock do so. This concentration in a single asset puts employees in a precarious position where both their job and their life savings can be wiped out by shocks to a single company—a sort of "double jeopardy" that is extremely unwise.

Yet another form of speculation is placing one's retirement plan bets on which managers will provide the highest returns in the future. Years ago, the betting was focused on individual stocks (company stock is a good example). But today it is largely speculation on future mutual fund performance where the past, alas, is rarely prologue to the future. Participants in DC plans are presently betting on an astonishing total of 562 different mutual funds, the vast majority of which are actively managed, often assuming extra market risk (see Box 7.3).

It is only in recent years that broadly diversified, passively managed index funds have come into their own. But despite their obvious suitability in DC plans, index funds represent but 25 percent of DC assets, albeit up from a 15 percent share 15 years ago. The increasingly popular "target date funds" (making portfolios gradually more conservative as the retirement date nears) are also beginning to make inroads. Despite their obvious sense, suitability, and low cost, target-date *index* funds have yet to dominate the field. (Most target date funds are actively managed.)

Excessive Costs. As noted earlier, excessive investment costs are the principal cause of the inadequate long-term returns earned by both stock mutual funds and bond mutual funds. The average equity fund carries an annual expense ratio of about 1.3 percent per year (somewhat lower when weighted by fund assets), consuming an incredible 65 percent of their current dividend yield of 2 percent, and leaving a puny yield of just 0.7 percent. But that is only part of the cost. Mutual funds also incur substantial transaction costs, reflecting the rapid turnover of their investment portfolios.

Last year, the average actively managed fund had a turnover rate of an astonishing 96 percent. Even if weighted by asset size, the turnover rate is still a shocking—if slightly *less* shocking—65 percent. Admittedly, the costs of this portfolio turnover cannot be measured with precision. But it is reasonable to assume that trading activity by funds adds costs of 0.5 percent to 1.0 percent to the dilution inflicted on returns by the expense ratio. So the all-in-costs of fund investing (*excluding* sales loads, which are generally waived for large retirement accounts) can run from, say, 1.5 percent to 2.3 percent per year. By contrast, low-cost market index funds—which I've discussed earlier—have expense ratios as low as 0.10 percent or less, with transaction costs that are close to zero.

In investing, costs truly matter, and they matter even more when related to real (after-inflation) returns. Let's assume again that future nominal investment return on a balanced retirement account were, say, 5.5 percent per year (3.5 percent nominal return for bonds, 7−8 percent for stocks). Adjusted for, say, 2.5 percent inflation, the real return would be just 3 percent. An annual cost of 2.0 percent would therefore consume fully 67 percent of that annual return, while a low-cost index fund with a cost of 0.1 percent would consume but 5 percent. Even worse, over an investment lifetime of, say, 50 years, these costs of active management would consume a staggering share of the potential wealth accumulation. It is an ugly picture.

Given the centrality of low costs to the accumulation of adequate purchasing power in retirement savings plans, it is high time that both the impact of inflation and the toll taken by costs are disclosed to participants. The disclosure must include the *all-in* costs of investing, not merely the expense ratios. However, I confess to being skeptical about a recent regulatory proposal that would apply cost-accounting processes to the

Box 7.3

Speculation: Betting on Mutual Funds by Retirement Plan Participants

When 401(k) thrift plans began to develop some 30 years ago, the list of choices was usually limited to those funds under a given sponsor's management, but what gradually developed was a sort of "open architecture" plan, in which—while a single sponsor was responsible for the record keeping of participant accounts—a whole range of other funds could be selected. It is now typical for mutual fund managers to offer a wide selection of their funds to retirement plan participants. If "the more the choices, the better the outcome" were the rule, that expansion in options would be called progress. But the history of fund choice suggests that the reverse is true.

Let's look at the record, and examine the amounts held by 401(k) participants in individual mutual funds in 1997, then in 2012. The table below shows the 20 largest fund holdings, and the cumulative returns provided by each during the past 15 years and in 2012.

Domestic Equity Funds Most Used by DC Plans

	1997				2012		
			Return: 15 Years Ending March 2012				Return: 1 Year March 2012
	Fund	Assets (billions)	Annual	Cumulative	Fund	Assets (billions)	
1	Fidelity Magellan	$30.3	4.5%	94.0%	1 American Funds Growth	$67.6	3.5%
2	Vanguard 500 Index	14.8	6.0	140.3	2 Vanguard 500 Index	62.2	8.3
3	Fidelity Growth & Income	11.4	3.1	58.3	3 Fidelity Contrafund	44.7	9.4
4	Fidelity Contra	9.5	9.2	276.7	4 Fidelity Spartan 500 Index	23.7	8.4
5	Fidelity Equity Income	9.0	5.4	122.5	5 Fidelity Growth Co.	22.4	12.6

	1997				2012		
		Return: 15 Years Ending March 2012					**Return: 1 Year March 2012**
Fund	**Assets (billions)**	**Annual**	**Cumulative**		**Fund**	**Assets (billions)**	
6 Twentieth Century Ultra	8.2	5.6	127.0	6	Fidelity Low-Priced Stock	17.0	7.2
7 Vanguard Windsor	7.7	5.9	137.9	7	Vanguard PRIMECAP	13.4	2.9
8 Fidelity Growth Co.	5.6	9.2	276.8	8	Fidelity Magellan	10.6	−2.3
9 Fidelity Spartan 500 Index	5.0	5.9	139.1	9	American Funds Fundamental	9.6	2.6
10 Vanguard Windsor II	4.0	6.9	174.0	10	Vanguard Windsor II	9.5	8.3
11 Investment Co. of America	4.0	7.1	180.2	11	American Funds Washington	9.5	8.4
12 Fidelity Blue Chip Growth	3.9	5.9	137.4	12	Investment Co. of America	8.5	4.6
13 Putnam Voyager	3.7	5.7	130.8	13	T. Rowe Price Midcap Growth	8.4	2.8
14 Capital Research Washington	3.6	6.8	169.1	14	Columbia Acorn	7.6	4.2
15 Merrill Lynch Basic Value	2.9	6.5	159.3	15	Neuberger Genesis	7.3	2.3
16 Twentieth Century Growth	2.7	6.5	159.3	16	Fidelity Equity Income	6.5	−1.2
17 Vanguard U.S. Growth Portfolio	2.5	2.2	38.6	17	T. Rowe Price Equity Income	5.6	4.5
18 T. Rowe Price Equity Income	2.4	6.8	170.5	18	Fidelity Midcap Stock	5.2	3.3
19 Neuberger & Berman Guardian	2.4	4.7	100.3	19	Fidelity Blue Chip Growth	5.1	9.2
20 Janus	2.4	5.0	110.3	20	Goldman Sachs Midcap Value	5.1	−0.06

SOURCE: Pensions & Investments.

(*Continued*)

Some Lessons

- There's a continuing change in leadership during the period. By 2011 six funds had disappeared from the 1997 list (often because of faltering performance), replaced by six new entrants (often with recent past returns that were superior).
- Magellan Fund, the top-performing fund of the 1970s and 1980s, stumbled badly (next to last performer during the past 15 years), and its long-time #1 rank in popularity fell to #10 in 2012. (Holdings by participants fell from $30 billion to $10 billion.)
- Index Funds rose sharply in popularity. Vanguard 500 rose from #8 to #2, with 401(k) holdings soaring from $9 billion to $62 billion. Similarly, Fidelity's Spartan U.S. Equity Index Fund jumped from #10 ($5 billion) to #4 ($24 billion.)
- Little magic can be found in the actively managed equity selections offered by 401(k) leaders Fidelity, Vanguard, and American Funds. During the 15-year period, these three firms had both winners and losers. For Fidelity, Magellan and Growth and Income stumbled badly, but Contrafund and Growth Fund enjoyed positive returns that were almost symmetrical, but in reverse. For Vanguard, Windsor II shone, but U.S. Growth failed badly. Both of the American Funds—Investment Company of America and Washington Mutual—had superlative records.
- The 15-year records illustrate the folly of believing that the past is prologue. It wasn't. In 2012, the returns for the top 20 funds were random. Magellan's earlier shortfall relative to the S&P 500 sharply accelerated. PRIMECAP did extremely well, and Vanguard's Windsor II continued to win. At Fidelity, Contrafund lagged slightly and Equity Income tumbled. At American, Growth, now the most popular fund in 401(K) plans ($67 billion), performed poorly, as did Investment Company of America, but Washington Mutual experienced a one-year return that was first rate.

The inability of plan participants (and their advisers) to predict, in advance, patterns of performance seems obvious. If we look to, not merely the top 20 choices, but to *all* of the funds selected by participants, that message is magnified. Currently, participants have selected 562 individual funds, more what one would expect of stock-pickers rather than fund-pickers. The winning number, as it were, for 2012 was the 400th largest fund, Federated Strategic Value, with an 11.5 percent gain for the year; the losing number, Columbia Acorn, with a 16.5 percent loss—a spread of nearly 30 percentage points from best to worst. (The gap between the top and bottom deciles was of course smaller—+6 percent versus −10 percent, a 16-percentage-points spread. But that spread still made a huge difference.)

The 500 index funds of Vanguard and Fidelity were, inevitably, the surest bet; that is, the safest way to avoid both the extremes of underperformance and, necessarily, of overperformance. But by minimizing speculation on who will win and who will lose, that safe course guarantees—as it always has—that 401(k) participants who chose index funds will garner their fair share of whatever returns the stock market earns (or fails to earn).

allocation of fund expenses among investment costs, administrative costs, marketing costs, and record-keeping costs. What's important to plan participants is the amount of *total* costs incurred, not necessarily the allocation of those costs among the various functions as determined by accountants and fund managers who have vested interests in the outcome.

Failure to Deal with Longevity Risk.   Even as most DC plan participants have failed to deal adequately with inflation risk, investment risk, and selection risk, so they (and employers and fund sponsors) have also failed to deal adequately with longevity risk. It must be obvious that at some point in an investment lifetime, most plan participants would be well served by having at least some portion of their retirement savings provide income that they cannot outlive. But despite the fact that the 401(k) plan has now been around for three full decades, systematic approaches to annuitizing payments are rare and often too complex to implement. Further, nearly all annuities carry grossly excessive expenses, often because of high selling and marketing costs. Truly low-cost annuities remain conspicuous by their absence from DC retirement plan choices. (TIAA-CREF, operating at rock-bottom cost and providing ease and flexibility for clients using its annuity program, has done a good job in resolving both the complexity issue and the cost issue.)

Lack of Investor Education. While defined contribution plans give investors the ability to customize their retirement accounts to their specific circumstances, far too often investors have not been given the tools that they need to make financial decisions that are in their own best interests. The shift towards defined contribution retirement plans has essentially thrust the head of each participating household into the role of pension plan manager, a role for which they are not properly prepared and are often reluctant to assume. As a result, retirement savers make many of the mistakes already discussed—not saving enough, being either too conservative or too aggressive in their asset allocation, taking loans from a 401(k), cashing out early—simply because they've received inadequate preparation for these critical investment decisions. The fund industry has not helped, marketing their hottest funds and giving inadequate attention to the critical role played by asset allocation.

The New Pension Plan

Given the tenuous funding of DB plans, the widespread failures in the existing DC plan structure—including both 401(k) plans and IRAs—we ought to carefully consider and then implement changes that move us to a retirement plan system that is simpler, more rational, and less expensive. The new system must be one that will be increasingly and inevitably focused on DC plans, albeit those that can to some degree emulate the security of DB plans. (Our Social Security System and, at least for a while, our state and local government systems would continue to provide the DB backup as a "safety net" for all participating U.S. citizens.) It is time for reform—a reform that serves, not fund managers and our greedy financial system, but plan participants and their beneficiaries.

I am hardly alone in my critique of today's retirement system, nor in my struggle to build a better one. Consider the words that follow from the respected pension strategist Keith Ambachtsheer, Director of the Rotman International Centre for Pension Management at the University of Toronto. In his remarks, prepared for a *FairPensions* event at Westminster Hall, Houses of Parliament, London, on November 15, 2011, he provides excellent ideas about how to assure wealth across the generations. Some excerpts are presented in Box 7.4.

Box 7.4

Wealth across Generations: Can Pension Funds Shape the Future of Capitalism?

By Keith Ambachtsheer

It is within our reach to move capitalism in a direction that is more wealth-creating, more sustainable, less crisis-prone, and more legitimate than the "headwinds" capitalism we have today. Why specifically pension funds (including both defined contribution and defined benefit plans)? Because they are the only global investor class which has a fiduciary duty to invest across generations. In determining their investment strategies, pension funds are duty-bound to be even-handed between the financial needs of today's pensioners and those of young workers whose retirement years lie 30, 40, 50 years ahead of them.

However, this transformation to "pension fund capitalism" will not be easy for two reasons: (1) It requires the redesign of pension systems so these systems themselves become more sustainable and intergenerationally fair. (2) It requires the redesign of pension fund organizations so that they *themselves* become more effective and hence more productive

(Continued)

stewards of the retirement savings of young workers and pensioners alike.

The designs of traditional DC and DB plans are both problematical:

1. Traditional DC plans force contribution rate and investment decisions on participants that they cannot, and do not want to make. Also, little thought has been given to the design of the post-work asset decumulation phrase. As a result, DC plan investing has been unfocused, and post-work financial outcomes have been, and continue to be highly uncertain, raising fundamental questions about the effectiveness and sustainability of this individualistic pension model.

2. Traditional DB plans lump the young and the old on the same balance sheet, and unrealistically assume they have the same risk tolerance and that property rights between the two groups are clear. These unrealistic assumptions have had serious consequences. Over the course of the last decade, aggressive return assumptions and risk-taking—together with falling asset prices, falling interest rates, and deteriorating demographics—have punched gaping holes in many DB plan balance sheets, to which unfocused responses have ranged the full spectrum—from complete de-risking at one end to piling on more risk at the other . . .

Pension systems have two goals: (1) a pension affordability for workers (and their employers), and (2) certainty for pensioners. Therefore they must offer participants two instruments: a long-horizon (LH) return maximization instrument to support the affordability goal, and an asset-liability matching instrument to support the payment certainty goal. Logically, younger workers should favor return maximization, and pensioners should favor payment certainty. Over the course of their working lives, participants should transition steadily from the former goal to the latter.

Unfortunately, there continues to be considerable resistance to adopting this more transparent, robust "two goals/two instruments" pension model. Some continue to defend traditional DB models for emotional rather than rational reasons; others continue to defend the "caveat emptor" philosophy of traditional DC plans because they profit from it. But the "two goals two instruments" design feature is critically important to pension funds ability to reshape capitalism. Without the existence and legitimacy of highly focused, well-managed long-horizon return-maximization instruments, pension funds *cannot* play the wise intergenerational investor role that we have cast them in. . . .

I put to you that if we could achieve that vision, we would not just create more wealth for current and future pensioners. We would in the process transform today's "headwinds" capitalism into a more sustainable, wealth-creating version that is less prone to generate the financial bubbles and crises of the last decade, and more legitimate in the skeptical eyes of today's occupiers of Wall Street.

What's to Be Done?

Where there are multiple sins and flaws, as there are in today's retirement system, there are multiple opportunities for improvement. So as we work toward the ideal of "The New Pension Plan" just described—with pension funds helping to shape the future of capitalism—here are five specific recommendations toward that end.

Simplify the DC System

Offer a single DC plan for tax-deferred retirement savings available to all of our citizens (with a maximum annual contribution limit), consolidating today's complex amalgam of traditional DC plans, IRAs, Roth IRAs, 401(k) plans, 403(b) plans, and the federal Thrift Savings Plan. I envision the creation of an independent Federal Retirement Board to oversee both the employer sponsors and the plan providers, assuring that the interests of plan participants are given the highest priority. This new system would remain in the private sector (as today), with asset managers and record keepers competing in costs and in services. (Such a board might also create a public sector DC plan for wage earners who are unable to enter the private system or whose initial assets are too modest to be acceptable in that system.)

Get Real about Stock Market Return and Risk

Financial markets, it hardly need be said today, can be volatile and unpredictable. But common stocks remain a perfectly viable—and necessary—investment option for long-term retirement savings. Yet stock returns have been oversold by Wall Street's salesmen and by the mutual fund industry's giant marketing apparatus. In their own financial interests, they ignored the fact that the great bull market we enjoyed during the final 25 years of the twentieth century was in large part an illusion, creating what I call "phantom returns" that would not recur. Think about it: From 1926 to 1974, the average annual real (inflation-adjusted) return on stocks was 6.1 percent. But during the following quarter-century, stock returns soared, an explosion borne, not of the return provided by corporations in the form of dividend yields and earnings growth, but of soaring price-to-earnings ratios, what I define as *speculative* return. By 1999, that long-term rate of real returns had jumped to 12 percent.

This higher market valuation reflected investor confidence—along with greed—produced an extra speculative return of 7 percent annually—resulting in a cumulative increase of 400 percent in final value for the full 25 years, a staggering accretion without precedent in financial history. This speculative return almost doubled the market's *investment* return (created by dividend yields and earnings growth), bringing the market's total real return to nearly 12 percent per year. From these speculative heights, the market had little recourse but to return to normalcy, by providing far lower returns in subsequent years. And in fact, the real return on stocks since the turn of the century in 1999 has been minus 7 percent per year, composed of a negative *investment* return of −1 percent and, as price-earnings multiples retreated to (or below) historical norms, a negative *speculative* return of another −6 percent.

The message here is that investors in their ignorance, and financial sector marketers with their heavy incentives to sell, well, "products," failed to make the necessary distinction between the returns earned by business (earnings and dividends) and the returns earned by irrational exuberance and greed. In retrospect, we now realize that much of the value we saw reflected on our quarterly 401(k) statements in 1999 (and again in 2007) was indeed *phantom wealth*. But as yesteryear's stewards of our investment management firms became modern-day salesmen of investment products, they had every incentive to disregard the fact that this wealth could not be sustained. Our marketers (and our investors) failed to recognize that only fundamental (investment) returns apply as time goes by. As a result, we misled ourselves about the realities that lay ahead, to say nothing of the risks associated with equity investing.

Reduce Participant Flexibility

Both the "open architecture" plan that I described earlier and the near-freedom to withdraw assets from DC plans have ill-served investors. Limiting choices is relatively easy to understand and to achieve. But it will take major reform to reduce the flexibility that plan participants presently enjoy to draw down their cash almost at will (albeit sometimes with tax penalties). If the DC plan is to reach its potential as a retirement savings vehicle, there must be substantial limits—including larger penalties—on cash-outs and loans, no matter how painful in the short term. (Just imagine what would have happened to our Social Security if participants had withdrawal rights!) Importantly, 401(k) plans were originally designed as *thrift savings plans*. They need to have far more emphasis on their role as *thrift retirement plans* than we expect them to play today.

A poignant example of the flaws in our 401(k) savings plans, shared by our IRA plans, came from financial writer (*A Piece of the Action: How the Middle Class Joined the Money Class*, Simon & Schuster, 1994) and *The New York Times* editorial board member Joe Nocera. In his April 28, 2012 column, entitled, "My Faith-Based Retirement," he identified many of the procedural and human barriers that stand between opening a retirement account, and building it into a meaningful asset to fund one's retirement. Box 7.5 presents some excerpts.

Box 7.5

My Faith-Based Retirement

By Joe Nocera

"My 60th birthday is less than a week and a half away. . . . The only thing I haven't dealt with on my to-do checklist is retirement planning . . . [But] I can't retire. My 401(k) plan, which was supposed to take care of my retirement, is in tatters. Like millions of other aging baby boomers, I first began putting money into a tax-deferred retirement account a few years after they were legislated into existence in the late 1970s. The great bull market, which began in 1982, was just gearing up.

"As a young journalist, I couldn't afford to invest a lot of money, but my account grew as the market rose, and the bull market gave me an inflated sense of my investing skills. I became an enthusiast of the new investing culture, and I argued that the little guy have the same access to the markets as the wealthy. In the boom, I didn't make much of the decline of pensions. After all, we were in the middle of the tech bubble by then.

"The bull market ended with the bursting of that bubble in 2000. My tech-laden portfolio was cut in half. A half-dozen years later, I got divorced, cutting my 401(k) in half again. A few years after that, I bought a house that needed some costly renovations. Since my retirement account was now hopelessly inadequate for actual retirement, I reasoned that I might as well get some use out of the money while I could. So I threw another chunk of my 401(k) at the renovation. That's where I stand today. . . .

"The 401(k) is a failed experiment. . . . It is time to rethink it. . . . Most human beings lack the skill and emotional wherewithal to be good investors. Linking investing and retirement has turned out to be a recipe for disaster."

Own the Stock Market

Investors seem to largely ignore the close link between lower costs and higher returns—what I have called earlier "The Relentless Rules of Humble Arithmetic." Plan participants and employers also ignore this essential truism: In the aggregate, we investors are all "indexers." That is, all of the equity owners of U.S. stocks together own the entire U.S. stock market. So our collective gross return inevitably equals the return of the stock market itself.

And because providers of financial services are largely smart, ambitious, aggressive, innovative, entrepreneurial, and, at least to some extent, greedy, it is in their own financial interest to have plan sponsors and participants ignore that reality. Our financial system pits one investor against another, buyer versus seller. Each time a share of stock changes hands (and today's daily volume totals some 10 billion shares), one investor is (relatively) enriched; the investor on the other side of the trade is (relatively) impoverished. That diverse collection of 562 equity funds now held in 401(k) plans, combined in the aggregate, in fact owns the stock market itself. In substance, the winning funds' excess returns are offset by the losing funds' shortfalls. The obvious conclusion: *We're all indexers now.*

But, as noted earlier, this is no *zero-sum game.* The financial system— the traders, the brokers, the investment bankers, the money managers, the middlemen, "Wall Street," as it were—takes a cut of all this frenzied activity, leaving investors as a group inevitably playing a *loser's game.* As bets are exchanged back and forth, our attempts to beat the market, and the attempts of our institutional money managers to do so, then, enrich only the croupiers, a clear analogy to our racetracks, our casinos, and our state lotteries.

So, if we want to encourage and maximize the retirement savings of our citizens, we must drive the money changers—or at least most of them—out of the temples of finance. *If we investors collectively own the markets, but individually compete to beat our fellow market participants, we lose. But if we abandon our inevitably futile attempts to obtain an edge over other market participants and all simply hold our share of the market portfolio, we win.* (Please re-read those two sentences!) Truth told, it *is* as simple as that. So our Federal Retirement Board should not only foster the use of broad-market index funds in the new DC system (and offer them in its own "fallback" system described earlier) but approve only private providers who offer their index funds at minimum costs.

Balance Risk and Return through Asset Allocation

The balancing of return and risk is the quintessential task of intelligent investing, and that task too would be the province of the Federal Retirement Board. If the wisest, most experienced minds in our investment community and our academic community believe—as they do—that the need for risk aversion increases with age; that market timing is a fool's game (and is obviously not possible for investors as a group); and that predicting stock market returns has a very high margin for error, then something akin to roughly matching the bond index fund percentage with each participant's age with the remainder committed to the stock index fund, is the strategy that is most likely to serve most plan participants with the most effectiveness. Under extenuating—and very limited—circumstances, participants could have the ability to opt out of that allocation.

This allocation pattern is clearly accepted by most fund industry marketers, in the choice of the bond/stock allocations of their increasingly popular "target retirement funds." However, too many of these fund sponsors apparently have found it a competitive necessity to hold stock positions that are significantly higher than the pure age-based equivalents described earlier. I don't believe competitive pressure should be allowed to establish the allocation standard, and would leave those decisions to broad policies set by the new Federal Retirement Board.

I also don't believe that past returns on stocks that include, from time to time, substantial phantom returns—born of swings from fear to greed to hope, back and forth—are a sound basis for establishing appropriate asset allocations for plan participants. Our market strategists, in my view, too often deceive themselves by their slavish reliance on past returns, rather than focusing on what returns may lie ahead, based on the projected discounted future cash flows that, however far from certainty, represent the intrinsic values of U.S. business in the aggregate.

Once we spread the risk of investing to investors as a group, we've accomplished the inevitably worthwhile goal: a low-cost financial system that is based on the wisdom of long-term investing, eschewing the fallacy of the short-term speculation that is so deeply entrenched in our markets today. To do so, we must first eliminate the risk of picking individual stocks, of picking market sectors, and of picking money managers, leaving only market risk, which cannot be avoided. Such a strategy effectively *guarantees* that all DC-plan participants will garner their fair share of whatever returns our stock and bond markets are generous enough to bestow on us (or, for that matter, mean-spirited enough to inflict on us). Compared to today's loser's game, that would be a signal accomplishment.

Under the present system, some of us will outlive our retirement savings and depend on our families. Others will go to their rewards with large savings barely yet tapped, benefiting their heirs. But like investment risk, longevity risk can be pooled. So as the years left to accumulate assets dwindle down, and as the years of living on the returns from those assets begin, we need to institutionalize, as it were, a planned program of conversion of a portion of our retirement plan assets into annuities. (It could well be integrated with a plan most of us already have, one that includes defined benefits, an inflation hedge, and virtually bulletproof credit standing. It is called "Social Security.")

This evolution will be a gradual process; it could be limited to plan participants with assets above a certain level; and it could be accomplished by the availability of annuities created by private enterprise and offered at minimum cost, again with providers overseen by the proposed Federal Retirement Board (just as the federal Thrift Savings Plan has its own board and management, and operates as a private enterprise).

Focus on Mutuality, Investment Risk, and Longevity Risk

The pooling of the savings of retirement plan investors in this new pension fund environment is the *only* way to maximize the returns of these investors as a group. The pool would feature a widely diversified, all-market strategy, a rational (if inevitably imperfect) asset allocation, and low costs, and be delivered by a private system in which investors automatically and regularly save from their own incomes, aided where possible by matching contributions of their employers, and would prove that an annuity-like mechanism to minimize longevity risks is the optimal system to assure maximum retirement plan security for our nation's families.

There remains the task of bypassing Wall Street's croupiers, an essential part of the necessary reform. Surely our Federal Retirement Board would want to evaluate the need for the providers of DC retirement plan service to be highly cost-efficient, or even to be *mutual* in structure; that is, management companies that are owned by their fund shareholders and operated on an "at-cost" basis; and annuity providers that are similarly structured. The arithmetic is there, and the sole mutual fund firm that is organized under such a mutual structure has performed with remarkable effectiveness.[5]

Of course that's my view! But this critical analysis of the structure of the mutual fund industry is not mine alone. Hear this from another investor, one who has not only produced one of the most impressive investment records of the modern era but who has an impeccable reputation for character and intellectual integrity, David F. Swensen, Chief Investment Officer of Yale University:

> The fundamental market failure in the mutual fund industry involves the interaction between sophisticated, profit-seeking providers of financial services and naïve, return-seeking consumers of investment products. The drive for profits by Wall Street and the mutual fund industry overwhelms the concept of fiduciary responsibility, leading to an all too predictable outcome: . . . the powerful financial services industry exploits vulnerable individual investors. . . . The ownership structure of a fund management company plays a role in determining the likelihood of investor success. . . .
>
> Mutual fund investors face the greatest challenge with investment management companies that provide returns to public shareholders or that funnel profits to a corporate parent—situations that place the conflict between profit generation and

---

[5]I'm only slightly embarrassed again to be referring to Vanguard, the firm I founded 35 years ago. But it's difficult to argue with Vanguard's leadership in providing superior investment returns, in operating by far at the lowest costs in the field, in earning shareholder confidence, and in developing positive cash flows into our mutual funds (even in the face of huge *outflows* from funds operated by our rivals).

fiduciary responsibility in high relief. When a fund's management subsidiary reports to a multi-line financial services company, the scope for abuse of investor capital broadens dramatically. . . .

Investors fare best with funds managed by not-for-profit organizations, because the management firm focuses exclusively on serving investor interests. No profit motive conflicts with the manager's fiduciary responsibility. No profit margin interferes with investor returns. No outside corporate interest clashes with portfolio management choices. Not-for-profit firms place investor interests front and center. . . . Ultimately, a passive index fund managed by a not-for-profit investment management organization represents the combination most likely to satisfy investor aspirations.

What Would an Ideal Retirement Plan System Look Like?

However difficult to implement, it is easy to summarize the five elements of an ideal system for retirement savings that I've presented.

1. Social Security would essentially remain in its present form, offering basic retirement security for our citizens at minimum investment risk. (However, policymakers must promptly deal with its longer-run deficits.)
2. For those who have the financial ability to save for retirement, there would be a single DC structure, dominated by low-cost—even mutual—providers, inevitably focused on all-market index funds investing for the long term, and overseen by a newly created Federal Retirement Board that would establish sound principles of asset allocation and diversification in order to ensure appropriate investment risk for plan participants, as well as stringent limits on participant flexibility.
3. Retirement savings would continue to be tax-deferred, but with a dollar limitation on aggregate annual contributions by any individual, and a similar limit on the amount that is tax-deductible.
4. Longevity risk would be mitigated by creating simple low-cost annuities as a mandatory offering in these plans, with some portion

of each participant's balance going into this option upon retirement. (Participants should have the ability to opt out of this alternative.)

5. We should extend the existing ERISA requirement that plan *sponsors* meet a standard of fiduciary duty to encompass plan *providers* as well as the corporations themselves. (As noted earlier, I also believe that a federal standard of fiduciary duty for all money managers should be enacted.)

The system I'd like to see may not be—indeed, it is not—a system free of flaws. But it is a radical improvement, born of common sense and elemental arithmetic, over the present system, which is driven by the interests of Wall Street rather than Main Street. With the creation of an independent Federal Retirement Board, we have the flexibility to correct flaws that may develop over time, and assure that the interests of workers and their retirement security remain paramount. But the central principle remains: *minimize the impact of all of the various forms of speculation that plague our complex present-day national retirement plan system, vastly simplify it, slash the costs of it, assure its fairness to society, and maximize its focus on long-term investment.*

*   *   *

The perils of speculation and the merits of investment are not merely concepts. They are real factors in determining how the process of asset allocation and portfolio management actually functions. My career has fortified my strong views of this distinction, made real and tangible by my first-hand experience in the management of Wellington Fund during 61 years of its 83-year history. The next chapter tells this tale of triumph and tragedy and triumph.

Chapter 8

The Rise, the Fall, and the Renaissance of Wellington Fund

A Case Study—Investment Wins, Speculation Loses

The name "Wellington" had a magical ring, a sort of indefinable air of quality about it that made it almost perfect as a name for a conservative financial organization.

—*Walter L. Morgan,* Business Decisions
That Changed Our Lives, *1964*

Introduction

The triumph of long-term investment over short-term speculation is not just a theory. It can be a meaningful reality. So I present in this chapter a real-world case study of the Wellington Fund, an actively managed balanced mutual fund that was founded by Walter L. Morgan in 1928. Not only have I been present during the past 61 years of that nearly

84-year history, but I was an active participant at the two crucial turning points, first when the Fund moved away from its focus on traditional investment policies to speculation, and then when it returned to those investment roots.

During its first four decades, Wellington's hallmark had been a conservative strategy of long-term investment. Then, in 1966, under new management that sought to earn higher returns, the Fund turned to an aggressive strategy. Over the subsequent decade, that strategy, heavily laden with speculative elements, proved an abject failure. The Fund's returns were abysmal, and assets plummeted from $2.1 billion in 1966 to $475 million in 1974, a staggering drop of more than 75 percent.

Then, beginning in 1978, Wellington Fund returned to the objectives stated at its founding: (1) Conservation of Capital, (2) Reasonable Current Income, and (3) Profits without Undue Risk. The Fund's traditional strategy, with its focus on the long term, has now been in place for more than three decades. Its demonstrated success in providing superior returns to shareholders has returned Wellington to the industry leadership that it held in the earlier era. By 2012, total assets had soared to $55 billion, making it once again the largest balanced fund in the field.

I write from firsthand knowledge: My first job in the mutual fund industry began at Wellington in 1951, and I've remained involved in its affairs ever since. I became chief executive of Wellington Management Company, the Fund's external investment advisor in 1965, and Chairman of the Fund's board of directors in 1970, a role in which I remained until 1996, when I became honorary chairman, a position I hold to this very day.

While I played no role in its remarkable rise in the fund's very early years, I was a member of its Investment Committee during the post-1960 era, through 1966. Perhaps I can take a modicum of credit for its success. But I also share a heavy responsibility for the fall that followed. That failure taught me the error of my ways, which in turn helped to give me the wisdom and determination to demand a return to the Fund's original long-term strategy, focused on current income, risk control, minimizing advisory fees and other costs of operation, and the enhancement of investment returns. The Fund's remarkable renaissance followed, and continues to this day.

I write this history in honor of my great mentor, Walter L. Morgan, mutual fund pioneer and in his later years the dean of the industry. He loved the name "Wellington"; he reveled in the Fund's rise to leadership; he must have despaired over its subsequent fall (though he never told me so); and he lived to revel again in its renaissance through 1998, when, at age 100, he met his Maker. I dedicate this chapter to his memory.

Part I

Walter Morgan: Wellington's Founding Genius[1]

December 27, 1928, was the day Wellington Fund was born, when the variety of drab legal documents that breathe life into a corporation were filed in the State of Delaware. It was at that moment that Walter Morgan turned an idea into a reality—a business in being. Small, humble, and insignificant to be sure, but with the potential for success in its future—a future that in many respects had been determined by what went before.

After graduating from Princeton University, Class of 1920, Mr. Morgan began his career with a major accounting firm. Then, in 1925, he founded his own accounting firm, Morgan and Company, an early sign of his entrepreneurial bent. It was not long before investment advice and tax counseling became the dominant part of his business. As he helped this diverse group of clients with the handling of their investments, it occurred to Mr. Morgan that there must be a better way to handle investment management than to advise a large number of individual accounts, a better way to diversify investments than the purchase of only a few securities, a better way to handle the problems of safekeeping and recording a large number of securities and their dividend and interest payments.

---

[1] The information summarized in this section is adapted from *Business Decisions that Changed Our Lives*, published by Random House in 1964. The chapter, "Main Street Comes to Wall Street—A New Investment Concept Is Born," was written by Mr. Morgan. Full disclosure: I worked closely with him as a sort of ghostwriter in the preparation of that chapter, which can be found at www.johncbogle.com.

The solution quickly became obvious: If substantially the same investment goals were shared by each of these individual accounts, why not consolidate them into a single fund? Like most good ideas, the notion that kept coming into Mr. Morgan's mind was the essence of simplicity: to combine a group of individual investment accounts into a single large fund, which could be diversified broadly over perhaps a hundred or more securities, and managed efficiently by trained and experienced investment experts. To develop such a "mutual fund," of course, would require managerial, analytical, and promotional abilities that were to come in part from his heredity, education, training, and values, and in part from his ability to pick good people with whom to work.

By July 1, 1928, Industrial and Power Securities Company (Wellington Fund's original name) had amassed slightly over $100,000 of client assets and began operations. While he had chosen the worst time in the financial history of the United States to launch a new investment vehicle, Walter Morgan had been blessed with the foresight to launch a *balanced* fund—owning not only equities but a substantial bond position—just a few brief months before the crash of the stock market in 1929.

In the Great Depression that followed, the merits of conservative investing were to be amply demonstrated. As a result of the conservative philosophy and the strategic moves of its managers at Morgan's Wellington Management Company, the Fund demonstrated considerable downside protection in the decline, providing a relative stability of value unmatched by virtually any other investment trust or mutual fund in the challenging second half of 1929. Little by little, new capital had started to flow into the Fund. As its first year ended, total assets had risen to $195,000.

What's in a Name?

Mr. Morgan chose the name "Wellington" for his management company for a variety of reasons. A student and admirer of the life of the Duke of Wellington, Morgan was fascinated by the history of his military campaigns. The Wellington name, furthermore, had not been used by other American financial institutions, which was not the case with famous United States heroes, such as Washington, Jefferson, Hamilton, and Lincoln. Most important of all, Wellington was a name easy to remember. It was distinctive. It had, Morgan felt, a magical ring, a sort of indefinable air of quality about it that made it almost perfect as a name for a conservative financial organization.

The Fund's original name—Industrial and Power Securities Corporation—had been chosen because it was in tune with the 1920s. For the 1930s, however, it was rather off-key. The trials and tribulations of the heavily leveraged closed-end trusts—many of which would go bankrupt in the cataclysm that shook the economy—had given the over-used "industrial" name a bad connotation. As a result of collapse of the huge public-utility holding companies of the day, "power" was also bad news. Perhaps even more important, no one seemed to be able to remember the Fund's original name, and the Philadelphia investment community began to refer to Industrial and Power Securities as "a Wellington fund," that is, one of the accounts under the supervision of its adviser, Wellington Management Company.

The solution soon became obvious. On July 11, 1935, Industrial and Power Securities Corporation became Wellington Fund, Inc. Not only easy to remember, the name was well suited to help accomplish one of Morgan's major objectives: to make Wellington a household name like "Cadillac," "Coca-Cola," or "Tiffany." The choice of the Wellington name was one of the cornerstones of its early success, and, despite the devastating bumps the Fund would experience along the long road that followed, its name has endured,[2] and remains a key component of the Fund's remarkable acceptance in the investor marketplace.

Part II

O Pioneers!

When Morgan founded Wellington Fund in December 1928, it was one of seven original mutual funds formed before the Great Crash that almost destroyed the embryonic fund industry. Today, Wellington

---

[2]While still known as Wellington Fund, its official name became "Vanguard Wellington Fund" in 1980.

Exhibit 8.1   Total Net Assets of Wellington Fund versus Its Fellow Pioneers

Fund	Total Net Assets (000)
Massachusetts Investors Trust	$3,247,913
State Street Investment Trust	0
Incorporated Investors (Now Putnam Investors)	$1,325,262
Scudder Balanced Fund (Now DWS Core-Plus Income Fund)	$323,314
Pioneer Fund	$6,308,697
Century Shares Trust	$178,217
Wellington Fund	$55,238,130

stands alone as by far the most successful of those seven early pioneers. That claim may seem extreme, or even self-serving, but as we compare the Fund's present asset base with those of the other pioneers, such a bias seems easily justified by the facts. Let's see how each fared over the eight-plus decades that followed, listing them in the order of the dates of their founding (see Exhibit 8.1).

Massachusetts Investors Trust (MIT)

Massachusetts Investors Trust (MIT), founded in 1924, was not only the first mutual fund. It held its position as the industry's largest fund for the next 45 years. Key to this equity fund's success during that period were its middle-of-the-road investment policies and its consistent standing as by far the industry's lowest-cost fund. Then, in 1969, it abandoned its original "mutual" type of structure (managed by its own trustees), and became part of the Massachusetts Financial Services group (MFS). In 1980, MFS was sold to Sun Life of Canada, and MIT's expense ratio soared five-fold—from 0.19 percent in 1968 to 0.97 percent in 2011. Its investment return declined commensurately, and even a solid performance record during recent years has not been enough to move its longer-term performance out of mediocrity. MIT's present assets of just $3.2 billion are but a shadow of their $15 billion peak, reached a full decade ago.

State Street Investment Trust

State Street Investment Trust was founded shortly after MIT in 1925, but went out of business in 2004. Its founding managers had sold their company to Metropolitan Life Insurance Company in 1982. A series of risk-oriented portfolio managers then altered the Fund's policies from its original conservative and prudent focus to a speculative focus. Its fate was sealed by the resulting performance failure—especially in the bear market of 2000–2003. In 2004, after its assets had tumbled to $1.4 billion from a high of $3.9 billion, the Met sold the firm to financial conglomerate BlackRock. The new owner of the management company quickly decided to put State Street out of its misery, merging it into the BlackRock Large Cap Core Fund. I was deeply saddened when State Street Investment Trust died, describing it as "a death in the family."[3]

Incorporated Investors

Incorporated Investors was formed in 1926. It gave up its independent existence in 1964, when it became part of the Putnam Group, which promptly changed its name to Putnam Investors. Its strategies and its record since then have been inconsistent. Even worse, as a heavy annual expense ratio of 1.2 percent took its toll, its return has lagged the S&P 500 index by more than 2 percentage points annually over the past 15 years. Present assets of $1.3 billion are but one-tenth of the $13 billion peak reached a decade earlier.

Scudder Stevens & Clark Balanced Fund

During the 40-plus years following its founding in 1928, this balanced fund, run by the venerable investment advisory firm of Scudder Stevens & Clark, was a worthy competitor to Wellington Fund. But in 1970, Scudder management abandoned the fund's original balanced strategy,

---

[3]It is in fact remarkable that among the seven pioneers, only one failed to survive. In recent decades, the industry-wide fund failure rate has averaged about 50 percent *per decade*.

changing it into a bond fund and renaming it Scudder Income Fund. This change did not work well. The management company was sold to new owners in 1997, and then resold in 2002. Its current owner, Deutsche Bank, renamed the fund "DWS Core-Plus Income." (It's not clear how such a moniker could help the fund to reclaim a leadership role among its new bond fund peers.) Burdened by its debilitating average expense ratio of 1.6 percent per year, even 10 changes (!) in portfolio managers in the past six years alone failed to improve its record. This fund's *negative* 18 percent return in 2008 left it 23 percentage points shy of the 5 percent *positive* return of the bond market index, and the fund's assets have dwindled to barely $300 million.

Century Shares Trust

With its initial focus on insurance stocks, this pioneer grew substantially during the great boom in insurance shares during the 1935–1945 era, reaching an asset high of $220 million in 1945. (While small in today's terms, Century Shares was then the industry's eighth largest mutual fund.) But the Fund has yet to find its niche in the industry. Whether by luck or necessity, the Fund changed its focus in 2001, becoming a growth-oriented equity fund focused on the health care, technology, and retail sectors of the market. Since then, the record has been solid but erratic, and finding a new identity has proved elusive. By 2012, assets had fallen to less than $200 million.

Pioneer Fund

Well-named as an industry pioneer, this fund was also founded in 1928. As a middle-of-the-road equity fund, Pioneer pretty much represents "the shoemaker who stuck to his last," sticking to its focus on long-term investing. Although its assets have tumbled from a peak of $8 billion in 2006 to the 2012 total of $4.6 billion, Pioneer has survived. Despite numerous changes in the ownership of its management company by financial conglomerates, and despite the Fund's high expense ratio (1.1 percent), its long-term focus (annual turnover usually below 10 percent), along with an historical return that has virtually matched the S&P 500, have helped to keep Pioneer an important player in the game. None-theless, it remains less than one-tenth of Wellington's size.

What Explains the Wellington Advantage?

What were the characteristics that distinguished Wellington Fund from the other pioneers? What strategy enabled the Fund not only to survive but to grow? First, it focused on a balanced, middle-of-the-road investment strategy and *never* changed the stated objectives noted earlier: conservation of capital; reasonable current income; and profits without undue risk. With the exception of the period 1968–1978 when Wellington strayed from those roots, the implementation of those objectives was quite consistent. Ever since 1978, Wellington has remained fundamentally a conservative balanced fund focused on the long term—the leopard that never changed its spots. Although, during the history that follows in Part III of this chapter, those spots, as it were, periodically changed their color, they finally returned to their original hue.

Despite that single decade-long failure over the Fund's 84-year life, its aggregate investment performance has nicely exceeded the returns of its peers. This success is largely a product of its focus on the long term, its consistent investment strategy, the quality of portfolio supervision provided by its investment adviser, and particularly its exceptionally low costs. With its generally solid returns—and especially by its consistent superiority over its peers during the past three-plus decades—Wellington's assets have burgeoned. Exhibit 8.2 shows the Fund's remarkable asset growth over its long history, interrupted only by that troublesome era, a decline that would soon be reversed—and then some.

Steady Long-Term Growth, Once Interrupted

So what's to be learned from this sharp contrast in how the winds of change—of fate and competition and strategy and judgment—treated these seven original industry pioneers at each step along the way? Why did Wellington Fund succeed? Why did the others lag, or even fail? Consider these lessons from that history.

Exhibit 8.2   Wellington Fund Assets under Management, 1929–2012[4]

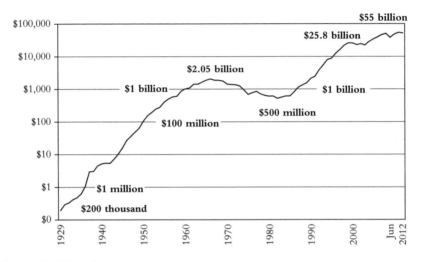

- Focus on the wisdom of long-term investment, and avoid the folly of short-term speculation.
- Never ignore a fund's stated objectives.
- Hold to a constant strategy. If something's broke in its implementation, fix it.
- Carefully measure risk, and control it.
- Never change advisers without a compelling case that it will serve the interests of fund shareholders.[5]

---

[4]The $475 million low in assets was reached in July 1982, after which Wellington Fund enjoyed the greatest asset growth in its long history. An important portion of this resurgence can be attributed to the decision, in February 1977, to eliminate sales commissions and thus our reliance on the broker-dealer network that had distributed Wellington shares to investors since the fund's inception, and rely solely on an investor-driven "no-load" shareholder strategy.

[5]When an adviser is sold to enrich its founders, beware. If the new adviser is a financial conglomerate, be scared.

- Keep the fund's name, enhance it, and treasure it.
- Minimize fund costs to the bare-bones essentials, not only operating expenses and advisory fees, but also the drag of high portfolio turnover.

Then, in the saying I've used for many decades, *stay the course!*

Part III

Wellington Fund Strategy and Returns 1929—2012

I've divided Wellington's history into three eras: the Rise (1929—1966), the Fall (1967—1978), and the Renaissance (1979 to date). Before I turn to that history, I want to discuss some of the challenges of earning superior returns in a competitive and largely efficient financial marketplace.

That long history has taught me, above all, that the wisdom of long-term investment is a winner's game; the folly of short-term speculation is a loser's game. History (and arithmetic) tell us that there are four factors that determine the returns that any mutual fund delivers: (1) investment policy and strategy; (2) risk exposure; (3) manager skill (or, in the short term at least, luck); and (4) the investment advisory fees and other costs paid for the fund's management. Over time, however, policy and strategy, risk exposure, and cost seem to dominate, and skill seems to average out, as hundreds of perfectly sound managers compete amongst one another in buying and selling stocks.[6] Thus, strategy, risk, and cost are the central factors in providing superior returns over like competitors.

Since risk can be quantified, I've measured Wellington Fund's risk exposure during its long history, using two basic metrics: the fund's equity ratio (equities and lower-grade bonds as a percentage of fund assets) and "Beta," a now-common measure of a fund's volatility relative to that of the stock market itself, as described in Box 8.1.

---

[6]The great Benjamin Graham was right on the mark describing the stock market as "a huge laundry in which institutions take in large blocks of each other's washing—nowadays to the tune of 30 million shares a day—without the rhyme or reason." That was in 1978. By 2012, a far huger laundry was often washing 8.5 billion shares each day. Talk about the dominance of speculation! In fact, fund managers buy their stocks *from* other managers, and sell their stocks *to* other managers—this trading, as I noted earlier, is obviously a zero-sum game before transaction costs and a loser's game thereafter.

Box 8.1
A History of Risk Measurement . . .
and Risk Preference

Wellington Fund's history as a balanced mutual fund—consistently allocating a substantial position of its investment portfolio to bonds and other fixed income securities—has been one of its most distinguishing characteristics. Yet during its eight-plus decades of existence, the fund has taken various approaches to control the risk inherent in owning common stocks.

During most of the Fund's first four decades of existence, the Fund's allocation of assets between equities—typically about 60–65 percent of resources—and corporate and government bonds—the remaining 35–40 percent—varied around these ratios. That balance provided a relatively predictable exposure to risk, one that shareholders could rely upon to moderate stock market swings as compared to all-stock portfolios.

As the 1960s unfolded, academics devised a new measure to supplement the equity ratio as the principal measure of a mutual fund's risk. The measure was called "Beta." It simply measured the volatility in a fund's net asset value per share relative to the volatility of the stock market itself, measured by the Standard & Poor's 500 Stock Index. A typical equity fund would score a Beta of about 1.00, meaning it was approximately as volatile as the market itself. Such a ratio implies an equity ratio of 100 percent. But since equity funds usually held a modest cash position, in the 5 percent range, their actual Betas were slightly lower.

During the 1929–1965 period, Wellington's Beta did a fine job as a proxy for the Fund's equity ratio. In fact, Wellington's equity ratio during that period averaged 62 percent; its Beta averaged 0.60, a solid confirmation of its typical risk exposure of

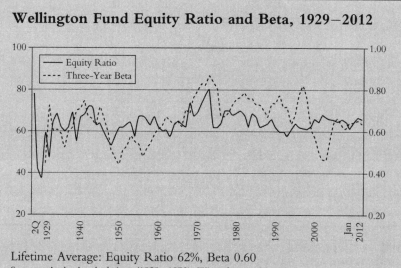

Wellington Fund Equity Ratio and Beta, 1929–2012

Lifetime Average: Equity Ratio 62%, Beta 0.60
SOURCE: Author's calculations (1929–1972), Wiesenberger; Morningstar.

less than two-thirds of the risk of the stock market, consistent with the Fund's long tradition of conservatism and balance.

But there are also variations in the character of a fund's equities that influence the difference between the equity ratio and the Beta. For example, if a given equity fund were to hold a 100 percent position in high-quality, income-producing stocks, its Beta might be as low as, say, 0.90. If it were to hold more speculative stocks, those with higher market valuations, or lower quality or smaller companies, or companies that pay little or no dividend, or those with uncertain growth prospects, its Beta might run to 1.10 or even 1.20—a portfolio fully one-third more volatile and risky than that 0.9 Beta for the more conservative equity funds.

Whichever measure one prefers, we are able to measure in real time (as we say today) the extent to which a fund controls its risk or changes its risk exposure over an extended period of years. The exhibit presented here shows Wellington's risk profile over its entire history, measuring both its equity

(Continued)

exposure, and (over a rolling three-year period) its Beta. For Wellington, far more often than not, the data in the two lines of Exhibit 8.1 reaffirm one another. And when they do not, the difference is likely to reflect either a change in equity ratio or in the character of the fund's equity holdings. (The complete history of Wellington Fund's equity ratio and beta is presented in Appendix IV.)

Risk and Return

Both the general stability of Wellington Fund's risk exposure—and the rare departures from the norm—have played a vital role in shaping the Fund's returns relative to its balanced fund peers. At first, the Fund was almost alone in its field, but by 2012 its number of peers had grown to more than 1,000 balanced funds. As a group, these rivals have maintained a risk exposure roughly comparable to that of Wellington.

In analyzing Wellington's performance, I've calculated the Fund's annual returns going back to 1929, and compared them with the returns earned by the average balanced mutual fund, focusing especially on three fairly distinct eras in the Fund's history:

1. **1929–1966,** when Wellington first carved out a singular advantage over its peers, an advantage that persisted through 1960, only to fall to the very bottom of the pack over the next six years.
2. **1967–1978,** beginning when Wellington Management Company merged with a group of aggressive, growth-oriented speculative managers, who moved the Fund to a risk-exposure level far higher than ever before.
3. **1978–2012,** an era that began when the newly independent Wellington Fund (now part of Vanguard) laid down the marching orders to Wellington Management Company that it return to its traditional values—an equity ratio mandated within the 60–70 percent range, emphasizing dividend-paying investment-grade stocks.

During this long era, as shown in Exhibit 8.3, the Fund outpaced its peers, by a growing cumulative margin. Despite the obvious bumps it

Exhibit 8.3   Wellington Fund versus Average Balanced Fund: Cumulative Returns, 1929–2012

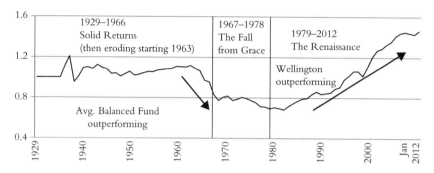

Average Annual Return: Wellington 8.2 Percent; Average Balanced
Fund 7.7 Percent

SOURCE: Wiesenberger, Vanguard. This chart represents the growth of an initial investment in
Wellington Fund relative to an equal investment in the average balanced fund. An upward slope
means Wellington Fund is outperforming its peers; a downward slope represents underperformance
of Wellington versus its peers. The full history is presented in Appendix V.

suffered along the way, from start to finish, it accumulated an extraordinary performance advantage—a solid achievement in the hard business
of investing Other People's Money.

The Rise: Solid Returns, Later Eroding (1929–1966)

In the aftermath of the Great Crash, the protective merits of balanced
investing became obvious. Beginning in 1929, the perilous lessons of equity
risk (and even worse, leveraged equity risk), had been learned. So during
the 1930s and 1940s, more and more balanced funds were formed.
While performance measures during the 1930–1960 period were crude,
they were a far cry from those we use today (for better or worse!). But
the data that we have show that during 1929–1962, Wellington gained a
nice edge on its rivals. Annual returns averaged 7.0 percent annually, versus
6.6 percent for its peers. While that small gap in percentage points
may appear small, compounded over the years it meant that each $1
invested at the outset had grown by 1962 to $9.33 in Wellington,
compared to $8.35 for the average balanced fund, a solid advantage.

In its formative years, essentially from 1929 through the end of
World War II in 1945, its ratio of equities to bonds varied rather widely,

beginning with a timely slash in the stock portion from 78 percent of resources in June of 1929 to 41 percent at the stock market's peak on September 3, 1929. During the 1930s, while the stock ratio varied around 50 percent of assets, the position in discounted bonds and pre-ferred stocks—bought for their appreciation potential—typically added roughly another 10 percentage points, bringing the equity position to the 60 percent range.

Raising cash for the portfolio and then reinvesting reserves on an opportunistic basis was not unusual for a small mutual fund during those volatile days. At the end of 1930, cash reserves accounted for but 3 percent of resources, increasing a year later to 28 percent. A similar swing—but in an upward direction—took place in 1935, with reserves rising from 2 percent in mid-year to 22 percent by year-end. Just before World War II broke out, reserves totaled 15 percent, but by the time the subsequent market drop was over, they had been cut to 6 percent.

Some of these substantial changes in allocation were timely and successful; some were not. But what was easily accomplished up until 1949, when Fund assets were generally below $100 million[7] (almost $1 billion in today's dollars), was less easily accomplished as Wellington grew and matured. Its assets crossed the $1 billion mark for the first time in 1959 (some $8 billion in today's dollars). Perhaps in part because the managers came to realize their fallibility, the Fund's rather aggressive changes in allocations would not recur during the sub-sequent decade.

During its first half-century, the Fund's dividend policy was one of the prime ingredients of Wellington's success in the marketplace of brokers who distributed the Fund's shares, and among the investors who owned them. Sadly, that same dividend policy became, in my judgment (and I was there), a major source of the Fund's failure during the 1960s and early 1970s—the gradual, yet unmistakable, deterioration of its investment performance relative to its balanced fund peers. I describe the genesis of this payout strategy in Box 8.2, "The Six Percent Solution."

---

[7]When I joined the small Wellington organization in 1951, the fund's assets totaled $140 million.

Box 8.2
"The Six Percent Solution"

The first formal mention of Wellington Fund's return objective of 6 percent came in its 1933 prospectus. This dividend policy was not a secret. Indeed, it was clearly described in 1945 in the Fund's marketing brochure "Beyond the Headlines": The Fund's policy is "to endeavor to pay dividends (sic) at such a minimum annual rate as would represent a reasonable return on asset value, including ordinary net income from interest and dividends, special dividends from security profits . . . and a portion from paid-in surplus (when necessary) to maintain a reasonable return to shareholders."[8] An accompanying table showed a 15-year string of total distributions averaging about $0.90 per share (unadjusted for the Fund's 2-for-1 stock split in 1956), ranging from $0.70 to $1.30. The sources of the distributions were undisclosed. Relating these distributions to the varying annual asset values produced "yields" of 5.5 percent to 6.2 percent, year after year through the 1930s and 1940s.

Despite Pennsylvania trust law that seemed to validate the distribution of realized capital gains to income beneficiaries ("life tenants"), giving them preference over the residual beneficiaries ("remaindermen"), this policy of regularly paying distributions from sources other than investment income and calling them "dividends" infuriated our competitors. Many believed that such

(Continued)

---

[8]Dividend income represents the interest payments and corporate dividends received from the fund's investments, less the fund's operating expenses. "Dividends" from security profits represent the capital gains realized on the sale of fund securities, net of any losses. "Special dividends" from paid-in surplus are distributed at management's discretion, based on an accounting principle in which the excess of the fund's net asset value over its par value of $1.00 per share may be distributed. In fact, such distributions are returning to the shareholders their own money, albeit without any tax consequences.

payouts of capital gains (and of course surplus) were not "income"; they were simply returns to investors of their own capital. Whatever the case, in 1950 regulatory authorities at the NASD banned the practice of combining income dividends with distributions from any other source. The Wellington distributions, accordingly, were restated. Later reports showed that the original average payment of $0.90 per share in fact included $0.60 of investment income, $0.27 of capital gains, and $0.03 from paid-in surplus.

But while the reporting rules changed, the Fund's policy did not. Shareholders and broker-dealers who distributed the Fund's shares had come to rely on the high payouts, and couldn't seem to be weaned away from relying on them. As the income dividend grew, so the capital gains distribution grew apace. In the 1940s, income dividends averaged $0.30 per share, capital gains distributions, $0.22. In the 1950s, $0.44 and $0.34. And in the 1960s, $0.47 and $0.43. Obviously, each payout of capital eroded the Fund's per share assets value, making it more difficult for the per share dividend income to be sustained.

The 1950s and 1960s were robust decades for corporate dividend growth, averaging annual increases of 5.2 percent. Rising stock prices, engendered in part by this dividend growth, meant that capital gains were relatively easy to realize, simply by selling the portfolio holdings with the largest appreciation. But by 1970, well before the bear market of 1973–1974, the string ran out.

By that time, as the Fund's new chairman, recommending the Fund's dividend policy to the Board was my responsibility. I'd been around long enough to realize that to terminate our high distribution policy would be ill-accepted by shareholders, causing severe liquidations that could be gravely harmful to the returns earned by Wellington Fund. So, when no unrealized capital gains remained in 1970, I recommended, and the Board reluctantly approved, a payment of $0.25 per share from surplus. While I wasn't keen about the idea, it seemed to do the job. At least such payments were tax-free to our shareholders.

But in 1971, a technicality in the Fund's tax status left us in a position where even a surplus distribution would have been taxable to our owners. I could no longer recommend such a payout. When we made no extra distributions in 1971, our worst fears were realized. Shareholder net redemptions doubled to 22 percent of assets in 1972 (cash outflow of $276 million), and continued in 1973 to 15 percent, and then 12 percent in 1974–1975, and again in 1976—yet another outflow during those three years of $420 million.

As 1976 began, Fund assets had fallen to $939 million, less than one-half of the $2.1 billion peak recorded in 1965. While we were able to resume the tax-free payments from surplus during 1972–1978, the damage had been done. Net redemptions continued to run at the 5 percent annual level during 1977–1981, another outflow of $475 billion. Wellington's assets would continue to decline, and by the third quarter of 1981 assets reached a low of $475 million, 75 percent below their peak.

In 1979, we abandoned the payout policy once and for all. But by 1983, the Fund was again realizing capital gains, not to force a given total payout but only in the normal course of the investment activities of our portfolio managers. Given the income-oriented policy that we had adopted in 1978, however, our payout from dividend income alone had risen sharply. When the capital gains payment dropped from $0.60 in 1989 to zero in 1990, it was a nonevent, as was its drop from $1.48 per share in 2000 to $1.13 in 2001 and to zero in 2002. We had successfully broken away from a policy that began, innocently enough, in the 1930s, a policy that became a Frankenstein monster in the 1960s and mid-1970s before finally being abandoned.

Let the long saga described in this history serve as a warning to future generations of Wellington Fund directors—indeed to all fund directors—to demand that the portfolio managers of the funds that they serve stick to producing income, and realize capital gains *only* for investment reasons. It was our decision to stop such payouts, along with the new income-oriented strategy described later in this chapter, that would begin the remarkable renaissance of Wellington Fund.

When 1963 began, an original $1.00 investment at the fund's inception had grown to $10.44, about 10 percent more than the value of a comparable investment return of $9.59 from our peers (see Appendix VI). During most of the post–World War II era, swings between the Fund's reserves and equities moderated, and the Fund's equity ratio, with only a few minor exceptions, remained in the narrow range of 62 to 67 percent for the next two decades, into the latter part of the 1960s. By that time, the opportunities for appreciation in fixed-income securities that were available during the 1930s and 1940s were behind us, and the Fund's equity position consisted almost entirely of common stocks.

Like its peers during that period, the Fund was run largely by an investment committee. When the industry's focus then turned to individual portfolio managers, Wellington followed suit. But the Fund's superiority was soon erased. By the close of 1966, while the cumulative value of that initial $1 back in 1929 had risen to $11.40, the cumulative value of an initial $1.00 in Wellington's average peer had risen to $11.92. The fund marketplace began to focus far more intensely on relative returns than in the earlier era. Performance data—lots of it!—had entered the game, and Wellington's lag was obvious.

From 1929 through 1964, Wellington Management Company's investment committee—determining the Fund's strategies and equity selections—had been led by Walter Morgan and investment chief A. Moyer Kulp. Brandon Barringer's early active participation gradually declined; during the 1950s and early 1960s Rawson Lloyd became the third major voice. But even as the fund industry was shifting its modus operandi from the collective judgment of an investment committee to the individual judgment of a portfolio manager, so, in 1960, did Wellington Management Company—first with Robert Cummin, then Robert Steinburgh, and then the firm's economist Daniel Ahearn. Their records, alas, speak for themselves, and they do not speak favorably.

The Fund's shortfall grew larger. It almost seemed as if the harder we tried, the less favorable the comparison became. In the stress of the tough Go-Go Years, traditional rules of sensible, long-term investment were forgotten. The fund industry was characterized by the rise of speculative equity funds and an increasing disregard of risk. Under my leadership, conservative Wellington Management Company consummated a merger with the aggressive Boston investment counseling firm of Thorndike,

Doran, Paine & Lewis. That leadership turned out to have been badly misguided.

The merger was designed to achieve three goals: (1) retain managers who could at last regain Wellington Fund's long-sought-after performance advantage, relying on new aggressive money managers who were products of the "New Era" in the financial markets,[9] (2) bring a new speculative growth fund (Ivest Fund) under the Wellington banner and build our marketing effort, and (3) through TDP&L gain an entry into the rapidly growing investment counseling business, a field in which advisory firms were rapidly growing at the expense of the giant trust companies that had held a virtual monopoly in the pension plan market. It all seemed too good to be true.

The Fall: Wellington Fund's Nadir (1967–1978)

It *was* too good to be true, at least for Wellington Fund. Our bullish and innovative new managers had set out to "modernize" Wellington Fund. Inappropriate as it may seem today, Wellington joined the new speculative parade. Walter M. Cabot became the Fund's investment director in 1967. (He would leave the firm in 1974 to become president of Harvard Management Company, running the college's huge endowment fund. He remained there until 1990.)

Cabot had left the Putnam fund organization to join Wellington Fund's partners in 1967. Acting quickly, he had raised the equity ratio from 62 percent in 1966 to 72 percent in 1967, and finally to an all-time high of 81 percent in 1972. Here's how Walter Cabot described the change in philosophy in the Fund's 1967 Annual Report:

> Change is a starting point for progress, and 1967 was a year of change for Wellington Fund. Obviously, times change. We decided we too should change to bring the portfolio more into line with modern concepts and opportunities. We have chosen "dynamic conservatism" as our philosophy, with emphasis on

---

[9]The TDP&L managers were featured in *The New Breed on Wall Street*, a 1969 book by Martin Mayer. Prophetically, the book was subtitled, "Today's stock market the way it is—in the words and through the personalities of the men who make the money GO."

companies that demonstrate the ability to meet, shape, and profit from change. (We have) increased our common stock position from 64 percent of resources to 72 percent, with a definite emphasis on growth stocks and a reduction in traditional basic industries.

A conservative investment fund is one that aggressively seeks rewards, and therefore has a substantial exposure to capital growth, potential profits and rising dividends . . . (one that) demands imagination, creativity, and flexibility. We will be invested in many of the great growth companies of our society. Dynamic and conservative investing is not, then a contradiction in terms. A strong offense is the best defense.

Cabot, encouraged by our firm's new partners/managers, had taken an aggressive stance that was without precedent in the Fund's long history. The traditional Beta in the 0.65 range rose into the high 0.70s, and then into the 0.80s. In a single year—unfortunately, right at the market's peak in 1972—the Fund's Beta reached a record high of 1.04. The once-conservative balanced fund was taking on greater risk than the stock market itself! Contributing to this risky position, the equity ratio had gradually risen from that earlier conservative norm of 62 percent to an all-time high of 81 percent as 1972 ended. The sharp increase in risk exposure was followed by a major bear market in stocks. The Standard and Poor's 500 Index fell by 48 percent and the Fund's asset value fell by 40 percent—nearly 80 percent of the decline in the Index, a shocking excess relative to Wellington's long history. The loss would not be recouped until 1983, 11 long years later. The "strong offense" proved no "defense" at all.

Rather than improving the Fund's record, the about-face in the Fund's character devastated it. Even as the market rose during 1967–1972, our cumulative return lagged that of our balanced fund peers by fully 30 percentage points (cumulative gain of 38 percent versus 68 percent for our peers). We didn't do any better during 1973–1978, which encompassed the great bear market and the partial recovery that followed, lagging our peers by another 12 percentage points (13 percent gain versus 25 percent gain for our peers). We had brought in new managers as partners to improve the lagging performance that

Wellington had delivered during the early 1960s, but we had succeeded only in making it worse. There is, of course, a profound lesson here!

In short, the conservative "blue-chip" Wellington Fund had indeed changed the color of its spots. It increased both its equity position and its risk exposure far beyond their traditional levels; it increased its exposure to stocks with below-investment grade quality, stocks selling at historically high market valuations, and stocks of less seasoned companies; it increased its focus on the short term, with annual portfolio turnover doubling, from 20 percent to 40 percent (a high figure in that ancient era). Investment, alas, had taken a back seat to speculation. This change in the Fund's character alarmed me, and I wrote a sharply worded memorandum to our investment executives, warning them about both the excessive risks and their all too likely unhappy consequences (see Box 8.3).

Box 8.3
1972: A Warning about Speculation

Memorandum
To: Wellington Management Company Senior Officers
From: John C. Bogle
Date: March 10, 1972
Subject: Some Thoughts about the Future of Wellington Fund[10]

What is the future of Wellington Fund? This is a question that has no easy answers, and involves the most complex kinds of conflicts and considerations, including how to improve performance, dividend policy, future marketing strategy, obligations to existing shareholders, fee structure, relationship to other funds in the Wellington group, and so on.

Before turning to these questions, I have to say a word about (of all things) "Beta." I am using Beta in this memorandum as a

(Continued)

---

[10]Excerpts. The entire memorandum is available at www.johncbogle.com.

simple index of volatility—probably the best single measure of analyzing the character of Wellington Fund.

   I. Wellington Fund has become a "different" fund than it was in the past. Wellington Fund's Beta (or risk exposure relative to the stock market) is now at the highest level in our 42-year history. From a figure of 0.62 during the 1930s and 0.65 during the 1960s, the Beta had risen to 0.81 and then 0.82 in the past two three-year periods. Expressed simply, this means if the S&P 500 Index were to decline by 20 percent, Wellington Fund would be expected to drop 16 percent, as compared to about 13 percent under Wellington's historical Beta averaging 0.65.

       Yet the one characteristic that Wellington Fund has consistently offered to its shareholders has been relatively good "downside protection" (the result of its balanced asset allocation between bonds and equities). I conclude that our failure to show reasonable stability in the next market decline—*and there will be one*—would be "the last straw."

  II. Wellington Fund, at the moment, can barely be considered a "balanced fund." The Wellington Fund prospectus (consistent with the SEC's policy guidelines with respect to "balanced funds") stated that ". . . the present intention of management is that generally the Fund will have no more than 75 percent of its assets in common stocks." Yet the fund's equity ratio is now 81 percent. I have grave doubts as to whether we are meeting the investment policy test specified in the Fund's prospectus. It is clear that Wellington Fund has departed from its traditional balanced posture of 55 percent to 70 percent in common stocks.

 III. Wellington Fund's income dividend, partly as a result of an increasing common stock ratio, is in serious jeopardy. If a bad downside performance would be "the last straw" for Wellington Fund, a reduction in the $.11 quarterly dividend would be the *very* last straw. In the face of the performance problems of the past and the demise of the capital distribution, a dividend cut would be a disaster. Yet, at present, Wellington Fund is earning income at the annual rate of $.42. It appears increasingly doubtful that, absent a policy change, we will have sufficient "adjustments" to meet our $.44 paid last year.

IV. I conclude that "surgery" is needed with respect to restructuring Wellington Fund. Specifically, I ask each of you to consider the wisdom of having the Wellington Fund return to its traditional policy of greater conservatism. If we moved, for example, to a "60 percent commons, 40 percent seniors" investment position, we would accomplish (a) a return of Wellington Fund to its traditional investment posture, with a consequent enhancement of its downside protection characteristics; and (b) preservation of Wellington Fund's identity as a balanced fund. If this is hardly a marketable concept *at the moment*, at least it is consistent with what 250,000 shareholders purchased in the first place.

I recognize that there are lots of risks in making a change like this—the worst of which, I suppose, would be a rampant bull market. But I believe the greater risk is doing nothing—ignoring the significant change that has developed in the Fund's investment characteristics, and disregarding a very serious income problem. In this change, in my judgment, is sown the seeds of a new future for Wellington Fund, even if in its old vestments.

What we appear to have done, perhaps unknowingly, is to turn Wellington Fund very nearly into an equity fund. Perhaps what we should have been doing is turning—or *returning*—Wellington Fund into an "income development fund"—that is to say, a fund with a realistic *current* yield, along with a *growing* dividend. Making such a change is risky, I repeat, but it seems a lot less risky with the Dow at 940 and bond yields at 7.25

(Continued)

percent—this is hindsight of course—than it might have been with the Dow at 400 and bond yields at 4.5 percent. In other words, my view is that this change *would* be good long-term strategy, and *may* even be good short-term tactics.

Wellington Fund has more than 43 years of history. Wellington Fund is the foundation upon which our Company is built. In Wellington Fund, to a major extent, lies the value and goodwill of the very name that we at Wellington Management Company apply to almost everything we do.

* * *

When I wrote this memorandum, the term *Beta* was an obscure academic concept designed to measure risk. Ever the statistical devotee, I introduced the concept to a skeptical audience at the General Membership Meeting of the Investment Company Institute in May 1971. It did not go over well. One journalist in the audience was particularly unimpressed. He wrote: "John Bogle gave an academic speech about mutual fund performance. It was likely of interest only to those with a mathematical turn of mind, and those who track the next reappearance of Halley's Comet." But I was stuck with the Beta identifier. One of our portfolio managers, who knew that the name "Bogle" was derived from a Scots word for devil or goblin, referred to me as "Beta Bogle, the data devil." (I took that as a compliment.)

Cabot responded promptly. He didn't agree with me, nor did he accept my conclusions. I found his response totally unsatisfactory, indeed barely responsive to the issues raised in my eight-page memorandum. Here are excerpts from his reply:

This, in my opinion, is a marketing problem and really has very little to do with the investment objectives or strategy for Wellington Fund. I would suggest that the fund currently has good downside protection and that I would not return it to its traditional investment posture. . . . The balanced concept is outmoded. . . . I don't think I would like to call for an increasing dividend indefinitely . . . but that hopefully over a period of time the list would shift gradually from higher income stocks to moving towards the growth segment of the market. Ultimately what this fund has sorely missed is a consistent long-term holding of quality, growth-oriented companies. It would seem to me that the shareholder of this fund could be reasonably well-serviced, receive a modestly increasing dividend, good protection on the downside, and an attempt to have his capital grow.

But the Wellington Fund problem was hardly the only problem created by the newly merged firm. In the bear market, Ivest Fund collapsed, along with three other similarly speculative funds we had created to share in the blessings of a "New Era" that never came into existence. (None of these four funds survived.) Our fund and counsel assets plummeted, and the once-happy partners of that original merger had a falling out. While these partners held the prime responsibility for our investment activities, it was they who fired me in January 1974. It was not a happy moment in my career.

During this era, the Fund's competitive shortfall grew ever greater, and the cumulative value of that initial $1.00 invested in Wellington at the outset, $11.40 at the end of 1966 rose to $15.76 at the 1972 peak, only to tumble to a mere $11.43 at the close of 1974, hard hit by the decline and by the new and risky strategy adopted seven years earlier. In the ensuing recovery, the gap got still worse, with Wellington underperforming its peers in five of the next six years. By the time that 1978 mercifully ended, the shortfall had reached boxcar proportions: cumulative value of that initial $1.00 in 1929, Wellington $17.78; average balanced fund, $25.20. For a moment, I entertained the idea that we should simply merge Wellington Fund, once the Grand Old Lady who was the paradigm of our high standing in the industry, into another of our funds, and get on with our business. But I couldn't do it. Rather, I would do whatever was necessary to restore Wellington to her former grandeur.

The Renaissance (1978–2012)

After that ghastly combination of terrible market conditions, a vastly diminished asset base, the collapse of our aggressive growth funds, and

278 THE CLASH OF THE CULTURES

the demise of Wellington Fund's performance, there seemed no way out. Yet, deeply disguised, lay the opportunity of a lifetime. For while I was "out" as Wellington Management's chief executive as 1974 began, I remained "in" as chairman and president of Wellington Fund and its sister funds, in a position of surprising strength. (A comprehensive account of this change is presented in Box 4.3 "How Did Vanguard Happen" in Chapter 4.)

In September 1974, after eight months of laborious study and give-and-take, I was able to persuade the Fund directors to retain me in my posts and build a small staff to administer the accounting, shareholder record keeping, and legal affairs of Wellington, and the seven other funds in what had become referred to as "The Wellington Group." We formed a new corporation to handle these responsibilities, wholly-owned by the funds themselves and operating on an at-cost basis—a truly *mutual* mutual fund structure, without precedent in the mutual fund industry. The name I chose for the new firm (as readers now must know) was The Vanguard Group, Inc. On September 24, 1974, *Vanguard* was born.

Under the new structure, the funds' staff would also oversee and evaluate the investment performance and marketing results of Wellington Management in its continuing role as adviser and distributor to the Vanguard funds. I was especially determined to return Wellington Fund to its roots, for I had failed, however unintentionally, to live up to Mr. Morgan's confidence in me. He had hired me, trusted my judgment, and promoted me again and again, finally naming me to lead the company in 1965. I owed everything to that marvelous mentor. I could not let him down.

Restructuring Wellington Fund would be no easy task, but, with a helping hand from Princeton professor Burton Malkiel, who had joined our Fund boards in 1977, we got the job done, and recommended the new plan to the Wellington Fund directors. The board promptly approved it, and we directed Wellington Management Company to implement the restructuring. Box 8.4 provides excerpts of the detailed 26-page memorandum that I wrote to our Fund's directors recommending the change.

Sometimes in life, we make the greatest forward progress by going backward. That is just what we did when we decided to take Wellington Fund back to its roots. Months later, the Board agreed to

Box 8.4

Urging a Return to Traditional Investment (1978)

Memorandum
To: Wellington Fund Directors
From: John C. Bogle
Date: October 9, 1978
Subject: Future Investment Policy for Wellington Fund[11]

Wellington Fund will soon celebrate the 50th anniversary of its founding by Walter L. Morgan on December 27, 1928. For the first 30 years—until Windsor Fund began in October 1958—it was the only Fund in what is now the 13-Fund Vanguard Group of Investment Companies. While it remains the largest Vanguard Fund, capital flow trends of recent years virtually assure that it will be replaced by Windsor as our "flagship" within a year or two.

Wellington Fund's asset erosion has been extreme and consistent. From a year-end high of $2,048,000,000 in 1965, assets have declined to $704,000,000 currently. The principal cause of this decline is capital outflow from the Fund, as these trends took hold:

1. An unremitting decline in investor purchases of Wellington shares, from $159,000,000 in 1965, to a projected $1,300,000 in 1978.
2. Continuing share liquidations vastly in excess of sales volume, and averaging about $100,000,000 per year over the past decade.
3. Net capital outflow since 1966 has totaled $1,070,000,000.

(Continued)

[11]Excerpts. The entire memorandum is available at www.johncbogle.com.

The performance problems faced by Wellington Fund since 1965 have been a contributing, but not a controlling factor, in the Fund's capital outflow picture. *All* balanced funds have experienced an ongoing and significant gap between sales volume and liquidations. In the 1960s and early 1970s, balanced funds lost "market share" to the more aggressive common stock and growth funds. After the failure of many of these funds to deliver on their performance promise, however, the marketing pendulum swept all the way over to the much more conservative corporate and municipal bond funds, totally bypassing the balanced funds in the process. This tabulation illustrates the point:

Market Share of Industry Sales

	Balanced	Stock	Bond
1955	40%	55%	5%
1960	20	72	8
1965	17	73	10
1970	5	85	10
1975	3	71	26
1977	1	32	67

There is little evidence—or even hope—that these trends will (soon) change in such a manner as to restore the traditional balanced fund to market share levels of 15 or 20 years ago. Thus, if Wellington is to remain in a viable position to keep its existing shareholders and to attract new investors, a change in its investment policy must be considered. It should be emphasized that such a change in *policy* should not be construed as a change in its fundamental investment *objectives*: (a) conservation of capital, (b) reasonable income return, and (c) profits without undue risk. Rather, the questions are: would Wellington Fund's shareholders be better served by readjusting the relative emphasis on each of these three objectives? And, if so, what would the nature of that adjustment be?

Shareholder Objectives

To help answer these two questions, we can rely with a high degree of confidence on recent surveys that were mutually confirmatory as to the objectives, requirements, and demographics of the Fund's 100,000 shareholders.

- 73 percent have an investment philosophy they consider "conservative," 26 percent are "moderate," and only 1 percent are "aggressive."
- 56 percent stated that "current income" best describes their investment objective, 33 percent stated "growth and income," and only 11 percent stated "long-term growth."
- 70 percent of shareholders are retired, and 60 percent have under $20,000 of annual income (27 percent under $10,000).

The surveys confirm what my shareholder correspondence indicates: that a greater emphasis on current income (which would in fact today come hand-in-hand with somewhat greater capital conservation) would meet the needs of our shareholders. If this higher income could be realized *without* an important sacrifice in total return (income plus capital growth) and *with* an ongoing growth in our dividend income, it is virtually inconceivable that it would not have an important and favorable impact on the Fund's present list of shareholders.

A Portfolio Approach to Higher Income

If, as it appears, higher income is the key goal to be sought by Wellington fund, the principal questions are these: how much higher? And at what, if any, sacrifice to the Fund's capital conservatism and profits objectives? We have examined a long-range analysis of the total performance of income stocks versus growth stocks to determine whether there was any sustainable historical differential between these two types of equities. In effect, we

(*Continued*)

wanted to answer the question as to whether there was any historical evidence that would suggest one strategy or the other as the
preferred route for Wellington in terms of total return.

So we analyzed portfolios of growth stock mutual funds
relative to portfolios of income stock funds, calculating the
average performance of the funds in each group over a period of
nearly 40 years—1940 to 1978 inclusive. Over this entire span,
the annual rate of total return (income plus capital) was 10.5
percent for the growth funds and 11.3 percent for the income
funds. Thus, the income funds enjoyed a rate of return that was
0.8 percent *higher*.

Of course, there were (extended) periods in which the
growth funds showed more advantageous performance (and vice
versa). Looked at on a decade-by-decade basis, growth stocks
had the best of the game in the 1950s (annual returns of 19.7
percent versus 16.5 percent). However, the two sets of portfolios
gave about the same performance in the 1940s (growth, 9 percent; income, 9 percent plus) and in the 1960s (income 10.5
percent; growth 10.1 percent). So far in the 1970s, income
stocks have done much better (7.7 percent versus 2.4 percent).
The important point is that there seems to be no systematic
long-term bias as between the two types of portfolios.

To avoid making changes deemed in the immediate interest
of Wellington Fund shareholder on the basis of "timing" various cycles would seem a hazardous sort of approach. So if we
want to adopt a long-run investment strategy emphasizing
income for Wellington Fund and its shareholders, it would
seem best to begin the work of adjusting the portfolio to such a
strategy without delay.

Implications of an Income Strategy

What tangible results would be involved in an income strategy
for Wellington Fund? First, we can examine the change in
dividend income. Let us assume, for the purposes of argument,
that we were to accept *in toto* the idea that Wellington Fund's

income stocks could provide a current yield of about 6.6 percent,[12] with a projected dividend growth of 52 percent over the next four years (based on Value Line projections), and without material sacrifice to the Fund's total (income-plus-growth) return.

What kind of current and future income might we be able to generate? Here are the projections, assuming a balance of 65 percent stock and 35 percent bonds: The analysis shows that such a change could produce sharply higher per share income dividends over the next five years.

Wellington Fund Annual Dividend Income

	1978	1979	1980	1981	1982	1983
Projection	$.54	$.67	$.73	$.78	$.84	$.91

Interestingly (again, based on the Value Line projections), the *total* projected return on the new portfolio[13] (16.1 percent), would compare quite favorably with the present portfolio (16.0 percent). While the new portfolio would have a lower earnings growth rate (9.5 percent versus 11.0 percent), it would make up for this deficiency with its higher income yield (6.6 percent versus 5.1 percent). Further, the new portfolio would carry a lower P/E ratio (7.1X versus 8.8X), than the current portfolio

(Continued)

---

[12]For comparison, the current yield [in 1978] on the equities in our Wellesley Income Fund portfolio is 6.9 percent.

[13]When I wrote the 1978 memorandum, I was no longer working as a security analyst (my early years at Wellington had included substantial training in that field) Still, I had the temerity to present a sample 50-stock portfolio with dividend yields, price-earnings ratios, earnings growth rates, and projected returns for each one. When I looked at the Fund's actual portfolio at the end of 1980, after most of the restructuring was implemented, 25 of those 50 stocks were held in Wellington's portfolio.

> and would have a higher "value" component (dividing P/E
> into total return).
>
> What we have, then, is a shift of the Fund's total return
> marginally away from its capital component toward its income
> component, without apparent sacrifice in total return, and with
> what would appear to be lower risk. In substance, the shift in
> emphasis increases the *more predictable* component of the Fund's
> return (income) and reduces the *less predictable* component
> (capital appreciation). Given the nature and objectives of the
> Wellington Fund shareholders set forth at the beginning of this
> paper, it is difficult to regard that shift as in any sense negative.

adopt my policy recommendations: (1) hold the equity ratio firmly within a range of 60 to 70 percent of assets; (2) emphasize seasoned dividend-paying blue-chip stocks, largely of investment-grade quality; and (3) sharply increase the Fund's dividend income. Given the limits set by the Fund's now mandatory position of 30 percent to 40 percent of assets in high-grade bonds, the new strategy would require the sale of many of the portfolio's low-yielding growth stocks. Here's how I announced these changes in Wellington Fund's 1978 Annual Report:

> We believe a greater emphasis on current income would
> enhance Wellington Fund's ability to meet the needs of its
> shareholders. Your Board of Directors has approved a change in
> investment approach which will increase the amount of divi-
> dends earned on the Fund's common stock investments. This
> goal should increase the likelihood of a growing dividend, and
> be accomplished without any material sacrifice of "total return"
> potential (income plus capital appreciation).
>
> This strategy does not contemplate any material change in
> the fund's stock/bond ratio (now 68 percent of assets), which
> will continue to represent between 60 percent and 70 percent of
> net assets. (The) additional investment income will be primarily
> generated by orienting portions of our common stock holdings
> to higher yielding issues with dividend growth potential. . . .
> We launched a vigorous program for increasing current income

in the closing months of 1978, and plan to further increase the emphasis on income in 1979.

"Back to Basics"

When I gave these marching orders—especially our insistence in raising the Fund's income dividend by fully 70 percent over the next five years (in fact, the increase was slightly larger than that)—to Wellington Management's next choice to run the Fund's portfolio, the late Vincent Bajakian was not pleased. He believed that growth stocks were the optimal choice, and that the emphasis on higher-yielding stocks would harm performance. Happily for the Fund's shareholders, however, he signed on to the new strategy and implemented it well. The portfolio veered away from growth and toward value, and the Fund's income dividends began a sharp and steady increase.

And as it turned out the actual annual dividends paid by the Fund during 1978–1983 were $.54, $.66, $.75, $.84, $.87, and $.92, astonishingly close to the original dividend projections in my memo—almost to the penny. Relative to Wellington's average net asset value of $12.39 in 1983, that $.92 payment happened to represent a dividend yield of 7.4 percent for the fund. (Those were the long-gone days of generous yields on both bonds and stocks. Today the Fund's yield is 2.5 percent.) This new strategy had obviated the need ever to return to the old (and discredited by experience) "Six Percent Solution."

Wellington Management Does the Job

Portfolio manager Vin Bajakian deserves great credit for adjusting to the new strategy and, by judicious stock selection, making it work so effectively for the Fund's shareholders. His tragic death while flying his own airplane in 1995 could have been a major setback. But Wellington Management chose his partner, investment veteran Ernst von Metzsch, to succeed him and, until his retirement in 2000, he continued to deliver returns under the new strategy that were generally superior to those of his balanced fund peers. Since then, under the management of Ernst's successor, Edward Bousa, Wellington Management has done an outstanding job in continuing to effectively implement the income-oriented equity strategy adopted by the Fund back in 1978.

The Fund's equity managers did their work well. And they were more than ably supported by Wellington's bond managers, who maintained a fixed-income portfolio for which investment-grade quality continued to be the watchword. Paul Sullivan led these professionals during 1972–1995, ably succeeded by Paul Kaplan, and then by John Keogh. The bond managers also share in the credit for the Fund's renaissance.

Wellington's portfolio managers continue to reaffirm the merit of the strategy adopted by the Fund's Board back in 1978. Here's what they wrote to the Fund's shareholders in the 2000 Annual Report

> A reasonable level of current income and long-term growth in capital can be achieved without undue risk by holding 60% to 70% of assets in equities and the balance in fixed income securities. Consistent with this approach, dividend-paying stocks dominate the fund's equity segment.

And in the 2010 Annual Report, manager Edward Bousa wrote:

> We continue to search diligently for attractively valued companies with strong operating characteristics. We are particularly interested in the stocks of companies whose business fundamentals are poised to improve. As always, an above-average dividend is central to our stock selection process.

Clearly, Wellington Management has "signed on" to that strategy. Even better, over the past 35 years, both the strategy and its implementation have met the test of time.

Taking into account the new shares that shareholders received by the reinvestment of the substantial capital gains distributions paid by Wellington since its inception, the Fund's income dividend totaled $0.94 per share in 1966 (see the right-hand column of Appendix IV). By 1977 it had increased only to $0.99, despite a 63 percent rise in the dividend of the S&P 500. When the new income-oriented policy was introduced in 1978, the Fund's dividend income leaped ahead—in 1979 to $1.30, $1.72 in 1982; $1.88 in 1985; and to $2.19 in 1990.

In just twelve years, with the Fund's bond position held constant in the 35 percent range, Wellington shareholders had received a 110 percent increase in dividend income. Despite the decline in interest rates from their peak in 1981, Wellington dividends held fairly steady through 1995, before rising to a then-peak-level of $2.74 in 1999. After a significant decline through 2003, the rise in dividend payments resumed, reaching $2.80 in 2008. Given lower interest rates and the substantial cut in corporate dividends in 2008, earning the dividend of $2.55 in 2011 seems a solid accomplishment. With its new strategy producing higher dividends, vastly improved performance, and careful control of risk, investors swarmed into the fund and it enjoyed an astonishing return to acceptance in the marketplace.

Asset Growth Rebounds

To say that the new strategy worked hardly captures the full extent of the Fund's remarkable rebound from its shriveled asset base. Wellington enjoyed a soaring rise in assets—first, to a new record high of $2.4 billion in 1990, with growth steadily continuing, year after year. As 2012 began, and assets reached an all-time peak of $55 billion, renaissance is hardly too strong a word to describe the change. Appendix IV also presents a tabulation of the fund's net assets, asset value, income dividends, and capital distributions since its 1928 founding.

During the early part of the past quarter-century, the Great Bull Market had been the dominant force shaping the investment world. Despite Wellington Fund's conservatism, the Fund gave a good account of itself relative to its peers in the long upsurge in stock prices through early 2000, and, given its conservative policies, an even better account during the ensuing painful bear markets, one in 2000—2003, the other in 2007—2009. With nice recoveries from both, and the good downside protection that had been our hallmark, Wellington had generated a cumulative 25-year total return of 886 percent during this challenging era, compared to 418 percent for its peers. Since the first bull market peak in 2000, Wellington Fund has actually generated a cumulative positive total return of 90 percent—a remarkable testimonial to the value of a balanced fund, especially in a stock market environment that proved virtually stagnant.

Wellington Fund's record of investment achievement is the result of three factors: (1) its investment policy and strategy, which is determined by *the Fund's* management; (2) the accomplishments of its portfolio managers, who are selected by the Fund's *investment adviser*, subject to the approval of the Fund's directors; and (3) by the substantial advantage that the Fund has enjoyed by operating at costs dramatically lower than its peers. Vanguard controls the contract with the adviser, Wellington

Management Company, which, with Vanguard's approval, names the portfolio manager. The two firms negotiate to establish the fee rates applicable to the Fund's assets. To get the best possible fee structure for Wellington's shareholders, I confess to having been a demanding negotiator. I present the history of the funds cost structure in Box 8.5.

Box 8.5
The Drive for Fair Advisory Fees

When I joined Wellington Management Company in 1951, the Fund's expense ratio of 0.55 percent was already well below the 0.74 percent average ratio of its balanced fund peers, a 19-basis-point annual advantage. A quarter-century later in 1976, the gap was somewhat larger: Wellington 0.56 percent, peer group 0.84 percent, a 28 basis point advantage. Then, as the Fund began to operate under Vanguard's at-cost mutual structure and, even more importantly, as the Fund gained the independence to negotiate at arm's-length the advisory fee rates it paid to Wellington Management Company, our cost advantage accelerated dramatically.

I remember those early negotiations as if they were yesterday. Simply put, prior to Vanguard's ascendancy, the advisory fee scale of 0.50 percent for the management of Wellington's portfolio had been scaled down to 0.25 percent on assets over $120 million—an effective fee rate of 0.35 percent on then-diminished-assets of $700 million in 1974. With Vanguard in charge, rate reductions took place in 1975, 1976, and again in 1978, bringing the advisory fee rate down to 0.16 percent by 1980. Fund assets, which had reached a high of $2 billion in 1965, continued to tumble as cash outflows continued unabated, finally leveling off in the $500–$600 million range during 1978–1984. By 1987, less than a decade later, when assets had risen to $1.3 billion, the effective base rate had been slashed to 0.12 percent.

Then the Fund began to grow at a rapid and sustained rate. Assets crossed $8 billion in 1993, and with no further change in the fee schedule the effective rate dropped to 0.06 percent. By 2005, as assets crossed the $35-billion-mark, the rate dropped by another 50 percent, to 0.03 percent. Yes, three basis points may seem like "small change," but consider that it generated a huge increase in revenue for Wellington Management Company— from $900 *thousand* in 1984 to $12.6 *million* in 2005. (I've excluded from the 2005 total an additional $2 million in incentive fees paid to the adviser, earned only when the Fund's performance exceeds certain market benchmarks.) Yes, when fund assets grow, as Wellington Fund's have, even when advisory fee rates are slashed, fee dollars can soar. And they did.

We negotiated further small reductions in rates in 1983 and 1986, with a final major fee cut in 1995—sort of my "swan song" as Vanguard's leader. Never mind that the effective fee rate had then fallen from 0.13 percent to 0.4 percent; the fees paid to Wellington Management Company had risen from $2.1 million in 1986 to $5.6 million in 1995 as fund assets leaped from $1.1 billion to $12.6 billion, and continued to grow. The table that follows presents the course of these fee negotiations, which are, I'm confident, without precedent in the mutual fund industry. The table also examines the relationship between the Fund's assets, the advisory fee schedule, and the resultant level of rates and fees.

Wellington Fund		
Year	**Advisory Fee Schedules**	**Millions**
1975	Fund Assets $771 million	
	0.445% first	$250
	0.375% next	200
	0.225% next	150
	0.150% next	100
	0.100% over	700
	Adv. Fee Ratio	0.311%
	Fee	**$2.36**

(Continued)

Wellington Fund		
Year	**Advisory Fee Schedules**	**Millions**
1976	Fund Assets $811 million	
	0.320% first	$250
	0.250% next	200
	0.150% next	150
	0.100% over	600
	Adv. Fee Ratio	0.293%
	Fee	**$2.39**
1978	Fund Assets $642 million	
	0.200% first	$100
	0.175% next	100
	0.150% next	500
	0.100% over	700
	Adv. Fee Ratio	0.192%
	Fee	**$1.31**
1983	Fund Assets $617 million	
	0.175% first	$100
	0.150% over	100
	Adv. Fee Ratio	0.160%
	Fee	**$0.98**
1986	Fund Assets $1,102 million	
	0.150% first	$500
	0.125% next	500
	0.075% next	1,000
	0.005% over	2,000
	Adv. Fee Ratio	0.151%
	Fee	**$1.49**
1995	Fund Assets $12,333 million	
	0.100% first	$1,000
	0.050% next	2,000
	0.040% next	7,000
	0.030% over	10,000
	Adv. Fee Ratio	0.051%
	Fee	**$5.26**

In 2005, with Fund assets now more than $38 billion, the board approved an increase in the base fee schedule, lifting the Fund's effective fee rate from 0.033 percent to 0.043 percent, an increase of 33 percent. I have no idea why or how that fee change occurred, for I was no longer serving on the Wellington Fund board. By 2011, the rate had doubled to 0.068 percent. Those extra three-plus basis points in seven years may seem insignificant. But those few basis points more than tripled the fees paid to Wellington Management Company from $12.6 million in 2005 to $38 million in 2011. Incentive fees added $1.3 million, bringing the total fee for the year to almost $40 million. Had the 2005 schedule remained in place, the fees paid to Wellington Management would have totaled just $18 million—less than half as much. While Wellington Fund's assets had grown by 67 percent—from $39 billion to $55 billion—the advisory fee paid by the Fund had grown by 200 percent above its level just six years earlier.

Unlike our earlier negotiations with Wellington Management Company, the Wellington Fund board "did not consider the profitability of the adviser in providing its services to the fund," according to the 2005 annual report. The huge fee increase was never submitted to the Fund's shareholders for approval— although, under an exception to the Investment Company Act specifically granted to Vanguard in 1993, such approval is neither required nor prohibited. (I accept responsibility for proposing that exemption.) I simply do not know the rationale for either of those Board decisions.

In all, with the Fund's assets now at $55 billion, the advisory fee *rate* has returned to its level of 1991, when Fund assets were less than $4 billion. But the *dollar amount* of the fee has risen 15-fold from $2.6 million to $38 million. My determination had always been to drive for advisory fees that were fair both to Vanguard fund shareholders and to our external advisers.

(Continued)

So I can't help but wonder, why *any* increase in rates would be paid by Wellington Fund shareholders, in the face of the huge dollar increases that these rates generate as the Fund grows.

I wasn't a participant in the recent negotiations, and I have no intention to criticize the Fund directors' decision to raise fee rates even as Wellington's assets were soaring, and generating even higher fee dollars. (Of course, the board has information that I'm not privy to.) Nonetheless, the apparent change in approach to advisory fee negotiations represents a reversal of almost four decades of reductions. For historical perspective, this table summarizes the appropriate data. (Data for the full 1975–2011 period are presented in Appendix VI.)

Wellington Fund Annual Expenses and Advisory Fees— Selected Years

	Total Net Assets $000	Expense Ratio	Advisory Fee Rate	Total Expenses $000	Investment Advisory Basic Fee	Investment Advisory Fee* $000
1966	$1,849,140	0.38%	0.252%	$7,287	$4,838	$4,838
1970	1,322,562	0.47	0.251	6,127	3,277	3,277
1977	704,128	0.48	0.276	3,682	2,115	2,115
1979	608,787	0.54	0.149	3,482	959	1,008
1984	604,359	0.59	0.153	3,529	917	1,029
1990	2,317,074	0.43	0.102	9,343	2,224	1,961
1996	16,505,373	0.31	0.043	43,298	6,042	6,121
2005	38,576,351	0.24	0.033	92,211	12,623	14,567
2011	54,790,055	0.23	0.068	126,950	38,030	39,413

SOURCE: Wellington Fund Annual Reports.
*Includes any incentive fees.

It is not easy to change the mutual fund industry's (self-interested) focus on fee rates rather than dollars. This focus goes back to the 1920s, when rates were reasonable and dollars modest. But the idea that a trustee might offer his investment services at 1 percent of assets to an individual investor with trust assets of $1 million—or $10 million—should be utterly irrelevant when the client is a mutual fund with assets of $1 billion—or $10 billion, or even $100 billion. (Magellan Fund's size when Fidelity Management was charging 0.75 percent.) Indeed, as I noted earlier, I couldn't even persuade the justices of the U.S. Supreme Court that the distinction between *actual fees paid* and *fee rates* was critical to evaluating advisory fee contracts. I hope that mutual fund directors everywhere will come to make the critical distinction between *rates* and *dollars*, for it is the fund shareholders who pay the bills.

Part IV

Strategy + Implementation − Costs = Superior Returns

Together, the combination of fund strategy, management tactics, and minimal cost has led to growth in each $1,000 invested when Wellington began operations in mid-1929 to an accumulation of $650,000 over the subsequent 83 years (through early 2012), compared to $440,000 for the average balanced fund—the magic of long-term compounding writ large. However, to use another favorite metaphor of mine: The long-term *magic* of compounding *returns* is all-too-often overwhelmed by the long-term *tyranny* of compounding *costs*. *Costs matter!* Wellington Fund, uniquely among its peers, has minimized the impact of the tyranny of costs, and its shareholders have prospered from the eternal magic of compounding returns.

Unarguably, it has been Wellington Fund's substantial cost advantage vis-à-vis its peers that has been the powerful mainspring of its comparative advantage—its superior record. It is those minimal costs—the significant margin of cost advantage that Wellington has earned over its balanced fund peers—that have enabled the Fund's cumulative return to explode

Exhibit 8.4   Wellington Long-Term Performance Tops Its Peers: Annual Returns, 1929–2012

	Gross Returns before Costs	Expense Ratio	Net Returns after Costs
Wellington Fund	8.78%	0.56%	8.22%
Average Balanced Fund	8.68	0.96	7.72
Wellington Advantage	+0.10%	−0.40%	+0.50%

over an 83-year span. In fact, as Exhibit 8.4 shows, the lion's share of Wellington's 50 basis-point edge over its peers in annual returns has resulted from this huge cost advantage of 40 basis points, with the other 10 basis points—encompassing both the Fund's good times and the bad— added by strategy and superior investment selection.

I should note that without the havoc wrought by the fund's foray into speculation in 1967–1978, Wellington Fund's average annual return during its two long eras of focus on investment would have totaled 9.01 percent, compared to 7.96 percent for its peers, an advantage of 1.05 percentage points per year, double the 0.50 percentage point positive margin shown in Exhibit 8.4.

Despite the recent increase in advisory fees described earlier, Wellington Fund's total expense ratio had declined from 34 basis points in 2003 to just 0.23 percent by 2011, largely because Vanguard's considerable economies of scale drove the Fund's operating costs down from 29 basis points in 2003 to 16 basis points in 2011. On the other hand, the expense ratio of the average balanced fund during that period, has gone *up* almost as fast as Wellington's has gone down, rising to a staggering 1.34 percent last year.

Result: Wellington Fund now enjoys *a* truly awesome *annual* edge of 100-plus basis points—*solely because of its low costs*—an advantage of one full percentage point per year in extra return. Over its long history, with Wellington's expense ratio averaging just 0.50 percentage points versus 0.96 percentage points for its peers, today's extra advantage at double that historical spread should auger well for the Fund's investment edge in the years ahead. *Yes, costs matter.*

I'm certain that Walter Morgan would be pleased—indeed, delighted—with the renaissance of his beloved Wellington Fund. His vision has been fully realized. Such an outcome would not have seemed very likely 40 years ago, when the traditions he had established were ignored. But a return to sound balance in asset allocation, and a renewed focus on the Fund's objectives of conservation of capital, reasonable current income, and profits without undue risk—originally stated way back in the 1930s—saved the day. Let all of us investors—and our institutional money managers too—remember this history, learn from it, celebrate it, and above all, honor it.

Wellington Fund's 100th anniversary in 2028 now lies just beyond the horizon, a time to celebrate reaching that mark with a strategy that is true to Wellington's traditional conservative principles and investment values. There may be—there will be!—bumps along the way, even severe ones, just as we have witnessed over past decades. But I have no doubt whatsoever that Wellington Fund will reach that 100th anniversary milestone, so rarely achieved among our nation's business corporations and financial institutions. When we reach that coveted anniversary, it will represent both a ringing endorsement of Walter Morgan's vision and the triumph—I reiterate—of the wisdom of long-term investment over the folly of short-term speculation.

Chapter 9

Ten Simple Rules for Investors and a Warning for Speculators

Many shall be restored that are now fallen and many shall fall that are now in honor.

—*Horace*[1]

Summing Up

In the course of this book, I've taken you through the hazards created in our financial system when short-term speculation takes precedence over long-term investment. When a value-destroying culture of salesmanship overwhelms a value-enhancing culture of stewardship, of course there's a clash. I've illustrated the problem that speculation engenders by describing its impact on today's financial environment and on our society at large, driven by our complicated new double-agency society in which a

---

[1]Benjamin Graham used this same quotation from *Ars Poetica* in the first edition of *The Intelligent Investor* in 1949.

powerful symbiotic relationship had developed between corporate executives and institutional money managers. It is high time that we challenge this happy conspiracy that focuses on short-term stock returns over long-term intrinsic values.

The solutions to these formidable problems begin with the development of a statutory federal standard of fiduciary duty outlined in Chapter 3. While I'm disinclined to advocate for further regulations that are detailed and precise, the present application of standards of fiduciary duty that have been on the books for decades has been weak, if not nonexistent. It's time to make it express and clear: *the agent has a duty to put the interests of his principal before his own interests.* (The Investment Company Act and the Investment Advisers Act, both enacted in 1940, establish this noble principle, but it's yet to be enforced.)

Until our government takes action—no mean challenge as long as our Congress is characterized by our intransigent, deadlocked, shockingly self-interested, parochial, and money-driven elected representatives— investors will have to look after their own interests. I have earlier explored how mutual fund investors can do so more effectively by seeking out funds that already measure up to essential fiduciary principles, presenting in Chapter 5 a "stewardship quotient" checklist that investors can use to establish guidelines for their selection of a mutual fund family, and choosing among the mutual funds it supervises.

Buy Broad Market Index Funds

Another major positive step is focusing on index funds as the core of your portfolio. Owning an index fund is simply a decision to buy and hold a diversified portfolio of stocks representing the entire stock market, both U.S. and possibly non-U.S. companies. Such an index fund is the paradigm of long-term investing, and the antithesis of short-term speculation. That was my concept when I created the first index mutual fund way back in 1975, and the growth of indexing over the past 37 years has attested to its soundness—and then some!—over the decades that followed.

But the inherent validity of broad market indexing represented by the traditional index fund (TIF) and its success in serving fund investors—as well as in the marketplace—have paved the way for a new and different kind of index fund—the exchange-traded fund (ETF)—notable for huge turnover of its shares and short-term investor focus (ironically, on long-term investment portfolios), which I describe as speculation. The vast majority of ETFs have high trading volumes day after day, and there are a plethora of ETFs that invest in narrow market segments: ETFs using new and unproven "beat-the-index" strategies, and now explicitly actively-managed ETFs; ETFs trading in currencies and commodities; and ETFs with high leverage. (They typically claim to triple the stock market return, up or down. Take your choice!) Consistent with the broad trends discussed earlier in this book, speculation has come to seriously challenge the original investment concept of the index fund—the total-stock-market-based fund, designed to be bought and held, well, forever.

Wellington Fund and the Index Fund

In the previous chapter on the history of the Wellington Fund, I've also shown that the clash of the cultures is anything but theoretical. It's a real-world chronicle that describes the impact on individual investors in the Fund as it moved from one culture to the other, and then came home again. Wellington's rise from 1928 to 1966 succeeded because it focused on long-term investment. When the Fund turned its focus to speculation in 1966, it was soon hit by the 1973–1974 market crash and experienced a dramatic decline in returns. Its renaissance began in 1978, when it went "back to the future," and returned to its original focus on investment, establishing firm guidelines on the balance between dividend-paying stocks and investment-grade bonds. That change worked wonders, and Wellington Fund has now reclaimed its status as the world's largest balanced fund.

My conviction remains that broad market indexing in stocks and bonds is the only sure way for you to capture your fair share of the returns of the stock market and/or the bond market. But the renaissance of the actively managed Wellington Fund provides some important lessons. Consider the ingredients of success:

• A long-term investment policy, focused on a broadly diversified portfolio of high-quality stocks and bonds and low portfolio turn-over, is essential.

- Clarity of investment strategy and dividend policy must be shared by fund directors (acting on behalf of fund shareholders), understood by the fund's investment adviser, and overseen by the fund's executives.
- Mutual understanding by both fund directors and the managers of the adviser that it is absolutely essential for advisory fees and other fund costs to be held to the bare-bones minimum.

As you review these standards for a successful actively managed fund, you probably observe how close they come to the standards for passively managed index funds: long-term focus, clarity of strategy, wide diversification, rigid rules for portfolio selection, and, yes, minimal costs.[2]

No less an investment icon than Jeremy Grantham, a founder and principal of institutional money manager GMO, echoes my conclusion about both indexing and active management in his fourth quarter 2011 letter to shareholders.

> To be at all effective investing as an individual, it is utterly imperative that you know your limitations as well as your strengths and weaknesses. If you can be patient and ignore the crowd, you will likely win. But to *imagine* you can, and to then adopt a flawed approach that allows you to be seduced or intimidated by the crowd into jumping in late or getting out early is to guarantee a pure disaster. You must know your pain and patience thresholds accurately and not play over your head.
>
> If you cannot resist temptation, you absolutely must not manage your own money. There are no Investors Anonymous meetings to attend. There are, though, two perfectly reasonable alternatives: either (1) hire a manager who has those skills—remembering that it's even harder for professionals to stay aloof from the crowd—or (2) pick a sensible, globally diversified index of stocks and bonds, put your money in, and try never to

---

[2]In fact, Wellington Fund shares nearly all of the performance characteristics of a balanced *index* fund holding a portfolio consisting of 65 percent of assets in the total stock market index and 35 percent in the total bond market index. The correlation of returns between Wellington and the balanced index over the past decade is a powerful 98 percent. (100 percent would mean perfect correlation.)

look at it again until you retire. Even then, look only to see how much money you can prudently take out.

Reversion to the Mean (RTM) is a Virtual Certainty

Time and again, I have tried to drive home to investors the need to select prudent stewards to manage their funds, and to rely heavily on low-cost market index funds as the core (or even 100 percent) of their portfolios. Yet too many investors believe that "it's easy to find funds that have done better, and I know how to do it," or, "it's easy to beat the market, so why settle for boring mediocrity." They don't realize how much better off they would be with the boring mediocrity that index funds offer. Sadly, when investors try to beat the market, they select funds that have done well in the past, with the expectation, or at least the hope, that the past will be prologue to the future.

But in the world of investing, the past is rarely, if ever, prologue. All throughout the modern history of the mutual fund industry, investors have been all too willing to "bet on the wrong horse." This behavior, alas, has been formulated and encouraged by too many fund sponsors focused on salesmanship of the latest "hot new idea." It began with "Go-Go" funds in the mid-1960s, and continued with the "Information Age" boom in technology funds and dot-com funds during the late 1990s.

It remains to be seen whether the boom in gold funds and emerging market funds in recent years, or the excitement of using funds to trade "all day long, in real time" that is reflected in so many of today's ETFs will result in the same unhappy outcome for fund owners. But history tells us that is exactly what has happened in the past. Experience shows that fund speculators who hopped on the bandwagon of "hot" performance have lost tens of billions of dollars by their counterproductive behavior. Logic and common sense tell us that the same patterns will recur in the future.

Let me be specific. On the next few pages, I present eight examples of how some of the top-performing funds of the past succeeded in achieving market-beating returns—often over long periods—but finally faltered: Reversion to the mean (RTM) writ large. Paraphrasing economist Herbert Stein, former head of the Council of Economic Advisers in both the Nixon and Ford administrations, "If something can't go on forever, it will stop."

Nothing Is Forever: Eight Sobering Examples of Reversion to the Mean

The "telltale charts" that follow present the past investment perfor-mance of some of the most successful funds of the industry's modern history. They are devised simply by dividing the cumulative return of each fund into the return of the broad stock market (in this case, the S&P 500). The line begins at 1.00. As it rises, the fund is outperforming the market. As it falls, the fund is underperforming. The funds presented in this analysis include many of the funds that are more prominent examples of the pervasive presence of RTM.

CGM Focus Fund (1998–2012)
Cumulative Return vs. S&P 500

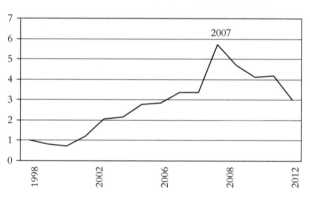

CGM Focus Fund is the classic short-term RTM fund. . . . Sole portfolio manager, Ken Heebner. . . . Assets grew from $100 million at start to $6 billion in 2007, only to tumble to $1.7 billion by 2012. . . . Fund return in 1998–2007, +917 percent; S&P 500 return, +78 percent; Great! . . . Then the music stops. . . . Fund return in 2007–2011 –51 percent, S&P 500 –6 percent. . . . Fund annual return for full period, 12.2 percent. . . . With a return of more than 18 percent per year, the Fund was the best performing U.S. stock fund of the decade. However, "the typical shareholder lost 11% annually." (*The Wall Street Journal*, December 31, 2009.)

Fidelity Magellan Fund (1981–2012)
Cumulative Return vs. S&P 500

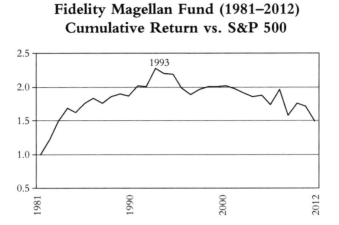

Fidelity Magellan Fund is the classic long-term RTM fund. . . . Offered publicly in 1980, following annual returns averaging 22 percent as a Fidelity "in-house" fund since 1964. . . . Managed by stock-picking legend Peter Lynch until 1990, with 588 percent return versus 268 percent for S&P 500. . . . In 1990 assets of $12 billion, rose to $106 billion in 1999. . . . Return 1990–2011, 368 percent; S&P 500 487 percent. . . . In 2012 assets of $15 billion, down 85 percent from high of $105. . . . Fund annual return has lagged S&P since 1983— 19 years. . . . Fund 9.7 percent, S&P 10.2 percent (for more detail, see Exhibit 5.5).

Janus Fund (1971–2012)
Cumulative Return vs. S&P 500

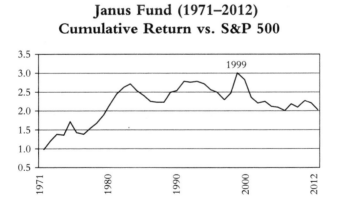

Janus Fund made its mark as one of the "hottest" funds of the Information Age bubble of the late 1990s. . . . An 18.5 percent annual return for 1971–1999. . . . Assets up from $400 million in 1998 to

$43 billion as 2000 began. . . . Investors jump on the bandwagon. . . . Becomes principal buyer of large-cap tech stocks. . . . Subsequent cumulative return −28 percent, with S&P 500 up 7 percent. . . . Investors depart in droves. . . . In 2012 assets $7.5 billion, off 82 percent from peak. . . . Since 1983, Fund annual return 9.6 percent, S&P 500 10.6 percent.

Legg Mason Value Trust Fund (1982–2012) Cumulative Return vs. S&P 500

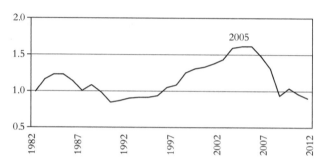

Legg Mason Value Trust Fund was managed by investment pro Bill Miller from inception through early 2012 . . . only portfolio manager in fund industry history to outpace S&P 500 for 15 consecutive years (1991–2005 inclusive). . . . Assets soar from $600 million to $20 billion. . . . In 2006–2008, Fund cumulative return −56 percent loss compared to −22 percent for S&P 500. . . . Assets collapse to $2.5 billion. . . . Over entire history, Fund almost matches the market; annual return of 10.3 percent versus 10.6 percent for S&P 500.

PBHG Growth Fund (1986–2004) Cumulative Return vs. S&P 500

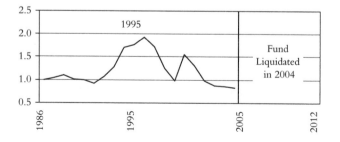

PGHG Growth Fund was run since inception in 1986 by Pilgrim Baxter's Gary Pilgrim. . . . When fund assets only $180 million in 1993 and turnover of 200 percent, validity of performance hard to establish. . . . As 671 percent cumulative return soars above S&P 500s 300 percent in 1988–1996, assets leap to $6 billion. . . . RTM strikes in 1996–1998, with a cumulative return of 6 percent versus 64 percent for S&P. . . . Even a monster (reported) gain of 92 percent in 1999 doesn't stem the tide. . . . In 2000–2003, Fund return of −56 percent far exceeds S&P 500s −20 percent drop. . . . In 2003 Pilgrim and partner Harold Bradley settle charges of fraud and breach of fiduciary duty brought by the SEC. . . . When assets shrink to $800 million in 2004, Fund ceases operation.

T. Rowe Price Growth Stock (1951–2012) Cumulative Return vs. S&P 500

T. Rowe Price Growth Fund is a classic growth fund managed by a classy organization, but couldn't avoid the ravages of RTM. . . . Started in 1950 by (yet another) investment legend, T. Rowe Price, by 1971 the fund's cumulative investment return of +1648 percent surpasses the S&P 500 return of +1021 percent by more than 600 percentage points. . . . Assets soar to $1.2 billion—first no-load fund to reach the $1 billion milestone . . . RTM then begins. . . . Huge shortfall in 1971–1988— fund +172 percent, S&P 500 +470 percent. . . . Since then, Fund reverts almost precisely to the market mean. . . . Fund lifetime annual return +9.5 percent versus +9.2 percent for S&P 500. . . . A fund's long-term return can't be too much closer to the market mean than that!

Vanguard Windsor Fund (1959–2012)
Cumulative Return vs. S&P 500

Vanguard Windsor Fund was Wellington Management's first equity fund. . . . Formation makes headlines in 1958. . . . A rare mutual fund that has made it through more than a half-century with objectives essentially intact. . . . A 7 percent annual return lagged the 10 percent return of the S&P 500 during 1958–1963. . . . Yet another legendary investor, John B. Neff, becomes the Fund's manager. . . . Returns soared through 1988 . . . with $4 billion of assets in 1985, became the industry's largest equity fund. . . . Then closed to new investors to avoid handicap of excessive assets. . . . With remarkable 31-year annual return of 14 percent versus 11 percent for S&P 500, Neff retires in 1995. . . . Assets grow to $21 billion in 1997, even as performance falters badly in 1997–1999, only to recover nicely in 1999–2000. . . . Assets dwindle to $12 billion in 2012. . . . Post-Neff annual returns: Fund 6.5 percent; S&P 500 6.5 percent. . . . Inferior returns turn to superior; then back to inferior; then average. Yet again, RTM strikes.

Vanguard U.S. Growth Fund (1960–2012)
Cumulative Return vs. S&P 500

Vanguard U.S. Growth Fund began in 1958 as Ivest Fund. . . . Wellington Management acquires its manager in 1966. . . . Cumulative return during 1961–1967 best in the entire mutual fund industry; 327 percent versus 108 percent for the S&P 500. . . . Pummeled in the 1973–1974 crash: −55 percent versus −35 percent for the S&P 500. Pedestrian recovery. . . . Cumulative return 1960–1976: Fund 238 percent; S&P 218 percent. RTM strikes again. . . . Name changed to Vanguard Growth Fund in 1980, then became a separate U.S. Growth portfolio. . . . New manager in 1987. . . . Fund and S&P 500 both rise 18 percent per year in 1987–1999. . . . Then fund falters again in 1999–2012. . . . Fund return −45 percent versus +7 percent for the S&P 500. From first in 1967 to worst in 2003.

Box 9.1
If You Pick Actively Managed Funds . . . The "Four Ps" in Evaluating Fund Managers

P + P + P + P (+ P)

Picking past fund winners—especially funds with outsized gains in short periods—has almost always proved to be a loser's game. So on what else can the investor who prefers actively managed funds to passively managed index funds rely? How can a motivated investor increase the odds of selecting a competent manager?

Way back in 1984, when Vanguard was seeking an active manager for a new growth fund, I faced this very question. We evaluated, and then hired, the young PRIMECAP Management Company, run by former portfolio counselors at the American Funds group, and agreed to use their firm's name for the new fund. In Vanguard PRIMECAP Fund's 1985 annual report, I explained our decision to shareholders, measuring the manager against a standard that I called "the four P's." Here are the four key questions I asked, and excerpts from my answers:

(Continued)

1. **People.** Who are the managers of the fund? "The people of PRIMECAP are outstanding investment professionals with a sterling reputation, who have, collectively, some 85 years of experience."

2. **Philosophy.** What are they seeking to accomplish? "The implementation of an investment philosophy with a growth orientation." (I also loved the managers' low portfolio turnover, reflecting their focus on the long term.)

3. **Portfolio.** How do they go about implementing their philosophy? "The pension portfolios managed by PRIMECAP include a mix of blue-chip stocks, some with a growth orientation; some with generous yields; companies deemed subject of takeover bids, and stocks in businesses deemed interest-sensitive."

4. **Performance.** What has their record been? I emphasized that "past performance wasn't the first criterion, but the last. Important, yes, but only in the context of the other three factors."

How did it all work out? At the end of the fund's first full year, as I reported to shareholders, PRIMECAP had outpaced 151 of the industry's 171 growth funds. A good start indeed, for a record, viewed in retrospect 26 years later, that began one of the highest-achieving—and most consistent—funds in Vanguard's history. Among the 94 growth funds that survived the quarter-century-plus-period, the Fund outpaced 89 of them. This record is a special tribute to Howard Schow, cofounder of the firm, who died at age 85 in early 2012. He deserves our salute and a hearty "thank you and bless you" from shareholders for the long partnership we enjoyed.[3]

---

[3]It was not all peaches and cream. In 1987 through 1990, the fund's return of 32 percent lagged the S&P 500's return of 57 percent, with later lags in 1996–1997, and again in 2010–2011. But the overall extraordinary annual return of 12.9 percent vs. 10.4 percent for the S&P speaks for itself.

Morningstar Ratings

In 2011, my "four P's" were eerily echoed by a new set of Analyst Ratings produced by Morningstar, the respected fund analysis organization. "Our (new) ratings (Gold, Silver, Bronze, Neutral, and Negative) reflect a synthesis of each fund's fundamentals, (grouped) into five pillars: People, Process, Parent, Performance, and Price." The first four "Ps" Morningstar listed were virtually reiterations of my own scorecard of a quarter-century earlier. (Simply because Vanguard had completed a tough negotiation on fees with the adviser leading to an extremely attractive scaled-down fee schedule, I hadn't mentioned that "fifth P"—"Price"—in my PRIMECAP Annual Report letter. So now we have *five* Ps.) A few excerpts from Morningstar's standards:

1. **People.** We think about what advantages they have over their peers along the lines of expertise, experience, and demonstrated skill, and assess how much a manager has invested in the fund; to assess firm-wide expertise; how much experience, and whether there's turmoil or stability in the ranks.

2. **Process.** Is the manager doing something that anyone can do or doing things that are hard to replicate? Is the strategy a proven one or a new, untested formula? Just as important is how well the process is matched to the manager and firm's skill set.

3. **Parent.** When you invest for the long haul, you realize just how important the company behind the fund is. We look at manager turnover at the firm, the investment culture, quality of research, ethics, directors, SEC sanctions, and more. . . . You want a partner you can trust for many years to come.

4. **Performance.** We focus on performance under the current manager. The longer the record, the more predictive of future relative performance. We care about the strategy and

(Continued)

> holdings, and how a fund has performed in different market environments, its risk profile, and consistency of returns over time.
>
> **5. Price.** Costs are a good predictor of future performance. They aren't everything, but they are a crucial piece in the puzzle. We look at a fund's expenses relative to its peer group, asset size and in some cases its trading costs.

The echoes of my "4 Ps" (really 5) and Morningstar's "5 Ps" continue to resonate. These touchpoints are sound, and can be helpful to investors selecting active fund managers. Following similar guidelines should provide investors the best opportunity to earn optimal returns on the actively managed funds in your portfolio, albeit with long odds *against* surpassing the after-cost, after-tax returns of an all-market index fund. Now, let's cut to the chase, and consider 10 rules for long-term investment in equity mutual funds, rules that ignore the noise created by short-term speculation.

Ten Simple Rules for Investment Success

The 10 elements of a simple strategy that follow should help you decide your optimal course of action for the years ahead. I wish I could assure you that the investment strategy outlined below is the best strategy ever devised. Alas, I can't promise that. But I can assure you that the number of strategies that are worse is infinite.

1. Remember Reversion to the Mean
2. Time Is Your Friend, Impulse Is Your Enemy
3. Buy Right and Hold Tight
4. Have Realistic Expectations: The Bagel and the Doughnut
5. Forget the Needle, Buy the Haystack
6. Minimize the Croupier's Take
7. There's No Escaping Risk

8. Beware of Fighting the Last War
9. The Hedgehog Bests the Fox
10. Stay the Course!

Rule 1: Remember Reversion to the Mean

After what I've focused on earlier in this chapter, it will not surprise you that "Remember RTM" is the first of these 10 rules. The message is that selecting your fund for tomorrow by picking a winner from yesterday is an exercise fraught with peril. No, the past is not prologue. This RTM concept applies not only to fund managers, but to fund objectives. Yesterday's growth fund leadership is often tomorrow's value fund leadership. The same is true with large-cap funds and small-cap, and with U.S. stocks and non-U.S. stocks.

RTM is also true of the stock market itself. Simply because of dividend yields and earnings growth, the fundamental value of stocks is highly likely to increase over time. But when stock market returns substantially exceed the investment returns generated by dividends and earnings during one era, the market tends to first revert to and then fall well short of that norm during the next era. Like a pendulum, stock

Exhibit 9.1   Stock Market Returns Revert to Fundamental Returns. Rolling 25-Year Periods, 1896–2011

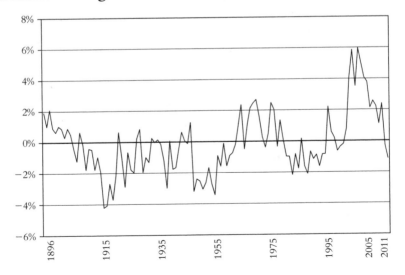

prices swing far above their underlying values, only to swing back to fair value and then far below it, and then converge again. When returns in the stock market get way ahead of the fundamentals—or way behind—RTM will strike again, sooner or later.

This illuminating chart makes it clear—admittedly, in retrospect—how attractive stock prices were before the great bull markets of 1954–1973 and 1977–1999, and how unattractive stock prices had become in the late 1990s. Only time will tell whether those patterns will repeat in the decades to come, but I am highly confident that this lesson of history—repeated over and over again in the past—will prevail. Finally, long-term value, not short-term price, rules the world, simply reinforcing the classic Graham principle about the voting machine and the weighing machine.

Rule 2: Time Is Your Friend, Impulse Is Your Enemy

Never forget that time is your friend. Take advantage of it, and enjoy the miracle that is compound interest. If, over the next 25 years, stocks produce an 8 percent return and a savings account produces a 2 percent return (in mid-2012, both are fairly aggressive numbers), $10,000 would grow by $58,500 in stocks versus $6,500 in savings. (After 2 percent inflation, $33,000 versus zero in real spendable dollars.) Give yourself all the time you can, and never forget the risk of inflation.

Impulse is your enemy. Realize that one of the greatest sins of investing is to be captivated by the siren song of the market, which can lure you into buying stocks when they are soaring and into selling stocks when they are plunging. Impulses like these can destroy even the best of portfolios. Why? Because market timing is impossible. Even if you turn out to be right when you sell stocks just before a decline (a rare occurrence!), where on earth would you ever get the insight that tells you the right time to get back in? One correct decision is tough enough. Two correct decisions in a row are nigh on impossible. And a dozen correct decisions over your investment lifetime is unimaginable.

When you think long term, you'll be less likely to allow transitory changes in stock prices to alter your investment program. There is a lot of noise in the moment-by-moment volatility of the stock market, which too often is, as Shakespeare wrote in a different context, "a tale told by an idiot, full of sound and fury, signifying nothing." If you allow your impulses to take over your rational expectations, of course impulse is your enemy.

Rule 3: Buy Right and Hold Tight

The next critical decision you face is getting the proper allocation of assets in your investment portfolio. Stocks are designed to provide growth of capital and growth of income, while bonds are for conservation of capital and current income. Once you get your balance right, then just hold tight, no matter how high a greedy stock market flies, nor how low a frightened market plunges. Change the allocation only as your investment profile changes. Begin by considering a 50/50 stock/bond balance, and then raise the stock allocation if:

- You have many years remaining to accumulate wealth.
- The amount of capital you have at stake is modest (for example, when you make your first investment in a thrift plan or an IRA).
- You have little need for current income.
- You have the courage to ride out booms and busts with reasonable equanimity.

As you age, *lower* your stock allocation accordingly. You have fewer years remaining to build your retirement; you likely have much more wealth; you'll soon need to spend your investment income rather than reinvest it; and (if you're like me) you're not quite so relaxed about violent market volatility. But, in your asset allocation, don't forget to include as a bond-like component of your wealth the value of any future pension and Social Security payments you expect to receive.

Rule 4: Have Realistic Expectations: The Bagel and the Doughnut

These two different kinds of baked goods—the bagel and the doughnut—symbolize the two distinctively different elements of stock market returns. It is hardly farfetched to consider that the bagel of the stock market is *investment* return—dividend yields plus earnings growth. The investment return on stocks reflects the bagel's underlying character: nutritious, crusty, and hard-boiled.

By the same token, the spongy doughnut of the market is *speculative* return wrought by any material change in the price that investors are willing to pay for each dollar of earnings. When public opinion about stock valuations changes from the soft sweetness of optimism to the acid sourness of pessimism and vice versa, that's evidence that the doughnut's essence has taken charge. While the substantive bagel-like economics of investing are almost inevitably productive, the flaky, doughnut-like emotions of investors are anything but steady. Indeed, as noted in Rule 2, these emotions are almost always counterproductive.

In the long run, it is investment return that rules the day. In the past 40 years, the annual investment return was 9 percent, almost precisely equal to the stock market's total return of 9.3 percent. The speculative return on stocks was just 0.3 percent. In both the first and last of those decades, as I noted in Chapter 2, investors soured on the economy's prospects, and tumbling price-earnings ratios provided a negative annual speculative return averaging −5.3 percent, reducing a solid annual investment return of 7.7 percent to a market return of just 2.4 percent. In the 1980s and 1990s, on the other hand, the outlook sweetened, and a soaring P/E ratio produced a sugary 7.4 percent annual speculative boost to an investment return of 10.1 percent. Result: an unprecedented total return on stocks averaging 17.5 percent per year during two consecutive decades.

Combining all four decades, the stock market return has averaged 9.3 percent annually, totally dominated by the 9 percent investment return, very close to the 100-year average of 9.0 percent. (Talk about the power of RTM!) The lesson: Enjoy the bagel's healthy nutrients, and don't expect the doughnut's sweetness either to enhance them or its sourness to erode them over the long run.

What does the future hold? Of course we can't be certain. But reasonable expectations for stocks suggest an annual return of about 7.5 percent for stocks and 3.5 percent for bonds in the decade that began on January 1, 2012. In Box 9.2, I explain where those numbers come from.

Box 9.2

Reasonable Investment Expectations
for the Coming Decade

Relying on the *sources* of market returns has proved in the past to be an exceptional way to establish reasonable expectations for the future returns on stocks. The initial dividend yield at the start of the decade is already a known factor, and corporate earnings are more likely than not to grow at a rate related to the growth of our nation's GDP.

While the level of the price-earnings multiple a decade hence can hardly be known in advance, we know more than we think. For RTM comes heavily into play once again. When the P/E was below 12 at the start of a past decade, it was highly likely (90 percent probability) to rise by its conclusion. If the P/E was above 18, it was highly likely (80 percent probability) to decline over the decade.

So let's look at what we might expect in the decade beginning in early 2012. The dividend yield on the S&P 500 is 2.1 percent. Annual earnings growth in the range of 5 to 6 percent (perhaps a bit less) seems a reasonable likelihood. Result: a possible *investment* return averaging 7 to 8 percent per year.

With outstanding earnings in 2011, the P/E now stands at around 16, close to the long-term historical average. I don't expect that P/E to be a lot different when 2022 begins. Result: a *speculative* return of zero, more or less. Combining the two sources, reasonable expectations suggest an annual *total stock market* return in the range of 6 to 9 percent during the coming decade.

A few words about bond returns. The interest rate at the beginning of a given decade has proved to be an exceptionally reliable basis for establishing reasonable expectations for the decade that follows. The entire source of the fundamental return over any subsequent decade has been the interest rate at the

(Continued)

outset. Assuming a bond portfolio composed of one-third U.S. Treasuries and agencies and two-thirds investment grade corporate bonds, with a combined average maturity of 10 to 12 years, you could expect a *fundamental* return near today's yield of around 3 percent. If held for the full 10 years, the final value of the bond portfolio is likely to center on its initial par value (assumed to be 100). So there should be no significant *speculative* return (positive or negative) affecting the calculation, and income will call the tune. Result: an annual *total return* on bonds of 2 percent to 4 percent.

Over the coming decade, that difference between stocks and bonds matters. If stocks return 7 percent, capital would increase by almost 100 percent. If bonds return 3.0 percent, capital would rise by about 35 percent. For a 60/40 balanced portfolio earning 6 percent, the increase would be about 70 percent.

CAUTION: These numbers reflect *nominal* returns. Should inflation average 2.5 percent annually, the return on the balanced portfolio would decline from 5.4 percent to about 3 percent before investment expenses. Should those all-in costs come to 2 percent—a typical number for mutual funds—only 1 percent would remain for the investor. That's largely why index funds (0.1 percent cost) are such a reasonable option.

All of these figures are merely my rational expectations. While I can easily guarantee an uneven path for such a balanced stock/bond portfolio along the way, I can't guarantee the final outcome. For in mid-2012, economic and market conditions together constitute as challenging a combination as I have seen at any time during my 61 years in finance (a milestone I reached on July 7, 2012).

Economic conditions in the U.S. and around the globe are, bluntly put, threatening. The battle has been joined between Keynesians demanding that governments borrow and spend to increase aggregate demand for goods and services, and Hayek-ites (disciples of the Austrian School of Economics) calling for fiscal austerity. It's premature to guess how a compromise might be reached. For the political will to save both the Euro from fragmenting and the dollar from inflation by taking strong action to redirect our nation's enormous overlay of debt seems stymied by partisan interests. Our economic future depends on resolving these seemingly intractable issues.

Financial market conditions, too, are unusually difficult. While the U.S. stock market seems reasonably valued, its long-term performance—let us never forget—is ultimately dependent on the course of our economy. In many earlier eras of challenge, bonds provided not only a haven against stock market risk, but solid yields while you waited. Today, bond yields are, well, awful. The yield on ten-year U.S. Treasury notes is just 1.6 percent, and the yield on the total bond market index is just 2.03 percent, only slightly above the stock yield of 2.0 percent.

My unvarying advice continues to be to accept the yield environment as it exists (no matter how painful). Most investors should avoid reaching out on the risky limbs of higher-yielding junk bonds and high-dividend stocks. With U.S. Treasury yields so low relative to investment-grade corporates, however, a holder of the total bond market index (72 percent in government-backed issues), might seek some increased exposure to corporate bonds, as suggested a few paragraphs earlier. Invest you must, however, for *not* investing is an iron-clad formula for failure.

The Academics Speak. I've been using the sources of return to establish reasonable expectations for future stock and bond returns for as long as I can remember. But it was not until early 1991 that I formally published my findings, spelled out in my article "Investing in the 1990s" in the spring issue of *The Journal of Portfolio Management*. In a follow-up article entitled "Occam's Razor Revisited" in the fall edition of *JPM*, I revisited the subject. Despite the demonstrated soundness of my methodology, it has been rarely noted in the academic literature.

Two exceptions: Writing in Barclay's *Investment Insights* in July 2002, Dr. Kenneth Kroner and Dr. Richard Grinold, former chairman of the management science faculty of the University of California at Berkeley, explained essentially my same thesis for stocks in this (to me, complex) equation:

$$R = D/P - \Delta S + i + g + \Delta PE$$

where:

$D/P - \Delta S$ is Yield (including share repurchases)
$i + g$ is Earnings Growth (inflation plus real earnings growth)
ΔPE is repricing (i.e., impact of change in P/E)

They also forecast that "the return to the 10-year government bond over the next 10 years is just the yield on that bond."

While Grinold and Kroner failed to mention my 1991 publication that introduced essentially the same methodology more than a decade earlier, Professor Javier Estrada of the IESE Business School was extremely gracious in this regard. In his article from the journal *Corporate Finance Review*, "Investing in the Twenty-First Century: With Occam's Razor and Bogle's Wit," he concluded "Sir William of Occam taught us to focus on the essentials, and Bogle showed us how to apply that lesson to forecasting the long-term returns of stock markets.[4] Taking a cue from both, I evaluate the forecasting ability of two simple models, and show that they are surprisingly successful."

Also generous in recognizing my methodology are Princeton professor Burton G. Malkiel and professors Earl Benson and Sophie Kong of Western Washington University, along with investment analyst Ben D. Bortner. In the Fall 2011 issue of *JPM*, Benson, Kong and Bortner applauded my 1991 formulation as "a rather elegant, yet simple, method of estimating the expected [long-term!] return on common stocks—using 'the Bogle model.'"

Rule 5: Forget the Needle. Buy the Haystack

It was Cervantes who warned us, "Look not for a needle in a haystack." While that phrase has become deeply imbedded in our language, it has yet to gain acceptance from most mutual fund investors. Too many of us spend countless time and effort poring over fund records, getting information from news articles and television interviews and friends, and from hyperbolic fund advertisements and well-intentioned fund rating

---

[4] I explain Occam's Razor more fully in Chapter 6.

services. In substance, all of these statistics describe the past returns of mutual funds with decimal-point precision, yet have no predictive power to forecast the future returns that a fund may earn. As it turns out, we are looking for a very small needle in a very large haystack.

When we look for the needle, we seem to rely in our search largely on finding fund needles based on past performance, ignoring the fact that what worked yesterday so often fails to work tomorrow. Investing in equities entails four risks: stock risk, style risk, manager risk, and market risk. You can easily eliminate the first three of these risks simply by owning the entire stock market—owning the haystack, as it were— and holding it forever.

Yes, market risk remains. It is quite large enough, thank you. So why pile those other three risks on top of it? If you're not certain that you're right (and who can be?), diversify. Owning the entire stock market is the ultimate diversifier for the stock allocation of the portfolio. When you understand how hard it is to find that needle, simply buy the haystack.

Rule 6: Minimize the Croupier's Take

The resemblance of the stock market to the casino is hardly far-fetched. Both beating the stock market and gambling in the casino are zero-sum games—but only before the costs of playing the game are deducted. After the heavy costs of financial intermediation (commissions, spreads, management fees, taxes, etc.) are deducted, beating the stock market is inevitably a loser's game for investors as a group. In the same way, after the croupiers' wide rakes descend, beating the casino is inevitably a loser's game for gamblers as a group. (What else is new?) I reiterate what I've emphasized often in this book, investors as a group must and do earn the market's return before costs, and lose to the market by the exact amount of those costs.

Your greatest chance of earning the market's return, therefore, is to own the market itself, and reduce the croupiers' take to the bare-bones minimum. When you read about stock market returns, realize that the financial markets are not for sale, except at a high price. The difference is crucial. If the stock market's return is 8 percent before costs, and inter-mediation costs are approximately 2 percent, then investors will capture a net return of 6 percent. Compounded over 50 years, a 6 percent return increases capital of $10,000 by $174,000. But if investors earn the full

8 percent, their final value would leap by $459,000—more than two and a half times as much, merely by eliminating the croupier's take. Yes, in mutual funds performance comes and goes, but expenses go on forever. So I reiterate that, in the mutual fund industry, *you not only don't get what you pay for, you get precisely what you don't pay for.* Therefore, if you pay *nothing,* you get *everything* (i.e., the stock market's gross return).

Rule 7: There's No Escaping Risk

When you decide to put your money to work to build long-term wealth, you are not deciding whether or not to take risk, for risk is everywhere. What you must decide is what kind of risk you wish to take. "Do what you will, the capital is at hazard," just as the Prudent Man Rule assures us. Written by Justice Samuel Putnam of Massachusetts way back in 1830, here's how he expressed that classic rule:

> All that can be required of a trustee to invest is that he shall conduct himself faithfully and exercise a sound discretion. He is to observe how men of prudence, discretion, and intelligence manage their own affairs, not in regard to speculation, but in regard to the permanent disposition of their funds, considering the probable income as well as the probable safety of the capital to be invested.

Yes, money in a savings account is dollar-safe, but the value of those safe dollars are virtually certain to be substantially eroded over time by inflation, a risk that almost guarantees that you will fail to reach your capital accumulation goals. And yes, money in the stock market is very risky over the short term. But if your portfolio is well diversified, it should provide remarkable growth over the long term. Why? Simply because our public corporations have huge amounts of capital to employ. They earn profits on that capital that can be distributed as dividends, reinvesting the remainder in the business to earn additional returns. So your capital is almost certain to be safer in real-dollar terms over the long term than those "safe" dollars in your savings account.

Rule 8: Beware of Fighting the Last War

Too many investors—individuals and institutions alike—are constantly making investment decisions based on the lessons of the recent, or even the remote, past. We seek technology stocks after they have emerged victorious in the great bull market of the "Information Age." We worry about high inflation after it becomes the accepted bogeyman, and it then recedes. We flee stocks after the stock market has plunged, and then miss the subsequent recovery.

You should not ignore the past, but neither should you assume that a particular cyclical trend will last forever. None does. Just because some investors insist on "fighting the last war," you don't need to do so yourself. It doesn't work for very long.

Rule 9: The Hedgehog Bests the Fox

The Greek poet Archilochus tells us that *the fox knows many things, but the hedgehog knows one great thing.* The fox—artful, sly, and astute— represents the financial institution with investment professionals who know many things (or at least sincerely believe that they do) about complex markets and sophisticated strategies. The hedgehog—whose sharp spines give it almost impregnable armor when it curls into a ball— is the financial institution that knows only one great thing: Long-term investment success is based on simplicity.

The wily foxes of the financial world justify their existence by propagating the notion that an investor can survive only with the benefit of their artful knowledge and professional expertise. Their assistance, alas, does not come cheap. The costs it entails tend to consume any value that even the most cunning of foxes can add. Result: The annual returns earned for investors by financial intermediaries such as actively managed mutual funds have averaged less than 80 percent of the stock market's annual return—a huge loss when compounded over decades.

The hedgehog, on the other hand, knows that the truly great investment strategy succeeds, not because of its complexity or its cleverness, but because of its simplicity and its low costs. The hedgehog diversifies broadly, buys and holds, and keeps expenses to the bare-bones minimum. The ultimate hedgehog is the all-market index fund, operated at minimal cost and with minimal portfolio turnover, which virtually guarantees that you will capture nearly 100 percent of the market's return. The index fund wins because its concept is both priceless and price-less. In the field of investment management, foxes come and go, but hedgehogs are forever.

Rule 10: Stay the Course!

The secret to investing is that there is no secret. When you consider the previous nine rules, you realize what they are *not* about. They are not about magic or legerdemain, nor about forecasting the unforecastable, nor about betting against long and ultimately insurmountable odds, nor about learning some great secret of successful investing. For there is no great secret. There is only the majesty of simplicity. These rules are about elementary arithmetic, about fundamental and unarguable principles. Yes, investing is simple. But it is not easy, for it requires discipline, patience, steadfastness, and that most uncommon of all gifts, common sense.

When you own the entire stock market through a broad stock index fund, all the while balancing your portfolio with an appropriate allocation to an all-bond-market index fund, you create the *optimal* investment strategy. While it is not necessarily the best strategy (as I conceded at the beginning of this chapter), the number of strategies that are worse is infinite. Owning index funds, with their cost-efficiency, their tax-efficiency, and their assurance that you will earn your fair share of the markets' returns, is, by definition a winning strategy. As the financial markets swing back and forth, do your best to ignore the momentary cacophony, and to separate the transitory from the durable. This discipline is best summed up by the most important principle of all investment wisdom:

Stay the course!

Appendix I: Performance Ranking of Major Mutual Fund Managers—March 2012

	Manager Name	Total Long-Term Assets (millions)	Number of Portfolios Rated						Percentage of Portfolios Rated		Net Rating	Expense Ratio
			1 Star	2 Stars	3 Stars	4 Stars	5 Stars	Total	1 and 2 Stars	4 and 5 Stars	4 and 5 Minus 1 and 2	
S	1 T Rowe Price	$303,424	2	7	25	43	10	87	10%	61%	51%	0.85%
P	2 TIAA-CREF	41,955	0	0	13	10	1	24	0	46	46	0.49
M	3 Vanguard	1,624,417	1	5	46	42	10	104	6	50	44	0.19
C	4 Delaware	34,237	2	6	23	23	10	64	13	52	39	1.43
C	5 USAA	40,483	1	3	15	12	1	32	13	41	28	0.97
S	6 Janus	91,106	2	5	8	13	2	30	23	50	27	1.23
P	7 NeubergerBerman	28,478	2	7	3	15	0	27	33	56	22	1.30
C	8 PIMCO/Allianz Glbl	519,612	2	21	35	24	22	104	22	44	22	1.01
P	9 DFA	153,870	1	8	27	16	5	57	16	37	21	0.39
S	10 Schwab	44,273	0	7	16	11	3	37	19	38	19	0.70
P	11 Grantham Mayo	58,108	1	5	10	10	1	27	22	41	19	0.59
C	12 Principal Funds	68,792	0	6	20	11	2	39	15	33	18	1.21
C	13 Northern Trust	39,822	0	5	29	13	0	47	11	28	17	0.71
C	14 American Century	84,586	0	16	27	23	2	68	24	37	13	1.23
S	15 Franklin Templeton	367,833	6	13	52	28	3	102	19	30	12	1.26
C	16 Morgan Stanley	23,776	3	5	10	7	4	29	28	38	10	1.23
C	17 JPMorgan Funds	151,607	6	12	37	22	3	80	23	31	9	1.20
C	18 BlackRock	667,967	21	63	126	90	19	319	26	34	8	1.03
P	19 American Funds	913,576	0	6	14	8	0	28	21	29	7	1.02
C	20 Russell Invst Grp	35,604	0	3	8	4	0	15	20	27	7	1.24
C	21 RidgeWorth Capital	20,215	0	8	13	9	1	31	26	32	6	1.04
P	22 Fidelity	858,794	12	51	83	66	9	221	29	34	5	1.14
C	23 MFS	95,196	2	11	35	13	2	63	21	24	3	1.37
C	24 Prudential Finl	46,318	1	12	15	12	2	42	31	33	2	1.49
C	25 Transamerica AM	25,795	3	12	30	13	3	61	25	26	2	1.20
C	26 John Hancock	74,456	1	21	45	19	4	90	24	26	1	1.25
C	27 Columbia MgmtInvst	158,966	1	21	52	20	2	96	23	23	0	1.28

(Continued)

	Manager Name	Total Long-Term Assets (millions)	Number of Portfolios Rated						Percentage of Portfolios Rated		Net Rating	Expense Ratio
			1 Star	2 Stars	3 Stars	4 Stars	5 Stars	Total	1 and 2 Stars	4 and 5 Stars	4 and 5 Minus 1 and 2	
S	28 Waddell & Reed	$72,048	3	10	18	12	1	44	30%	30%	0%	1.64%
C	29 Dreyfus	68,250	5	19	59	22	2	107	22	22	0	1.33
C	30 Legg Mason/Western	108,224	7	23	40	26	3	99	30	29	−1	1.33
S	31 Nuveen	95,103	5	56	88	46	10	205	30	27	−2	1.29
C	32 MainStay Funds	45,033	0	9	15	7	1	32	28	25	−3	1.42
C	33 Wells Fargo	97,602	5	23	37	17	7	89	31	27	−4	1.24
P	34 Van Eck	32,818	6	4	3	7	2	22	45	41	−5	0.84
C	35 State Street Glbl	105,290	11	19	36	21	4	91	33	27	−5	0.46
C	36 NGAM Advisors LP	40,330	0	7	8	4	1	20	35	25	−10	1.51
S	37 Virtus Invst Ptnrs	25,572	4	12	8	9	3	36	44	33	−11	1.59
C	38 AllianceBernstein	65,156	6	14	17	10	4	51	39	27	−12	1.41
S	39 Federated	53,660	2	22	23	12	3	62	39	24	−15	1.31
C	40 DWS Investments	50,539	8	19	23	12	5	67	40	25	−15	1.34
P	41 Lord Abbett	75,526	2	11	11	6	1	31	42	23	−19	1.19
S	42 SEI	25,661	4	7	15	4	1	31	35	16	−19	0.90
C	43 OppenheimerFunds	147,925	8	11	23	6	3	51	37	18	−20	1.39
C	44 Invesco/PowerShares	146,154	21	62	57	38	7	185	45	24	−21	1.20
C	45 Pioneer	37,161	2	11	17	4	1	35	37	14	−23	1.47
C	46 Putnam	54,275	10	21	24	6	0	61	51	10	−41	1.44
C	47 Goldman Sachs	59,817	3	26	19	6	0	54	54	11	−43	1.34
S	48 Eaton Vance	98,882	8	50	37	7	3	105	55	10	−46	1.37
C	49 The Hartford	49,162	2	14	11	2	0	29	55	7	−48	1.26
P	50 ProFunds	20,621	34	20	8	1	0	63	86	2	−84	1.57
	Total	$8,148,075	226	809	1,414	862	183	3,494	30%	30%	0%	1.16%

C	Conglomerate (30)	$3,162,349	39%
S	Publicly Traded (10)	$1,177,563	14%
	Total (40)	$4,339,912	53%
P	Privately Held (9)	$2,183,746	27%
M	Mutual Structure (1)	$1,624,417	20%

Appendix II: Annual Performance of Common Stock Funds versus S&P 500, 1945–1975

From Memorandum Presented to Vanguard Directors, September 1975

Year	1945–1975 Common Stock Funds	S&P 500	S&P 500 Better	S&P 500 Worse
1945	33.6%	36.4%	2.8%	
1946	−4.5	−8.1		−3.6%
1947	0.5	5.7	5.2	
1948	0.4	5.6	5.2	
1949	19.9	18.8		−1.1
1950	22.3	31.7	9.4	
1951	17.8	24.0	6.2	
1952	12.9	18.3	5.4	
1953	−0.4	−1.1		−0.7
1954	45.1	52.1	7.0	
1955	20.1	31.4	11.3	
1956	8.9	6.6		−2.3
1957	−9.5	−10.8		−1.3
1958	40.7	44.6	3.9	
1959	9.7	11.9	2.2	
1960	1.9	0.5		−1.4
1961	25.8	26.8	1.0	
1962	−11.0	−8.7	2.3	
1963	18.8	22.7	3.9	
1964	15.6	16.3	0.7	
1965	16.7	12.4		−4.3
1966	−5.1	−10.1		−5.0
1967	23.8	23.9	0.1	
1968	13.3	11.0		−2.3
1969	−10.4	−8.4	2.0	
1970	0.9	3.9	3.0	
1971	14.9	14.3		−0.6
1972	12.7	18.9	6.2	

(*Continued*)

325

| Year | 1945—1975 | | S&P 500 | |
	Common Stock Funds	S&P 500	Better	Worse
1973	−16.2%	−14.8%	1.4%	
1974	−21.5	−26.4		−4.9
1975 (6 mos.)	31.9	36.9	5.0	
30½ years*	9.7%	11.3%	1.6%	

JCB
3/15/1976

*Compounded annually.

Appendix III: Growth in Index Funds—Number and Assets, 1976–2012

Year End	Number Traditional Index Funds	Number Exchange Traded Funds	Total Assets (in millions) Traditional Index Funds	Total Assets (in millions) Exchange Traded Funds	Total Index Funds	Indexing Share of Equity Fund Assets
1976	1	–	$14	–	$14	0%
1977	1	–	34	–	34	0
1978	1	–	79	–	79	0
1979	1	–	91	–	91	0
1980	1	–	113	–	113	0
1981	1	–	103	–	103	0
1982	1	–	135	–	135	0
1983	1	–	275	–	275	0
1984	2	–	322	–	322	0
1985	5	–	511	–	511	0
1986	7	–	623	–	623	0
1987	11	–	1,208	–	1,208	1
1988	12	–	1,528	–	1,528	1
1989	14	–	3,125	–	3,125	1
1990	28	–	4,857	–	4,857	2
1991	38	–	10,735	–	10,735	3
1992	54	–	17,323	–	17,323	3
1993	71	1	26,311	$464	26,774	3
1994	85	1	30,943	424	31,367	3
1995	86	2	53,919	1,052	54,971	4
1996	101	19	91,194	2,411	93,605	5
1997	135	19	155,020	6,707	161,727	7
1998	160	29	241,374	15,568	256,942	9
1999	209	30	356,617	33,873	390,491	10
2000	262	80	352,643	65,702	418,345	11
2001	247	101	340,904	82,930	423,834	13
2002	249	113	299,276	102,022	401,299	14
2003	239	121	413,804	151,656	565,459	15
2004	237	154	504,561	228,221	732,782	16
2005	225	206	567,072	302,194	869,267	16
2006	229	365	695,315	423,372	1,118,687	17
2007	249	656	808,969	613,661	1,422,631	19
2008	248	835	572,458	535,696	1,108,154	24
2009	239	910	758,270	785,984	1,544,254	24
2010	251	1,082	937,642	1,005,628	1,943,270	26

(Continued)

Year End	Number		Total Assets (in millions)			Indexing Share of Equity Fund Assets
	Traditional Index Funds	Exchange Traded Funds	Traditional Index Funds	Exchange Traded Funds	Total Index Funds	
2011	256	1,372	998,882	1,061,803	2,060,685	28
2012 (3/31)	258	1,441	1,129,993	1,210,876	2,340,869	28

SOURCE: Bogle Financial Markets Research Center, Strategic Insight, Morningstar.

Appendix IV: Wellington Fund Record, 1929–2012

		Per Share Results				Results with Reinvested Capital Gains	
(1) Year	(2) Total Net Assets (mil)	(3) Net Asset Value	(4) Income Dividends	(5) Capital Gains Distributions	(6) Return of Capital	(7) Adjusted Asset Value	(8) Income Dividends Received*
1929	$0.2	$12.29	–	–	–	$12.29	–
1930	0.3	9.26	$0.50	–	–	9.26	$0.50
1931	0.3	6.40	0.50	–	–	6.40	0.50
1932	0.4	5.75	0.50	–	–	5.75	0.50
1933	0.5	5.78	0.29	–	$0.06	5.78	0.29
1934	0.6	6.59	0.32	$0.03	0.01	6.62	0.32
1935	1.1	8.42	0.29	0.09	0.05	8.54	0.29
1936	3.0	10.38	0.30	0.29	0.02	10.81	0.30
1937	3.1	6.20	0.39	0.26	–	6.72	0.41
1938	4.5	6.98	0.28	–	0.07	7.56	0.30
1939	5.2	7.21	0.18	0.27	–	8.08	0.19
1940	5.5	6.80	0.23	0.17	–	7.79	0.26
1941	5.4	6.13	0.34	0.08	–	7.10	0.39
1942	7.3	6.69	0.32	0.10	–	7.85	0.37
1943	10.4	7.85	0.31	0.20	–	9.41	0.36
1944	16.1	8.77	0.30	0.28	–	10.79	0.35
1945	26.9	10.01	0.26	0.49	–	12.81	0.32
1946	36.5	9.13	0.25	0.41	–	12.09	0.31
1947	48.9	8.32	0.29	0.21	–	11.22	0.38
1948	64.1	8.14	0.33	0.18	–	11.16	0.44
1949	105.4	8.95	0.39	0.11	–	12.38	0.53
1950	154.5	9.51	0.40	0.15	–	13.30	0.55
1951	193.9	10.01	0.40	0.25	–	14.25	0.56
1952	246.2	10.44	0.40	0.25	–	15.11	0.57
1953	280.9	9.99	0.40	0.23	–	14.69	0.58
1954	401.7	12.30	0.41	0.32	–	18.40	0.60
1955	496.6	13.31	0.44	0.44	–	20.35	0.65
1956	578.8	12.99	0.55	0.45	–	20.31	0.84

(Continued)

(1) Year	(2) Total Net Assets (mil)	(3) Net Asset Value	Per Share Results			Results with Reinvested Capital Gains	
			(4) Income Dividends	(5) Capital Gains Distributions	(6) Return of Capital	(7) Adjusted Asset Value	(8) Income Dividends Received*
1957	$604.6	$11.56	$0.46	$0.43	—	$18.51	$0.72
1958	858.0	13.88	0.45	0.45	—	22.67	0.72
1959	1,017.2	14.15	0.46	0.48	—	23.59	0.75
1960	1,087.0	13.89	0.47	0.48	—	23.64	0.78
1961	1,419.1	15.53	0.47	0.51	—	26.94	0.80
1962	1,413.4	13.81	0.46	0.44	—	24.40	0.80
1963	1,642.0	14.48	0.46	0.49	—	26.07	0.80
1964	1,883.2	15.04	0.47	0.52	—	27.60	0.85
1965	2,047.5	14.84	0.48	0.53	—	27.76	0.88
1966	1,867.5	12.95	0.50	0.40	—	24.63	0.94
1967	1,856.6	13.07	0.49	0.42	$0.01	25.27	0.93
1968	1,754.5	13.20	0.45	0.35	0.10	25.88	0.87
1969	1,416.3	11.34	0.45	0.15	0.25	22.38	0.88
1970	1,376.9	11.30	0.45	—	0.25	22.30	0.88
1971	1,356.6	11.84	0.44	—	—	23.37	0.87
1972	1,229.5	12.42	0.44	—	0.25	24.51	0.87
1973	938.6	10.26	0.47	—	0.25	20.25	0.93
1974	687.8	7.73	0.50	—	0.25	15.26	0.99
1975	775.9	8.91	0.48	—	0.25	17.58	0.95
1976	846.8	10.19	0.49	—	0.25	20.11	0.97
1977	705.7	8.98	0.50	—	0.25	17.72	0.99
1978	639.8	8.65	0.54	—	0.25	17.07	1.07
1979	607.2	9.13	0.66	—	—	18.02	1.30
1980	612.6	10.38	0.75	—	—	20.49	1.48
1981	521.1	9.80	0.84	—	—	19.34	1.66
1982	567.9	11.21	0.87	—	—	22.12	1.72
1983	613.5	12.46	0.91	0.44	—	25.03	1.80
1984	613.9	12.32	0.92	0.48	—	25.23	1.85
1985	812.6	14.50	0.92	0.30	—	29.99	1.88
1986	1,134.8	15.85	0.94	0.34	—	33.13	1.94
1987	1,331.4	15.15	0.98	0.14	—	31.80	2.05
1988	1,526.9	16.01	0.96	0.58	—	34.19	2.02
1989	2,099.2	17.78	1.02	0.60	—	38.57	2.18
1990	2,449.2	16.26	1.01	—	—	35.27	2.19

(1) Year	(2) Total Net Assets (mil)	Per Share Results (3) Net Asset Value	(4) Income Dividends	(5) Capital Gains Distributions	(6) Return of Capital	Results with Reinvested Capital Gains (7) Adjusted Asset Value	(8) Income Dividends Received*
1991	$3,818.4	$18.81	$0.96	$0.23	–	$41.03	$2.08
1992	5,570.0	19.16	0.94	0.16	–	41.96	2.05
1993	8,075.8	20.40	0.92	0.38	–	45.05	2.01
1994	8,809.4	19.39	0.88	0.03	–	42.85	1.94
1995	12,656.0	24.43	0.97	0.28	–	54.27	2.14
1996	16,189.8	26.15	1.06	1.11	–	59.20	2.35
1997	21,811.8	29.45	1.12	1.57	–	68.24	2.54
1998	25,760.9	29.35	1.13	2.44	–	70.45	2.62
1999	25,528.5	27.96	1.14	1.50	–	68.61	2.74
2000	22,799.0	28.21	1.07	1.48	–	70.71	2.63
2001	24,293.0	27.26	0.95	1.13	–	69.45	2.38
2002	22,389.0	24.56	0.84	–	–	62.57	2.14
2003	28,513.4	28.81	0.77	–	–	73.40	1.95
2004	33,929.8	30.19	0.88	0.91	–	77.83	2.23
2005	38,949.5	30.35	0.90	0.97	–	79.21	2.32
2006	45,719.0	32.44	0.98	1.40	–	86.07	2.56
2007	50,293.4	32.62	1.08	1.42	–	87.97	2.87
2008	38,363.3	24.43	1.04	–	–	65.88	2.80
2009	47,742.2	28.85	0.90	–		77.80	2.42
2010	53,870.8	31.10	0.85	–	–	83.87	2.30
2011	55,644.7	31.34	0.94	–	–	84.52	2.55
2012 (3/31)	61,090.2	33.48	0.23	–	–	90.29	0.61
Total			$51.22	$28.77	$2.57		$103.19

*Assumes capital distributions are reinvested at year-end NAV.

Appendix V: Wellington Fund Equity Ratio and Risk Exposure (Beta), 1929–2012

Year	Equity Ratio	Three-Year Beta	Year	Equity Ratio	Three-Year Beta
2Q 1929	78%	–	1961	61%	0.67%
3Q 1929	42	–	1962	58	0.65
1929	37	–	1963	63	0.63
1930	60	0.45	1964	65	0.65
1931	47	0.73	1965	64	0.62
1932	65	0.60	1966	62	0.71
1933	69	0.61	1967	74	0.69
1934	62	0.59	1968	67	0.76
1935	60	0.52	1969	69	0.79
1936	62	0.60	1970	73	0.83
1937	70	0.62	1971	77	0.82
1938	55	0.70	1972	81	0.87
1939	67	0.71	1973	62	0.83
1940	68	0.75	1974	62	0.80
1941	72	0.67	1975	64	0.67
1942	72	0.66	1976	70	0.67
1943	63	0.63	1977	70	0.69
1944	64	0.72	1978	68	0.73
1945	60	0.67	1979	69	0.76
1946	56	0.60	1980	70	0.77
1947	53	0.51	1981	68	0.79
1948	59	0.48	1982	62	0.76
1949	62	0.44	1983	69	0.76
1950	62	0.51	1984	67	0.73
1951	64	0.53	1985	62	0.73
1952	64	0.58	1986	63	0.70
1953	58	0.55	1987	64	0.66
1954	67	0.54	1988	66	0.74
1955	67	0.48	1989	62	0.73
1956	66	0.52	1990	60	0.78
1957	63	0.54	1991	60	0.72
1958	67	0.59	1992	58	0.72
1959	62	0.61	1993	61	0.63
1960	60	0.63	1994	64	0.68

(Continued)

Year	Equity Ratio	Three-Year Beta	Year	Equity Ratio	Three-Year Beta
1995	62	0.78	2004	66	0.64
1996	61	0.83	2005	65	0.67
1997	61	0.76	2006	66	0.63
1998	62	0.61	2007	65	0.61
1999	66	0.58	2008	61	0.64
2000	64	0.50	2009	65	0.64
2001	68	0.47	2010	67	0.65
2002	66	0.46	2011	66	0.64
2003	66	0.57	2012 (3/31)	65	0.65

NOTE: Equity ratio refers to the fund's equity position as a percentage of total assets. Beta is the variability in the fund's net asset value versus the S&P 500.

SOURCES: 1929–1951, Author's calculations from Wellington Fund Annual Reports; 1952–1995, Wiesenberger; 1996–2012, Vanguard.

Appendix VI: Wellington Fund Performance versus Average Balanced Fund, 1929-2012

Date	Annual Return Wellington Fund	Annual Return Average Balanced Fund	Cumulative Growth of $1 Wellington Fund	Cumulative Growth of $1 Average Balanced Fund	Ratio: Wellington/ Average Balanced Fund
1929			$1.00	$1.00	1.00
1930	−21.2%	−21.2%	0.79	0.79	1.00
1931	−26.4	−26.4	0.58	0.58	1.00
1932	−1.8	−1.8	0.57	0.57	1.00
1933	6.8	6.8	0.61	0.61	1.00
1934	20.4	20.4	0.73	0.73	1.00
1935	35.4	21.5	0.99	0.89	1.11
1936	31.3	21.2	1.30	1.08	1.21
1937	−35.4	−18.2	0.84	0.88	0.95
1938	19.1	12.6	1.00	0.99	1.01
1939	10.3	1.9	1.10	1.01	1.09
1940	0.1	−0.5	1.11	1.01	1.10
1941	−3.9	−2.5	1.06	0.98	1.08
1942	16.6	12.5	1.24	1.10	1.12
1943	24.9	27.9	1.55	1.41	1.10
1944	19.4	21.0	1.85	1.71	1.08
1945	23.1	28.7	2.27	2.20	1.03
1946	−2.4	−3.0	2.22	2.13	1.04
1947	−3.5	−0.5	2.14	2.12	1.01
1948	3.9	1.5	2.23	2.15	1.03
1949	16.5	13.9	2.59	2.45	1.06
1950	12.8	16.9	2.92	2.87	1.02
1951	12.4	11.4	3.29	3.20	1.03
1952	11.0	9.3	3.65	3.49	1.04
1953	1.9	0.8	3.72	3.52	1.06
1954	31.0	31.2	4.87	4.62	1.05
1955	15.5	13.6	5.63	5.25	1.07
1956	4.4	4.0	5.88	5.46	1.08
1957	−4.3	−5.0	5.62	5.19	1.08
1958	28.5	28.2	7.22	6.65	1.09
1959	8.9	6.7	7.87	7.10	1.11
1960	5.2	5.4	8.27	7.48	1.11
1961	19.0	19.3	9.84	8.93	1.10
1962	−5.2	−6.4	9.33	8.35	1.12
1963	11.9	14.8	10.44	9.59	1.09
1964	10.8	13.2	11.57	10.86	1.07
1965	5.4	15.6	12.20	12.55	0.97
1966	−6.6	−5.0	11.40	11.92	0.96
1967	8.2	24.4	12.32	14.83	0.83

(Continued)

Date	Annual Return		Cumulative Growth of $1		Ratio: Wellington/ Average Balanced Fund
	Wellington Fund	Average Balanced Fund	Wellington Fund	Average Balanced Fund	
1968	7.9%	16.0%	$13.30	$17.20	0.77
1969	−7.8	−11.5	12.26	15.22	0.81
1970	6.4	4.9	13.04	15.97	0.82
1971	8.9	14.9	14.20	18.36	0.77
1972	11.0	9.3	15.76	20.06	0.79
1973	−11.8	−13.9	13.90	17.27	0.80
1974	−17.7	−16.5	11.43	14.42	0.79
1975	25.2	28.4	14.31	18.52	0.77
1976	23.4	26.6	17.66	23.45	0.75
1977	−4.4	0.9	16.88	23.67	0.71
1978	5.3	5.7	17.78	25.02	0.71
1979	13.5	16.5	20.19	29.15	0.69
1980	22.6	20.6	24.75	35.16	0.70
1981	2.9	4.0	25.47	36.57	0.70
1982	24.5	27.1	31.72	46.49	0.68
1983	23.6	17.6	39.20	54.67	0.72
1984	10.7	6.6	43.39	58.29	0.74
1985	28.5	24.2	55.77	72.42	0.77
1986	18.4	15.3	66.03	83.50	0.79
1987	2.3	1.5	67.54	84.79	0.80
1988	16.1	10.8	78.42	93.96	0.83
1989	21.6	17.9	95.36	110.83	0.86
1990	−2.8	−0.1	92.68	110.68	0.84
1991	23.6	22.6	114.60	135.74	0.84
1992	7.9	7.1	123.68	145.36	0.85
1993	13.5	8.7	140.40	157.94	0.89
1994	−0.5	−2.2	139.71	154.52	0.90
1995	32.9	22.4	185.71	189.20	0.98
1996	16.2	12.3	215.77	212.46	1.02
1997	23.2	17.7	265.91	250.14	1.06
1998	12.1	12.1	297.97	280.39	1.06
1999	4.4	9.2	311.10	306.16	1.02
2000	10.4	1.2	343.46	309.78	1.11
2001	4.2	−4.4	357.84	296.06	1.21
2002	−6.9	−11.4	333.16	262.21	1.27
2003	20.7	19.1	402.28	312.26	1.29
2004	11.2	7.9	447.23	337.02	1.33
2005	6.8	4.7	477.75	352.83	1.35
2006	15.0	10.6	549.27	390.30	1.41
2007	8.3	5.9	595.05	413.45	1.44
2008	−22.3	−23.0	462.39	318.48	1.45
2009	22.2	23.2	565.02	392.46	1.44
2010	10.9	11.8	626.81	438.89	1.43
2011	2.8	0.5	644.36	440.97	1.46
2012 (3/31)	7.6	7.9	693.02	475.67	1.46

Appendix VII: Wellington Fund Expense Ratios, 1966–2011

	Total Net Assets $000	Expense Ratio	Advisory Fee Rate	Performance Adjustment Fee Rate*	Total Advisory Fee Rate	Total Expenses $000	Advisory Basic Fee $000	Advisory Performance Adjustment $000	Total Advisory Fee $000
1966	$1,849,140	0.38%	0.252%	—	0.252%	$7,287	$4,838	—	$4,838
1967	1,825,725	0.39	0.253	—	0.253	7,452	4,829	—	4,829
1968	1,842,588	0.41	0.253	—	0.253	7,299	4,502	—	4,502
1969	1,451,564	0.44	0.252	—	0.252	6,988	4,007	—	4,007
1970	1,322,562	0.47	0.251	—	0.251	6,127	3,277	—	3,277
1971	1,271,101	0.45	0.256	—	0.256	6,229	3,546	—	3,546
1972	1,243,771	0.42	0.257	—	0.257	5,402	3,309	—	3,309
1973	935,238	0.47	0.283	—	0.283	5,105	3,069	—	3,069
1974	703,143	0.56	0.349	—	0.349	4,569	2,849	—	2,849
1975	770,669	0.56	0.311	—	0.311	4,241	2,356	—	2,356
1976	811,207	0.49	0.293	—	0.293	4,008	2,395	—	2,395
1977	704,128	0.48	0.276	—	0.276	3,682	2,115	—	2,115
1978	642,018	0.56	0.192	—	0.192	3,830	1,311	—	1,311
1979	608,787	0.54	0.149	0.008%	0.156	3,482	959	$49	1,008
1980	637,705	0.54	0.156	0.019	0.174	3,263	940	113	1,053
1981	541,775	0.62	0.163	0.022	0.185	3,500	922	124	1,046
1982	554,805	0.69	0.165	0.023	0.188	3,480	834	115	949
1983	617,036	0.64	0.160	0.014	0.174	3,906	979	84	1,063
1984	604,359	0.59	0.153	0.019	0.172	3,529	917	112	1,029
1985	778,486	0.64	0.153	0.005	0.157	4,486	1,071	32	1,103

(Continued)

337

Year	Total Net Assets $000	Expense Ratio	Advisory Fee Rate	Performance Adjustment Fee Rate*	Total Advisory Fee Rate	Total Expenses $000	Advisory Basic Fee $000	Advisory Performance Adjustment $000	Total Advisory Fee $000
1986	$1,102,272	0.53%	0.151%	0.000%	0.151%	$5,234	$1,493	$0	$1,493
1987	1,273,706	0.43	0.122	−0.013	0.108	5,958	1,684	−182	1,502
1988	1,527,337	0.47	0.120	−0.004	0.116	6,754	1,721	−54	1,667
1989	2,034,707	0.42	0.112	−0.004	0.107	7,461	1,982	−77	1,905
1990	2,317,074	0.43	0.102	−0.012	0.090	9,343	2,224	−263	1,961
1991	3,473,346	0.35	0.088	−0.014	0.074	10,475	2,640	−421	2,219
1992	5,359,060	0.33	0.068	−0.013	0.055	14,653	3,006	−572	2,434
1993	7,916,668	0.34	0.059	−0.003	0.056	22,627	3,913	−177	3,736
1994	8,638,273	0.35	0.055	0.000	0.055	29,195	4,570	0	4,570
1995	12,332,614	0.33	0.051	0.000	0.051	34,314	5,261	0	5,261
1996	16,505,373	0.31	0.043	0.001	0.044	43,298	6,042	79	6,121
1997	21,340,282	0.29	0.040	−0.001	0.038	54,556	7,447	−244	7,203
1998	25,829,221	0.31	0.038	−0.009	0.029	74,625	9,157	−2,102	7,055
1999	25,846,313	0.30	0.036	−0.009	0.027	79,406	9,658	−2,480	7,178
2000	22,524,394	0.31	0.037	−0.012	0.025	72,012	8,607	−2,700	5,907
2001	24,149,929	0.35	0.039	0.008	0.047	84,364	9,447	1,927	11,374
2002	22,929,125	0.35	0.038	0.011	0.049	82,725	8,948	2,682	11,630
2003	26,985,256	0.34	0.038	0.011	0.049	81,501	9,006	2,651	11,657
2004	32,895,324	0.29	0.036	0.009	0.046	85,838	10,894	2,802	13,696
2005	38,576,351	0.24	0.033	0.005	0.039	92,211	12,623	1,944	14,567
2006	45,169,054	0.25	0.043	0.011	0.054	105,698	17,827	4,433	22,260
2007	50,774,449	0.23	0.049	0.009	0.058	109,593	23,637	4,163	27,800
2008	37,181,459	0.25	0.059	0.013	0.072	116,996	27,785	6,364	34,149
2009	47,324,976	0.30	0.067	0.017	0.084	120,494	27,424	6,887	34,311
2010	51,339,515	0.26	0.067	0.013	0.081	131,928	34,158	6,766	40,924
2011	54,790,055	0.23	0.068	0.001	0.069	126,950	38,030	1,383	39,413

*Incentive/penalty fee created in 1978, based on three-year moving average of the Fund's return relative to a similarly balanced portfolio of stock and bond index funds.

Index

339